# Tolley's Capital Gains Tax Workbook 1999/2000

by

David Smailes FCA
Kevin Walton BA(Hons)

Tolley Publishing

Published by Tolley
2 Addiscombe Road
Croydon Surrey CR9 5AF
England
0181–686 9141
020–8686 9141

Photoset by Interactive Sciences Ltd, Gloucester

Printed in Great Britain by
Hobbs the Printers Ltd, Totton, Hampshire

© Reed Elsevier (UK) Limited 1999

ISBN 0 7545 0328–3

# About This Book

Tolley's Capital Gains Tax Workbook illustrates the practical application of UK capital gains tax and corporation tax on chargeable gains legislation through worked examples. The computations aid understanding of complex areas of the law and provide guidance on layout. Detailed explanatory notes and statutory references are provided wherever appropriate. The comprehensive index and table of statutes make it easy to find a particular computation quickly.

The Workbook is designed to be used on its own or in conjunction with Tolley's Capital Gains Tax, and so the chapters follow the order of the commentary in that volume.

This 1999/2000 edition is fully up to date and includes the provisions of Finance Act 1999. Cross-references prefixed 'IT' and 'CT' refer to the companion volumes Tolley's Income Tax Workbook 1999/2000 and Tolley's Corporation Tax Workbook 1999/2000.

Comments and suggestions for improvements are always welcome.

**TOLLEY PUBLISHING**

# Abbreviations and References

## ABBREVIATIONS

| | | |
|---|---|---|
| ACT | = | Advance Corporation Tax |
| Art | = | Article |
| b/f | = | brought forward |
| C/A | = | Court of Appeal |
| CCAB | = | Consultative Committee of Accountancy Bodies |
| C/D | = | Chancery Division |
| c/f | = | carried forward |
| CGT | = | Capital Gains Tax |
| CGTA | = | Capitals Gains Tax Act 1979 |
| CT | = | Corporation Tax |
| DTR | = | Double Tax Relief |
| EIS | = | Enterprise Investment Scheme |
| ESC | = | Extra-Statutory Concession |
| FA | = | Finance Act |
| F(No 2)A | = | Finance (No 2) Act |
| FIFO | = | First In, First Out |
| FYA | = | First-Year Allowance |
| H/L | = | House of Lords |
| HMIT | = | Her Majesty's Inspector of Taxes |
| ICTA | = | Income and Corporation Taxes Act 1988 |
| IRPR | = | Inland Revenue Press Release |
| IT | = | Income Tax |
| LIFO | = | Last In, First Out |
| NBV | = | Net Book Value |
| para | = | paragraph |
| PAYE | = | Pay As You Earn |
| P/e | = | Period ended |
| Reg | = | Regulation |
| s | = | section |
| SC/S | = | Scottish Court of Session |
| Sch | = | Schedule |
| Sec | = | Section |
| SI | = | Statutory Instrument |
| SSAP | = | Statement of Standard Accounting Practice |
| TCGA | = | Taxation of Chargeable Gains Act 1992 |
| TMA | = | Taxes Management Act 1970 |
| Y/e | = | Year ended |

## REFERENCES

| | | |
|---|---|---|
| STC | = | Simon's Tax Cases, (Butterworth & Co (Publishers) Ltd, Halsbury House, 35 Chancery Lane, London, WC2A 1EL |
| TC | = | Official Tax Cases, (H.M. Stationery Office, P.O. Box 276, SW8 5DT) |

# Contents

| CHAPTER | | PAGE |
|---|---|---|
| 201 | Annual Rates and Exemptions | 2 |
| 202 | Anti-Aviodance | 6 |
| 203 | Assets held on 6 April 1965 | 11 |
| 204 | Assets held on 31 March 1982 | 27 |
| 205 | Companies | 33 |
| 206 | Disposal | 35 |
| 207 | Enterprise Investment Scheme | 49 |
| 208 | Exemptions and Reliefs | 54 |
| 209 | Hold-Over Reliefs | 57 |
| 210 | Indexation | 64 |
| 211 | Interest on Overpaid Tax | 72 |
| 212 | Interest and Surcharges on Unpaid Tax | 73 |
| 213 | Land | 74 |
| 214 | Losses | 86 |
| 215 | Married Persons | 88 |
| 216 | Mineral Royalties | 91 |
| 217 | Overseas Matters | 93 |
| 218 | Partnerships | 103 |
| 219 | Private Residences | 110 |
| 220 | Qualifying Corporate Bonds | 113 |
| 221 | Retirement Relief | 116 |
| 222 | Rollover Relief — Replacement of Business Assets | 131 |
| 223 | Settlements | 138 |
| 224 | Shares and Securities | 146 |
| 225 | Shares and Securities — Identification Rules | 169 |
| 226 | Taper Relief | 178 |
| 227 | Wasting Assets | 184 |
| | Table of Statutes | 188 |
| | Index | 193 |

## 201 Annual Rates and Exemptions

### 201.1 GAINS CHARGEABLE AT INCOME TAX RATES

**(A) General—1999/2000 onwards** [*TCGA 1992, s 4; F(No 2)A 1997, s 34, 4 Sch 24; FA 1998, s 120, 27 Sch Pt III(29); FA 1999, s 26*]

M, a single person and established sole trader, had trading income of £14,500 for the year ended 30 April 1999, but made a trading loss of £11,000 for the year ended 30 April 2000. He had no other source of income, but realised a capital gain of £36,500 in 1999/2000 from the sale of a country cottage. He claims relief for the trading loss under *ICTA 1988, s380(1)(b)* against his income for 1999/2000.

**M's income tax position for 1999/2000 is as follows**

|  | £ |
|---|---:|
| Schedule D, Case I | 14,500 |
| *Less:* Loss relief | 11,000 |
|  | 3,500 |
| *Less:* Personal allowance (maximum £4,335) | 3,500 |
| Taxable income | Nil |

**His capital gains tax computation is as follows**

|  | £ |
|---|---:|
| Gain | 36,500 |
| Annual exemption | 7,100 |
| Gain chargeable to tax | £29,400 |
| Capital gains tax payable | £ |
|   28,000 at 20% | 5,600.00 |
|   1,400 at 40% | 560.00 |
| £29,400 | £6,160.00 |

**Notes**

(*a*) For 1999/2000 and subsequent years, an individual's gains are chargeable at a rate equivalent to the lower rate of income tax (20%). The starting rate band for income tax does not apply for CGT. However, to the extent if any that gains, if treated as the top slice of income, exceed the basic rate limit (£28,000 for 1999/2000), they are chargeable at 40%.

(*b*) The unused personal allowance of £835 is not available to reduce the chargeable gain. If M's trading losses had exceeded his total income, he could have claimed, under *FA 1991, s 72*, to have the gain reduced by the unused losses (see IT 10.2 LOSSES).

# Annual Rates and Exemptions 201.1

**(B) With savings income otherwise within the lower rate band—1998/99 and earlier years** [*TCGA 1992, s 4; F(No 2)A 1992, s 23; FA 1993, 6 Sch 22; FA 1996, 6 Sch 27; FA 1998, s 120, 27 Sch Pt III(29); FA 1999, s 26*]

N, a single person, has the following income and gains for 1998/99

|  | £ |
|---|---:|
| Dividends and other savings income (net) | 19,200 |
| Schedule D, Case I | 4,955 |
| Capital gains | 11,300 |

**Disregarding the capital gains, N's income tax liability is computed as follows**

|  | £ | £ |
|---|---:|---:|
| Savings income | 19,200 |  |
| Tax credits (£19,200 × $\frac{1}{4}$) | 4,800 | 24,000 |
| Schedule D, Case I |  | 4,955 |
|  |  | 28,955 |
| *Deduct* Personal allowance |  | 4,195 |
| Taxable income |  | £24,760 |

| Tax payable: |  |
|---|---:|
| 760 @ 20% (lower rate band — maximum £4,300) | 152.00 |
| 24,000 @ 20% (savings income) | 4,800.00 |
| £24,760 |  |
|  | 4,952.00 |
| Tax at source (£24,000 × 20%) | 4,800.00 |
| Net liability | £152.00 |

Because part (£3,540) of the lower rate band of £4,300 is unused (other than by savings income chargeable at 20% in any case), the income tax position is revised, and the capital gains position computed, as follows

*Income tax position* (basic rate limit reduced by £3,540)

| Taxable income as above | £24,760 |
|---|---:|

| Tax payable: |  |
|---|---:|
| 760 @ 20% (lower rate band) | 152.00 |
| 22,800 @ 20% (savings income) | 4,560.00 |
| 23,560 |  |
| 1,200 @ 40% (savings income) | 480.00 |
| £24,760 |  |
|  | 5,192.00 |
| Tax at source as above | 4,800.00 |
| Net liability | £392.00 |

## 201.2 Annual Rates and Exemptions

*Capital gains position*

|  | £ |
|---|---:|
| Capital gains | 11,300 |
| *Deduct* Annual exemption | 6,800 |
| Taxable gains | £4,500 |

Tax payable:
| | |
|---|---:|
| 3,540 @ 20% (unused part of lower rate band) | 708.00 |
| 960 @ 40% (taxable income exceeds revised basic rate limit) | 384.00 |
| £4,500 | |

| | |
|---|---:|
| CGT liability | £1,092.00 |
| **Total net liability** £(392 + 1,092) | £1,484.00 |

201.2 **ANNUAL EXEMPTION** [*TCGA 1992, ss 2(2)(4)(5), 3; FA 1998, s 121(3)(4), 21 Sch 2,3*]

### (A) Interaction with losses

For 1999/2000, R has chargeable gains (after indexation but before taper relief) of £14,800 and allowable losses of £4,500. He also has allowable losses of £10,700 brought forward.

|  | £ |
|---|---:|
| Adjusted net gains (£14,800 – £4,500) | 10,300 |
| Losses brought forward (part) | 3,200 |
|  | 7,100 |
| Annual exempt amount | 7,100 |
| Taxable gains | Nil |
| Losses brought forward | 10,700 |
| *Less* utilised in 1998/99 | 3,200 |
| Losses carried forward | £7,500 |

**Note**

(*a*) TAPER RELIEF (226), if otherwise available in respect of the 1999/2000 chargeable gains, is effectively lost as the taxable gains are reduced to nil in any case.

# Annual Rates and Exemptions 201.2

**(B) Interaction with losses and attributed settlement gains**

**(i)**
For 1999/2000, P has the same gains and losses (including brought-forward losses) as R above, but is also a beneficiary of an offshore trust. Trust gains of £8,000 are attributed to her for 1999/2000 under *TCGA 1992, s 87*.

|  | £ |
|---|---:|
| Adjusted net gains (£14,800 − £4,500 + £7,100 (note (*a*)) | 17,400 |
| Losses brought forward (part) | 10,300 |
|  | 7,100 |
| Annual exempt amount | 7,100 |
|  | Nil |
| *Add:* Sec 87 gains not brought in above | 900 |
| Taxable gains | £900 |
| Losses brought forward | 10,700 |
| *Less* utilised in 1999/2000 | 10,300 |
| Losses carried forward | £400 |

**(ii)**
Q is in the same position as P except that his attributed gains are only £6,000.

|  | £ |
|---|---:|
| Adjusted net gains (£14,800 − £4,500 + £6,000) | 16,300 |
| Losses brought forward (part) | 9,200 |
|  | 7,100 |
| Annual exempt amount | 7,100 |
| Taxable gains | Nil |
| Losses brought forward | 10,700 |
| *Less* utilised in 1999/2000 | 9,200 |
| Losses carried forward | £1,500 |

**Notes**

(*a*) Attributed gains are included in adjusted net gains *only* to the extent that they do not exceed the annual exempt amount. Such gains cannot be covered by personal losses and will already have been reduced by any taper relief available to the trustees. The exempt amount is effectively allocated to attributed gains in priority to personal gains.

(*b*) 'Attributed gains' include, for these purposes, non-resident settlement gains attributed to a beneficiary under *TCGA 1992, s 87* (as in this example), those similarly attributed under *TCGA 1992, s 89(2)*, and gains charged on a settlor under *TCGA 1992, s 77* (UK trust) or *s 86* (non-resident trust).

## 202.1 Anti-Avoidance

## 202 Anti-Avoidance

202.1 **VALUE SHIFTING** [*TCGA 1992, s 29*]
J owns the whole £1,000 £1 ordinary shares of K Ltd. The shares were acquired on subscription in 1971 for £1,000 and had a value of £99,000 on 31 March 1982. In December 1999, the trustees of J's family settlement subscribed at par for 3,000 £1 ordinary shares in K Ltd, thereby acquiring 75% of the voting power in the company. It is agreed that the price an unconnected party would have paid for 75% of the equity in a transaction at arm's length is £150,000. J's remaining 25% holding is valued at £15,000.

**J will have a capital gain for 1999/2000 as follows (subject to indexation allowance to April 1998 plus any available TAPER RELIEF (226))**

|  | £ |
|---|---|
| Proceeds of deemed disposal | 150,000 |
| Allowable cost $\dfrac{150,000}{150,000 + 15,000} \times £99,000$ | 90,000 |
| Unindexed gain | £60,000 |

202.2 **VALUE-SHIFTING TO GIVE TAX-FREE BENEFIT** [*TCGA 1992, s 30, 11 Sch 10(1); FA 1996, 20 Sch 46, 47(a)*]
M owns the whole of the issued share capital in C Ltd, an unquoted company. He is also a director of the company. M receives an offer from a public company for his shares. Prior to sale, C Ltd pays M £30,000 for loss of his office as director. M then sells the shares for £100,000.

**On the sale of M's shares**, the Inland Revenue may seek to adjust the consideration in computing M's chargeable gain on the grounds that M has received a tax-free benefit and the value of his shares has thereby been materially reduced.

202.3 **VALUE SHIFTING: DISTRIBUTION WITHIN A GROUP FOLLOWED BY A DISPOSAL OF SHARES** [*TCGA 1992, ss 30, 31, 11 Sch 10(2); FA 1996, 20 Sch 46, 47(a)*]
Topco Ltd owns 100% of A Ltd, which owns 100% of B Ltd. Both A and B were acquired for negligible amounts. A bought some land in 1988 for a relatively small sum. It is now worth £100,000. In an attempt to realise the proceeds of the land at a tax saving, Topco arranges for B to borrow £100,000. In June 1999, A sells the land to B for this amount, and A, which previously had no undistributed reserves, then pays a dividend of £100,000 to Topco. Topco then sells all of its shares in A Ltd to an unconnected person at their market value which is now a nominal sum.

**On the sale of the A Ltd shares**, the Revenue may seek to apply *TCGA 1992, ss 30, 31* to increase the consideration on the sale by Topco Ltd to £100,000.

**Anti-Avoidance 202.4**

202.4 **ASSETS DISPOSED OF IN A SERIES OF TRANSACTIONS** [*TCGA 1992, ss 19, 20*]

L purchased a set of 6 antique chairs in June 1988 at a cost of £12,000. He gave 2 chairs to his daughter in February 1994, another pair to his son in November 1997, and sold the final pair to his brother for their market value in August 1999.

The market value of the chairs at the relevant dates were

|  | 2 chairs £ | 4 chairs £ | 6 chairs £ |
|---|---|---|---|
| February 1994 | 6,000 | 14,000 | 26,000 |
| November 1997 | 7,800 | 18,000 | 34,200 |
| August 1999 | 10,400 | 24,000 | 46,200 |

Indexation factors are

| | |
|---|---|
| June 1988 – February 1994 | 0.333 |
| June 1988 – November 1997 | 0.497 |
| June 1988 – April 1998 | 0.525 |

**The capital gains tax computations are as follows**

**February 1994**
*Disposal to daughter*

| | |
|---|---|
| Deemed consideration | £6,000 |

As the consideration does not exceed £6,000, the disposal is covered by the chattel exemption (see note (*a*)).

**November 1997**
(i) *1993/94 disposal to daughter recomputed*

| | |
|---|---|
| Original market value (deemed disposal consideration at February 1994) | £6,000 |
| Reasonable proportion of aggregate market value as at February 1994 of all assets disposed of to date £14,000 × $\frac{2}{4}$ | £7,000 |

| | £ |
|---|---|
| Deemed consideration (greater of £6,000 and £7,000) | 7,000 |
| Cost $\dfrac{7,000}{7,000 + 14,000} \times £12,000$ | 4,000 |
| Unindexed gain | 3,000 |
| Indexation allowance £4,000 × 0.333 | 1,332 |
| Chargeable gain 1993/94 | £1,668 |

7

## 202.4 Anti-Avoidance

(ii) *1997/98 disposal to son*

| | |
|---|---:|
| Original market value (deemed disposal consideration) | £7,800 |
| Reasonable proportion of aggregate market value as at November 1997 of all assets disposed of to date £18,000 × $\frac{2}{4}$ | £9,000 |

| | £ |
|---|---:|
| Deemed consideration (greater of £7,800 and £9,000) | 9,000 |
| Cost $\dfrac{9,000}{9,000 + 7,800}$ × (£12,000 − £4,000) | 4,286 |
| Unindexed gain | 4,714 |
| Indexation allowance £4,286 × 0.497 | 2,130 |
| Chargeable gain 1997/98 | £2,584 |

**August 1999**
(i) *Gain on 1993/94 disposal to daughter recomputed*

| | |
|---|---:|
| Original market value (deemed consideration in recomputation at November 1997) | £7,000 |
| Reasonable proportion of aggregate market value as at February 1994 of all assets disposed of to date £26,000 × $\frac{2}{6}$ | £8,667 |

| | £ |
|---|---:|
| Deemed consideration (greater of £7,000 and £8,667) | 8,667 |
| Cost $\dfrac{8,667}{8,667 + 14,000}$ × £12,000 | 4,588 |
| Unindexed gain | 4,079 |
| Indexation allowance £4,588 × 0.333 | 1,528 |
| Revised chargeable gain 1993/94 | £2,551 |

(ii) *Gain on 1997/98 disposal to son recomputed*

| | |
|---|---:|
| Original market value (deemed consideration in computation at November 1997) | £9,000 |
| Reasonable proportion of aggregate market value as at November 1997 of all assets disposed of to date £34,200 × $\frac{2}{6}$ | £11,400 |

|  | £ |
|---|---|
| Deemed consideration (greater of £9,000 and £11,400) | 11,400 |
| Cost $\dfrac{11,400}{11,400 + 7,800} \times (£12,000 - £4,588)$ | 4,401 |
| Unindexed gain | 6,999 |
| Indexation allowance £4,401 × 0.497 | 2,187 |
| Revised chargeable gain 1997/98 | £4,812 |

(iii) *Gain on 1999/2000 disposal to brother*

| | |
|---|---|
| Original market value (actual consideration) | £10,400 |
| Reasonable proportion of aggregate market value as at August 1999 of all assets disposed of to date £46,200 × $\frac{2}{6}$ | £15,400 |

|  | £ |
|---|---|
| Deemed consideration (greater of £10,400 and £15,400) | 15,400 |
| Cost (£12,000 − £4,588 − £4,401) | 3,011 |
| Unindexed gain | 12,389 |
| Indexation allowance £3,011 × 0.525    note (*d*) | 1,581 |
| Chargeable gain 1999/2000 (subject to any available TAPER RELIEF (226)) | £10,808 |

**Notes**

(*a*) The disposal in February 1994 is at first covered by the chattel exemption of £6,000. As the second disposal in November 1997 is to a person connected with the recipient of the first disposal, the two must then be looked at together for the purposes of the chattel exemption, and, as the combined proceeds exceed the chattel exemption limit, the exemption is not available. [*TCGA 1992, s 262*]. See also 208.1(C) EXEMPTIONS AND RELIEFS.

(*b*) The three disposals are linked transactions within *TCGA 1992, s 19* as they are made by the same transferor to persons with whom he is connected, and take place within a six-year period.

(*c*) It is assumed in the above example that it is 'reasonable' to apportion the aggregate market value in proportion to the number of items. In other instances a different basis may be needed to give the 'reasonable' apportionment required by *TCGA 1992, s 20(4)*.

(*d*) Other than for the purposes of corporation tax on chargeable gains, indexation allowance is frozen at its April 1998 level. Therefore, the indexation factor for April 1998 is used in respect of disposals in a later month (and expenditure incurred in April 1998 or later does not attract indexation allowance at all). See 210 INDEXATION.

## 202.5  Anti-Avoidance

202.5 **DEPRECIATORY TRANSACTIONS: GROUPS OF COMPANIES** [*TCGA 1992, s 176; FA 1996, 20 Sch 57*]

G Ltd owns 100% of the share capital of Q Ltd, which it acquired in June 1986 for £75,000. Q Ltd owns land which it purchased in 1982 for £50,000. In 1991, the land, then with a market value of £120,000, was transferred to G Ltd for £50,000. In April 1999, Q Ltd was put into liquidation, and G Ltd received liquidation distributions totalling £30,000.

**The loss on the Q Ltd shares** is £45,000 (£75,000 − £30,000). The Inland Revenue are likely to disallow the whole or part of the loss on the grounds that it resulted from the depreciatory transaction involving the transfer of land at less than market value.

# 203 Assets held on 6 April 1965

## 203.1 QUOTED SHARES AND SECURITIES [*TCGA 1992, s 109(4)(5), 2 Sch 1–8; FA 1996, 21 Sch 42(1)(2)*]

### (A) Basic computation of gain

H acquired 3,000 U plc ordinary shares in 1962 for £15,000. Their market value was £10 per share on 6 April 1965 and £12 per share on 31 March 1982. In September 1999, H sells 2,000 of the shares for £30 per share. The indexation factor for March 1982 to April 1998 is 1.047 (see note (*e*)).

|  | £ | £ | £ |
|---|---:|---:|---:|
| Sale proceeds | 60,000 | 60,000 | 60,000 |
| Cost | 10,000 | | |
| 6 April 1965 value | | 20,000 | |
| 31 March 1982 value | | | 24,000 |
| Unindexed gain | 50,000 | 40,000 | 36,000 |
| Indexation allowance: | | | |
| £24,000 × 1.047 | 25,128 | 25,128 | 25,128 |
| Indexed gain | £24,872 | £14,872 | £10,872 |

Chargeable gain (subject to any available TAPER RELIEF (226))  £10,872

### Notes

(*a*) The comparison is firstly between the gain arrived at by deducting cost and that arrived at by deducting 6 April 1965 value. The smaller of the two gains is taken. If, however, an election had been made under either *TCGA 1992, 2 Sch 4* or *TCGA 1992, s 109(4)* for 6 April 1965 value to be used in computing all gains and losses on quoted shares held at that date, this comparison need not be made and the taxable gain, subject to (*b*) below, would be £14,872.

(*b*) The second comparison is between the figure arrived at in (*a*) above and the gain using 31 March 1982 value. As the latter is smaller, it is substituted for the figure in (*a*) above by virtue of *TCGA 1992, s 35(2)*. If, however, an election had been made under *TCGA 1992, s 35(5)* for 31 March 1982 value to be used in computing all gains and losses on assets held at that date, neither this comparison nor that in (*a*) above need be made and the taxable gain would still be £10,872.

(*c*) Indexation is based on 31 March 1982 value in all three calculations as this gives the greater allowance. [*TCGA 1992, s 55(1)(2)*].

(*d*) All comparisons should be made between gains *after* indexation.

(*e*) Other than for the purposes of corporation tax on chargeable gains, indexation allowance is frozen at its April 1998 level. Therefore, the indexation factor for April 1998 is used in respect of disposals in a later month (and expenditure incurred in April 1998 or later does not attract indexation allowance at all). See 210 INDEXATION.

### (B) Basic computation—no gain/no loss disposals

J acquired a holding of quoted shares in 1953 for £1,000. The market value of the holding at 6 April 1965 and 31 March 1982 respectively was £19,000 and £20,000. J sells the holding in September 1999 for £18,000. The indexation factor for the period March 1982 to April 1998 is 1.047.

## 203.1 Assets held on 6 April 1965

*(i) Assuming no elections made to use 1965 value or 1982 value*

|  | £ | £ |
|---|---:|---:|
| Sale proceeds | 18,000 | 18,000 |
| Cost | 1,000 | |
| 6 April 1965 value | | 19,000 |
| Unindexed gain/(loss) | 17,000 | (1,000) |
| Indexation allowance: | | |
| £20,000 × 1.047 (see below) = £20,940 but restricted to | 17,000 | — |
| Indexed gain/(loss) | Nil | £(1,000) |
| Chargeable gain/allowable loss | | Nil |

As one computation shows no gain/no loss and the other a loss, the disposal is a no gain/no loss disposal. [*TCGA 1992, 2 Sch 2(1)*]. There is no need to compute the gain or loss using 31 March 1982 value as re-basing cannot disturb a no gain/no loss position. [*TCGA 1992, s 35(3)(c)*]. Other than for the purposes of corporation tax on chargeable gains, indexation allowance is frozen at its April 1998 level. Therefore, the indexation factor for April 1998 is used in respect of disposals in a later month (and expenditure incurred in April 1998 or later does not attract indexation allowance at all). See 210 INDEXATION.

*(ii) Election made to use 6 April 1965 value*

|  | £ | £ |
|---|---:|---:|
| Sale proceeds | 18,000 | 18,000 |
| 6 April 1965 value | 19,000 | |
| 31 March 1982 value | | 20,000 |
| (Loss) | (1,000) | (2,000) |
| Allowable loss | £1,000 | |

The allowable loss is £1,000 as re-basing cannot increase a loss. [*TCGA 1992, s 35(3)(b)*].

*(iii) Election made to use 31 March 1982 value*

There is an allowable loss of £2,000.

### (C) Parts of holding acquired at different times

L has the following transactions in shares of A plc, a quoted company

| Date | Number of shares bought/(sold) | Cost/(proceeds) £ |
|---|---:|---:|
| 9.1.55 | 1,500 | 1,050 |
| 10.11.62 | 750 | 600 |
| 15.7.69 | 1,200 | 3,000 |
| 12.10.80 | 1,400 | 5,000 |
| 16.12.83 | 850 | 5,950 |
| 17.9.93 | 1,150 | 5,200 |
| 19.12.99 | (6,000) | (63,000) |
| | 850 | |

Market value of A shares at 6 April 1965 was £1.60
Market value of A shares at 31 March 1982 was £4.00

# Assets held on 6 April 1965  203.1

Indexation factors  March 1982 to April 1998 (note (*c*))  1.047
December 1983 to April 1985  0.091
April 1985 to September 1993  0.497
September 1993 to April 1998 (note (*c*))  0.146

### (i) No election made to substitute 1965 market value

Identify 6,000 shares sold on a LIFO basis as follows

*Section 104 holding*

| | Shares | Qualifying Expenditure £ | Indexed Pool £ |
|---|---|---|---|
| 16.12.83 acquisition | 850 | 5,950 | 5,950 |
| £5,950 × 0.091 | | | 541 |
| 6.4.85 pool | 850 | 5,950 | 6,491 |
| Indexed rise: April 1985 to September 1993 | | | |
| £6,491 × 0.497 | | | 3,226 |
| 17.9.93 acquisition | 1,150 | 5,200 | 5,200 |
| | 2,000 | 11,150 | 14,917 |
| Indexed rise: September 1993 to April 1998 | | | |
| £14,917 × 0.146 | | | 2,178 |
| | | | 17,095 |
| 19.12.99 disposal | (2,000) | (11,150) | (17,095) |
| Balance of pool | — | — | — |

| | £ |
|---|---|
| Sale proceeds (2,000 × £10.50) | 21,000 |
| Cost (as above) | 11,150 |
| Unindexed gain | 9,850 |
| Indexation allowance (£17,095 − £11,150) | 5,945 |
| Chargeable gain (subject to any available TAPER RELIEF (226)) | £3,905 |

*1982 holding*

| | £ | £ |
|---|---|---|
| Sale proceeds (1,200 + 1,400) × £10.50 | 27,300 | 27,300 |
| Cost (£3,000 + £5,000) | 8,000 | |
| Market value 31.3.82 (2,600 × £4) | | 10,400 |
| Unindexed gain | 19,300 | 16,900 |
| Indexation allowance £10,400 × 1.047 | 10,889 | 10,889 |
| Gain after indexation | £8,411 | £6,011 |
| Chargeable gain (subject to any available TAPER RELIEF (226)) | | £6,011 |

## 203.1 Assets held on 6 April 1965

| | £ | £ | £ |
|---|---|---|---|
| *10.11.62 acquisition* | | | |
| Sale proceeds (750 × £10.50) | 7,875 | 7,875 | 7,875 |
| Cost | 600 | | |
| Market value 6.4.65 (750 × £1.60) | | 1,200 | |
| Market value 31.3.82 (750 × £4) | | | 3,000 |
| Unindexed gain | 7,275 | 6,675 | 4,875 |
| Indexation allowance £3,000 × 1.047 | 3,141 | 3,141 | 3,141 |
| Gain after indexation | £4,134 | £3,534 | £1,734 |
| Chargeable gain (subject to any available TAPER RELIEF (226)) | | | £1,734 |

| | £ | £ | £ |
|---|---|---|---|
| *9.1.55 acquisition (part)* | | | |
| Sale proceeds (650 × £10.50) | 6,825 | 6,825 | 6,825 |
| Cost (650 × £0.70) | 455 | | |
| Market value 6.4.65 (650 × £1.60) | | 1,040 | |
| Market value 31.3.82 (650 × £4) | | | 2,600 |
| Unindexed gain | 6,370 | 5,785 | 4,225 |
| Indexation allowance £2,600 × 1.047 | 2,722 | 2,722 | 2,722 |
| Gain after indexation | £3,648 | £3,063 | £1,503 |
| Chargeable gain (subject to any available TAPER RELIEF (226)) | | | £1,503 |

| *Summary of chargeable gains* | Number of shares | Chargeable gain £ |
|---|---|---|
| Section 104 holding | 2,000 | 3,905 |
| 1982 holding | 2,600 | 6,011 |
| 10.11.62 acquisition | 750 | 1,734 |
| 9.1.55 acquisition (part) | 650 | 1,503 |
| | 6,000 | £13,153 |

*Remaining shares*
850 acquired on 9.1.55 for £595

# Assets held on 6 April 1965 203.1

## (ii) Election made to substitute 1965 market value

Identify 6,000 shares on a LIFO basis as follows

*Section 104 holding*
Disposal of 2,000 shares as in (i) above £3,905

| *1982 holding* | Shares | | Pool cost £ |
|---|---|---|---|
| 9.1.55 | 1,500 × £1.60 | | 2,400 |
| 10.11.62 | 750 × £1.60 | | 1,200 |
| 15.7.69 | 1,200 | | 3,000 |
| 12.10.80 | 1,400 | | 5,000 |
| | 4,850 | | 11,600 |
| 19.12.99 Disposal | 4,000 | 4,000/4,850 × £11,600 | 9,567 |
| *Remaining shares* | 850 | | £2,033 |

| | £ | £ |
|---|---|---|
| Sale proceeds (4,000 × £10.50) | 42,000 | 42,000 |
| Cost (as above) | 9,567 | |
| Market value 31.3.82 (4,000 × £4) | | 16,000 |
| Unindexed gain | 32,433 | 26,000 |
| Indexation allowance £16,000 × 1.047 | 16,752 | 16,752 |
| Gain after indexation | £15,681 | £9,248 |
| Chargeable gain (subject to any available TAPER RELIEF (226)) | | £9,248 |

| *Summary of chargeable gains/allowable losses* | Number of shares | Chargeable gain/(loss) £ |
|---|---|---|
| *Section 104* holding | 2,000 | 3,905 |
| 1982 holding | 4,000 | 9,248 |
| | 6,000 | £13,153 |

### Notes

(a) Because re-basing to 31 March 1982 applies in this case, the result is the same whether or not the election to substitute 6 April 1965 value has been made, but with a lower 31 March 1982 value the computations could produce differing overall gains/losses.

(b) Note that indexation is based on 31 March 1982 value whenever this gives the greater allowance, and that comparisons are made between gains *after* indexation.

(c) Other than for the purposes of corporation tax on chargeable gains, indexation allowance is frozen at its April 1998 level. Therefore, the indexation factor for April 1998 is used in respect of disposals in a later month (and expenditure incurred in April 1998 or later does not attract indexation allowance at all). See 210 INDEXATION.

(d) See 225.1 SHARES AND SECURITIES (IDENTIFICATION RULES) for rules for matching disposals after 5 April 1998 with acquisitions after that date (not illustrated in this example).

## 203.2 Assets held on 6 April 1965

203.2 **LAND REFLECTING DEVELOPMENT VALUE** [*TCGA 1992, 2 Sch 9–15*]

K sells a building plot, on which planning permission has just been obtained, in November 1999 for £200,000. He acquired the plot by gift from his father in 1955 when its value was £2,000. The market value was £5,000 at 6 April 1965 and £10,000 at 31 March 1982, and the current use value in November 1999 is £15,000. The indexation factor for March 1982 to April 1998 is 1.047 (see note (*d*)).

|  | £ | £ | £ |
|---|---:|---:|---:|
| Sale proceeds | 200,000 | 200,000 | 200,000 |
| Cost | 2,000 | | |
| Market value 6.4.65 | | 5,000 | |
| Market value 31.3.82 | | | 10,000 |
| Unindexed gain | 198,000 | 195,000 | 190,000 |
| Indexation allowance | | | |
| £10,000 × 1.047 | 10,470 | 10,470 | 10,470 |
| Gain after indexation | £187,530 | £184,530 | £179,530 |
| Chargeable gain (subject to any available TAPER RELIEF (226)) | | | £179,530 |

**Notes**

(*a*) Time apportionment would have substantially reduced the gain of £179,530, using cost, such that re-basing to 31 March 1982 would have given a greater gain than that based on cost and would not therefore have applied. However, as the plot has been sold for a price in excess of its current use value, no time apportionment can be claimed.

(*b*) Gains must be compared after applying the indexation allowance, which is based on 31 March 1982 value, this being greater than either cost or 6 April 1965 value.

(*c*) Other than for the purposes of corporation tax on chargeable gains, indexation allowance is frozen at its April 1998 level. Therefore, the indexation factor for April 1998 is used in respect of disposals in a later month (and expenditure incurred in April 1998 or later does not attract indexation allowance at all). See 210 INDEXATION.

(*d*) In this case, the gain is computed in accordance with the rules in 204 ASSETS HELD ON 31 MARCH 1982 as the gain by reference to 31 March 1982 value is lower than the gain by reference to 6 April 1965 value which in turn is lower than the gain by reference to cost.

### Assets held on 6 April 1965    203.3

**203.3 OTHER ASSETS** [*TCGA 1992, 2 Sch 16–19; FA 1996, 21 Sch 42(1)(3)*]

**(A) Chattels**

M inherited a painting on the death of his mother in 1944, when it was valued for probate at £5,000. On 5 October 1999 he sold the painting for £270,000 net. The painting's value was £130,000 at 6 April 1965, but only £125,000 at 31 March 1982. The indexation factor for March 1982 to April 1998 is 1.047 (see note (*d*)).

**(i) Time apportionment**

| | | |
|---|---|---|
| Period of ownership since 6 April 1945   note (*a*) | | 54 years 6 months |
| Period of ownership since 6 April 1965 | | 34 years 6 months |

| | £ |
|---|---|
| Unindexed gain (£270,000 – £5,000) | 265,000 |
| Indexation allowance £125,000 × 1.047   note (*b*) | 130,875 |
| | £134,125 |

Gain after indexation £134,125 × $\dfrac{34y\ 6m}{54y\ 6m}$   note (*c*)     £84,905

**(ii) Election for 6.4.65 value**

| | £ |
|---|---|
| Sale proceeds | 270,000 |
| Market value 6.4.65 | 130,000 |
| Unindexed gain | 140,000 |
| Indexation allowance £130,000 × 1.047   note (*b*) | 136,110 |
| Gain after indexation | £3,890 |

Election for 6.4.65 value is beneficial, subject to re-basing.

**(iii) Re-basing to 1982**

| | £ |
|---|---|
| Sale proceeds | 270,000 |
| Market value 31.3.82 | 125,000 |
| Unindexed gain | 145,000 |
| Indexation allowance £130,000 × 1.047   note (*b*) | 136,110 |
| Gain after indexation | £8,890 |

**Re-basing cannot increase a gain.** [*TCGA 1992, s 35(3)(a)*]. **Therefore, the gain of £3,890 stands** (subject to any available TAPER RELIEF (226), and see note (*e*)) **and the election for 6.4.65 value is beneficial.**

**Notes**

(*a*)   Under time apportionment, the period of ownership is limited to that after 5 April 1945.

(*b*)   In (i) above, indexation is based on 31.3.82 value, being greater than cost — it cannot be based on 6 April 1965 value as this does not enter into the calculation. In (ii), indexation is on the higher of 31.3.82 value and 6.4.65 value. This is also the case in (iii) as one is comparing the position using 6.4.65 value and 31.3.82 value. See *TCGA 1992, s 55(1)(2)*.

(*c*)   The time apportionment calculation is applied to the gain *after* indexation (*Smith v Schofield* HL 1993, 65 TC 669, [1993] STC 268).

## 203.3   Assets held on 6 April 1965

(d)   Other than for the purposes of corporation tax on chargeable gains, indexation allowance is frozen at its April 1998 level. Therefore, the indexation factor for April 1998 is used in respect of disposals in a later month (and expenditure incurred in April 1998 or later does not attract indexation allowance at all). See 210 INDEXATION.

(e)   Any available taper relief should be computed by reference to the *chargeable* gain. Therefore, if time apportionment had produced the lower gain (disregarding taper relief at this stage), it is the time-apportioned gain that would be tapered. This is because taper relief comes after all other reliefs apart from the annual exemption. [*TCGA 1992, s 2A(1)(2); FA 1998, s 121(1)(4)*].

### (B) Land and buildings

X acquired land on 5 June 1960 as a distribution in specie on liquidation of his company. The value of the land was then £7,250. He acquired access land adjoining the property for £2,750 on 1 January 1961 and, having obtained planning consent, on 30 July 1963 incurred expenditure of £15,000 in building houses on the land, which were let. On 6 September 1999, X sells the houses with vacant possession for £300,000, net of expenses. The value of the houses and land is £20,000 at 6 April 1965 and £100,000 at 31 March 1982. The indexation factor for March 1982 to April 1998 is 1.047 (see note (*d*)).

**The gain using time apportionment is**

|  | £ | £ |
|---|---:|---:|
| Net proceeds of sale |  | 300,000 |
| *Deduct* Cost of land | 7,250 |  |
| Cost of addition | 2,750 |  |
| Cost of building | 15,000 | 25,000 |
| Unindexed gain |  | 275,000 |
| Indexation allowance £100,000 × 1.047 |  | 104,700 |
| Gain after indexation |  | £170,300 |

Apportion to allowable expenditure   note (*c*)

|  | £ | £ |
|---|---:|---:|
| (i) Land $\dfrac{7{,}250}{25{,}000} \times £170{,}300$ | 49,387 |  |
| Time apportion £49,387 × $\dfrac{34\text{y } 5\text{m}}{39\text{y } 3\text{m}}$ |  | 43,306 |
| (ii) Addition $\dfrac{2{,}750}{25{,}000} \times £170{,}300$ | 18,733 |  |
| Time apportion £18,733 × $\dfrac{34\text{y } 5\text{m}}{38\text{y } 8\text{m}}$ |  | 16,674 |
|  |  | c/f 59,980 |

# Assets held on 6 April 1965 203.3

|  |  |  |
|---|---|---|
|  |  | b/f 59,980 |
| (iii) Building $\dfrac{15{,}000}{25{,}000} \times £170{,}300$ | 102,180 |  |
| Time apportion $£102{,}180 \times \dfrac{34\text{y } 5\text{m}}{36\text{y } 1\text{m}}$ |  | 97,462 |
| Gain after indexation and time apportionment |  | £157,442 |

**The gain using re-basing to 1982 is**

|  | £ |
|---|---|
| Net proceeds of sale | 300,000 |
| Market value at 31.3.82 | 100,000 |
| Unindexed gain | 200,000 |
| Indexation allowance | |
| £100,000 × 1.047 | 104,700 |
| Gain | £95,300 |

**Chargeable gain** (subject to any available
TAPER RELIEF (226), and see note (*e*))                              £95,300

## Notes

(*a*) An election for 6 April 1965 valuation could not be favourable, even were it not for the effect of re-basing, as the value is less than historic costs.

(*b*) It is the gain/loss *after* time apportionment that is compared with the gain/loss produced by re-basing. [*TCGA 1992, 3 Sch 6*].

(*c*) The time apportionment calculation is applied to the gain *after* indexation (*Smith v Schofield HL 1993, 65 TC 669, [1993] STC 268*).

(*d*) Other than for the purposes of corporation tax on chargeable gains, indexation allowance is frozen at its April 1998 level. Therefore, the indexation factor for April 1998 is used in respect of disposals in a later month (and expenditure incurred in April 1998 or later does not attract indexation allowance at all). See 210 INDEXATION.

(*e*) Any available taper relief should be computed by reference to the *chargeable* gain. Therefore, if time apportionment had produced the lower gain (disregarding taper relief at this stage), it is the time-apportioned gain that would be tapered. This is because taper relief comes after all other reliefs apart from the annual exemption. [*TCGA 1992, s 2A(1)(2); FA 1998, s 121(1)(4)*].

## 203.3  Assets held on 6 April 1965

**(C) Unquoted shares**
On 6 April 1951, A acquired 5,000 shares in C Ltd, an unquoted company, for £15,201. At 6 April 1965, the value of the holding was £15,000. A sells the shares (his entire holding in the company) on 6 April 1999 for £75,000. The indexation factor for the period March 1982 to April 1998 is 1.047 (note (*b*)). No election for universal 31 March 1982 re-basing is made but the market value of the holding at that date is agreed at £17,000.

**The gain using time apportionment is as follows**

| | | |
|---|---|---|
| Total period of ownership: | 48 years | |
| Period after 6 April 1965: | 34 years | |
| | | £ |
| Proceeds | | 75,000 |
| Cost | | 15,201 |
| Unindexed gain | | 59,799 |
| Indexation allowance: | | |
| 31.3.82 value £17,000 × 1.047 | | 17,799 |
| Gain after indexation | | £42,000 |
| Gain after time apportionment: £42,000 × 34/48 | | £29,750 |

**The gain with an election to use 6.4.65 value is as follows**

| | £ |
|---|---|
| Proceeds | 75,000 |
| 6.4.65 value | 15,000 |
| Unindexed gain | 60,000 |
| Indexation allowance: | |
| 31.3.82 value £17,000 × 1.047 | 17,799 |
| Gain after indexation | £42,201 |

**The gain with re-basing to 1982 is as follows**

| | £ |
|---|---|
| Proceeds | 75,000 |
| 31.3.82 value | 17,000 |
| Unindexed gain | 58,000 |
| Indexation allowance: | |
| 31.3.82 value £17,000 × 1.047 | 17,799 |
| Gain after indexation | £40,201 |

Time apportionment is more beneficial than an election for 6 April 1965 value. Re-basing does not apply as it cannot increase a gain. The chargeable gain is therefore **£29,750** (subject to note (*a*)).

**Notes**

(*a*)  Any available taper relief should be computed by reference to the *chargeable* gain. Therefore, if, as in this example, time apportionment produces the lower gain (disregarding taper relief in making the comparison), it is the time-apportioned gain that is tapered. This is because taper relief comes after all other reliefs apart from the annual exemption. [*TCGA 1992, s 2A(1)(2); FA 1998, s 121(1)(4)*]. See generally 226 TAPER RELIEF.

(*b*)  Other than for the purposes of corporation tax on chargeable gains, indexation allowance is frozen at its April 1998 level. See 210 INDEXATION.

# Assets held on 6 April 1965   203.3

**(D) Unquoted shares — share exchange before 6 April 1965** [*TCGA 1992, 2 Sch 19(1)(3)*]

N purchased 5,000 £1 ordinary shares in R Ltd, an unquoted company, on 1 January 1961. The purchase price was £3 per share, a total of £15,000. On 1 December 1964, R Ltd was acquired by D Ltd, an unquoted company, as a result of which N received 10,000 8% convertible preference shares in D Ltd in exchange for his holding of R shares. In November 1999, N sold the D Ltd shares for £4.45 per share. The market value of the D Ltd shares was £2.03 per share at 6 April 1965 but only £1.50 per share at 31 March 1982. The indexation factor for March 1982 to April 1998 is 1.047 (see note (*e*)).

**The gain, disregarding re-basing, is**

|  | £ |
|---|---|
| Disposal consideration 10,000 at £4.45 | 44,500 |
| Allowable cost       10,000 at £2.03 | 20,300 |
| Unindexed gain | 24,200 |
| Indexation allowance £20,300 × 1.047 | 21,254 |
| Gain after indexation | £2,946 |

**The gain using re-basing to 1982 is**

|  | £ |
|---|---|
| Disposal consideration (as above) | 44,500 |
| Market value 31.3.82 10,000 at £1.50 | 15,000 |
| Unindexed gain | 29,500 |
| Indexation allowance £20,300 × 1.047 | 21,254 |
| Gain after indexation | £8,246 |

**The overall result is**

Chargeable gain (subject to any available TAPER RELIEF (226))       £2,946

**Notes**

(*a*) Subject to re-basing, allowable cost must be taken as 6.4.65 value.

(*b*) Indexation is based on the greater of 31.3.82 value and 6.4.65 value. [*TCGA 1992, s 55(1)(2)*].

(*c*) Where the effect of re-basing would be to increase a gain, re-basing does not apply. [*TCGA 1992, s 35(3)(a)*].

(*d*) By concession (ESC D10), CGT is not charged on a disposal of the *entire* new shareholding on more than the actual gain realised, i.e. by reference to original cost but without time apportionment.

(*e*) Other than for the purposes of corporation tax on chargeable gains, indexation allowance is frozen at its April 1998 level. Therefore, the indexation factor for April 1998 is used in respect of disposals in a later month (and expenditure incurred in April 1998 or later does not attract indexation allowance at all). See 210 INDEXATION.

## 203.3 Assets held on 6 April 1965

**(E) Unquoted shares — share exchange after 5 April 1965** [*TCGA 1992, 2 Sch 19(2)(3)*]

S purchased 10,000 £1 ordinary shares in L Ltd for £5,000 on 31 May 1959. The shares are not quoted, and their value at 6 April 1965 was £6,000. On 1 September 1989, the shares were acquired by R plc, in exchange for its own ordinary shares on the basis of 1 for 2. The offer valued L ordinary shares at £2.23 per share. In February 2000, S sells his 5,000 R shares for £8.60 per share. The agreed value of the L Ltd shares at 31 March 1982 was £2.05 per share.

| Indexation factors | March 1982 to September 1989 | 0.468 |
|---|---|---|
| | September 1989 to April 1998 (note (*c*)) | 0.395 |
| | March 1982 to April 1998 ((note (*c*)) | 1.047 |

**The gain without re-basing to 1982 is computed as follows**

*(i) Using time apportionment*

Deemed disposal at 1.9.89:

| | £ |
|---|---:|
| Proceeds (market value £2.23 × 10,000) | 22,300 |
| Cost | 5,000 |
| Unindexed gain | 17,300 |
| Indexation allowance | |
| MV 31.3.82 10,000 × £2.05 × 0.468 | 9,594 |
| Gain after indexation | £7,706 |

Gain after time apportionment:

$$£7{,}706 \times \frac{24y\ 5m}{30y\ 3m} \qquad £6{,}220$$

Actual disposal in February 2000:

| | £ |
|---|---:|
| Proceeds 5,000 × £8.60 | 43,000 |
| Deemed acquisition cost at 1.9.89 | 22,300 |
| Unindexed gain | 20,700 |
| Indexation allowance £22,300 × 0.395 | 8,809 |
| Gain after indexation | 11,891 |

| | |
|---|---:|
| Total gain 1999/2000 £(6,220 + 11,891) | £18,111 |

*(ii) With election for 6.4.65 value*

| | £ |
|---|---:|
| Disposal consideration | 43,000 |
| Allowable cost | 6,000 |
| Unindexed gain | 37,000 |
| Indexation allowance 10,000 × £2.05 × 1.047 | 21,463 |
| Gain | £15,537 |

The election is beneficial.

# Assets held on 6 April 1965 203.3

**The gain using re-basing to 1982 is**

|  | £ |
|---|---|
| Disposal consideration | 43,000 |
| Market value 31.3.82 10,000 × £2.05 | 20,500 |
| Unindexed gain | 22,500 |
| Indexation allowance £20,500 × 1.047 | 21,463 |
| Gain after indexation | £1,037 |

**The overall result is**

Chargeable gain (subject to any available TAPER RELIEF (226))                £1,037

Re-basing applies as it produces a smaller gain than that using 6 April 1965 value.

**Notes**

(*a*)   The deemed disposal on 1 September 1989 is *only* for the purposes of *TCGA 1992, 2 Sch 16* (time apportionment).

(*b*)   If an election is made for 6 April 1965 value, no valuation is required at 1 September 1989.

(*c*)   Other than for the purposes of corporation tax on chargeable gains, indexation allowance is frozen at its April 1998 level. Therefore, the indexation factor for April 1998 is used in respect of disposals in a later month (and expenditure incurred in April 1998 or later does not attract indexation allowance at all). See 210 INDEXATION.

## 203.3 Assets held on 6 April 1965

**(F) Part disposals after 5 April 1965** [*TCGA 1992, s 42, 2 Sch 16(8)*]
H bought land for £15,000 on 31 October 1960. Its value at 6 April 1965 was £17,200. On 1 February 1990, H sold part of the land for £50,000, the balance being then worth £200,000. In April 1999, H gives the remaining land to his daughter. Its value is then £300,000. The agreed value of the total estate at 31 March 1982 was £150,000 and H made a claim on the February 1990 disposal for that value to be used for indexation purposes.

| Indexation factors | March 1982 to February 1990 | 0.513 |
|---|---|---|
| | March 1982 to April 1998 (note (*e*)) | 1.047 |

**1990 disposal**

| | £ |
|---|---|
| Proceeds of part disposal | 50,000 |
| *Deduct* allowable cost $\dfrac{50,000}{50,000 + 200,000} \times £15,000$ | 3,000 |
| Unindexed gain | 47,000 |

Indexation allowance $£150,000 \times \dfrac{50,000}{50,000 + 200,000} = £30,000$

| | |
|---|---|
| £30,000 × 0.513 | 15,390 |
| Gain after indexation | £31,610 |

*Time apportionment*

Chargeable gain $\dfrac{24y\ 10m}{29y\ 3m} \times £31,610$ £26,837

If an election were made to substitute 6 April 1965 valuation, the computation would be

| | £ |
|---|---|
| Proceeds of part disposal | 50,000 |
| *Deduct* allowable cost $\dfrac{50,000}{50,000 + 200,000} \times £17,200$ | 3,440 |
| Unindexed gain | 46,560 |

Indexation allowance $£150,000 \times \dfrac{50,000}{50,000 + 200,000} = £30,000$

| | |
|---|---|
| £30,000 × 0.513 | 15,390 |
| Chargeable gain | £31,170 |

An election would not be beneficial.

# Assets held on 6 April 1965 203.3

**1999 disposal**

**The gain without re-basing to 1982 is as follows**

Computation of entire gain over period of ownership:

|  | £ |
|---|---|
| Proceeds | 300,000 |
| Cost £(15,000 − 3,000) | 12,000 |
| Unindexed gain | 288,000 |
| Indexation allowance | |
| MV 31.3.82 £(150,000 − 30,000) × 1.047 | 125,640 |
| Gain after indexation | £162,360(A) |

Computation of gain for period 31.10.60 − 1.2.90:

|  | £ |
|---|---|
| Market value at date of part disposal | 200,000 |
| Cost £(15,000 − 3,000) | 12,000 |
| Unindexed gain | 188,000 |
| Indexation allowance £(150,000 − 30,000) × 0.513 | 61,560 |
| Gain after indexation | £126,440(B) |

Time apportionment £126,440 × $\dfrac{24y\ 10m}{29y\ 3m}$ — £107,346(C)

Balance of gain (1.2.90 to April 1999) ((A) − (B)) — £35,920(D)

Chargeable gain (subject to re-basing) ((C) + (D)) — £143,266

**The gain using re-basing to 1982 is as follows**

|  | £ |
|---|---|
| Disposal proceeds | 300,000 |
| Market value 31.3.82 £150,000 × $\dfrac{12,000}{15,000}$  note (*b*) | 120,000 |
| Unindexed gain | 180,000 |
| Indexation allowance £120,000 × 1.047 | 125,640 |
| Gain after indexation | £54,360 |

**The overall result is**

| Chargeable gain | £54,360 |
|---|---|

Re-basing applies as it produces neither a larger gain nor a loss.

## 203.3 Assets held on 6 April 1965

**Notes**

(a) The deemed disposal on 1 February 1990 is only for the purposes of *TCGA 1992, 2 Sch 16(3)–(5)* (time apportionment). For re-basing purposes, the asset is still regarded as having been held at 31 March 1982.

(b) Where there has been a part disposal after 31 March 1982 and before 6 April 1988 of an asset held at 31 March 1982, the proportion of 31 March 1982 value to be brought into account in the re-basing calculation is that which the cost previously unallowed bears to the total cost, giving the same effect as if re-basing had applied to the part disposal. [*TCGA 1992, 3 Sch 4(1)*].

(c) The Revenue will also accept an alternative basis of calculation on the part disposal of land. Under this method, the part disposed of is treated as a separate asset and any fair and reasonable method of apportioning part of the total cost to it will be accepted e.g. a reasonable valuation of that part at the acquisition date. (Revenue Statement of Practice SP D1.)

(d) The time apportionment calculation is applied to the gain *after* indexation (*Smith v Schofield HL 1993, 65 TC 669, [1993] STC 268*).

(e) Other than for the purposes of corporation tax on chargeable gains, indexation allowance is frozen at its April 1998 level. See 210 INDEXATION.

# 204  Assets held on 31 March 1982

## 204.1 GENERAL COMPUTATION OF GAINS/LOSSES [*TCGA 1992, s 35, 3 Sch*]

**(A)**
Rodney purchased a painting on 1 October 1979 for £50,000 (including costs of acquisition) and sold it at auction for £160,000 (net of selling expenses) on 15 August 1999. Its value at 31 March 1982 was £70,000 and the indexation factor for the period March 1982 to April 1998 is 1.047 (see note (*f*)).

|  | £ | £ |
|---|---:|---:|
| Net sale proceeds | 160,000 | 160,000 |
| Cost | 50,000 |  |
| Market value 31.3.82 |  | 70,000 |
| Unindexed gain | 110,000 | 90,000 |
| Indexation allowance £70,000 × 1.047 | 73,290 | 73,290 |
| Gain after indexation | £36,710 | £16,710 |
| Chargeable gain |  | £16,710 |

**Notes**

(*a*) The asset is deemed to have been sold and immediately re-acquired at its market value at 31 March 1982. [*TCGA 1992, s 35(1)(2)*].

(*b*) Re-basing does not apply if it would produce a larger gain or larger loss than would otherwise be the case, nor if it would turn a gain into a loss or vice versa, nor if the disposal would otherwise be a no gain/no loss disposal. [*TCGA 1992, s 35(3)(4)*].

(*c*) An *irrevocable* election may be made to treat, broadly speaking, *all* assets held on 31 March 1982 as having been sold and re-acquired at their market value on that date, in which case the restrictions in (*b*) above will not apply. [*TCGA 1992, s 35(5)*]. If the election had been made in this example, the gain would still be £16,710, but there would have been no need to compute the gain by reference to cost and make a comparison with that using re-basing.

There are some minor exclusions from the rule that the election must extend to all assets. [*TCGA 1992, 3 Sch 7*]. There are also special rules for groups of companies. [*TCGA 1992, 3 Sch 8, 9*].

(*d*) Indexation is automatically based on 31 March 1982 value, without the need to claim such treatment, unless a greater allowance would be produced by reference to cost. [*TCGA 1992, s 55(1)(2)*]. See also 210.1(C) INDEXATION.

(*e*) See also 203 ASSETS HELD ON 6 APRIL 1965 for the general application of the re-basing provisions to such assets. See 210.2(A)(C) INDEXATION for the position as regards an asset acquired by means of a no gain/no loss transfer from a person who held it at 31 March 1982.

(*f*) Other than for the purposes of corporation tax on chargeable gains, indexation allowance is frozen at its April 1998 level. Therefore, the indexation factor for April 1998 is used in respect of disposals in a later month (and expenditure incurred in April 1998 or later does not attract indexation allowance at all). See 210 INDEXATION.

(*g*) Any available taper relief should be computed by reference to the *chargeable* gain after making the comparison illustrated by this example.

# 204.1 Assets held on 31 March 1982

**(B)**
The facts are as in (A) above, except that net sale proceeds amount to £60,000.

|  | £ | £ |
|---|---:|---:|
| Net sale proceeds | 60,000 | 60,000 |
| Cost | 50,000 | |
| Market value 31.3.82 | | 70,000 |
| Unindexed gain/(loss) | 10,000 | (10,000) |
| Indexation allowance (as in (A)) but restricted to | 10,000 | — |
| Gain/(loss) | Nil | £(10,000) |
| Chargeable gain/(allowable loss) | Nil | |

**Notes**
(a) Re-basing does not apply as it cannot disturb a no gain/no loss position. [*TCGA 1992, s 35(3)(c)*].

(b) An election under *Sec 35(5)* would produce an allowable loss of £10,000 (but must extend to all assets).

**(C)**
The facts are as in (A) above, except that net sale proceeds amount to £135,000.

|  | £ | £ |
|---|---:|---:|
| Net sale proceeds | 135,000 | 135,000 |
| Cost | 50,000 | |
| Market value 31.3.82 | | 70,000 |
| Unindexed gain | 85,000 | 65,000 |
| Indexation allowance (as in (A)) | 73,290 | |
| Indexation allowance (as in (A)) but restricted to | | 65,000 |
| Gain | £11,710 | Nil |
| Chargeable gain/(allowable loss) | | Nil |

**Note**
(a) Re-basing applies as it produces a no gain/no loss position compared to a gain.

# Assets held on 31 March 1982

**(D)**
Albert acquired a holding of D Ltd shares for £11,000 net in January 1980. At 31 March 1982, their value had fallen to £8,000. On 29 April 1999, Albert sold the entire holding for £25,000 net. The indexation factor for the period March 1982 to April 1998 (note (d)) is 1.047.

|  | £ | £ |
|---|---:|---:|
| Proceeds | 25,000 | 25,000 |
| Cost | 11,000 |  |
| Market value 31.3.82 |  | 8,000 |
| Unindexed gain | 14,000 | 17,000 |
| Indexation allowance £11,000 × 1.047 | 11,517 | 11,517 |
| Gain after indexation | £2,483 | £5,483 |
| Chargeable gain | £2,483 |  |

**Notes**
(a) Re-basing does not apply as its effect would be to increase a gain.

(b) Indexation is based on cost as that is greater than 31 March 1982 value.

(c) If a universal re-basing election had been made (under *Sec 35(5)*), the chargeable gain would have been £5,483.

(d) Other than for the purposes of corporation tax on chargeable gains, indexation allowance is frozen at its April 1998 level. See 210 INDEXATION.

**(E)**
Albert in (D) above also acquired a holding of E Ltd shares for £14,000 net in January 1980. At 31 March 1982, their value stood at £17,000. Albert sold the shares in April 1999 for £10,000 net.

|  | £ | £ |
|---|---:|---:|
| Proceeds | 10,000 | 10,000 |
| Cost | 14,000 |  |
| Market value 31.3.82 |  | 17,000 |
| Unindexed loss (no indexation due) | £4,000 | £7,000 |
| Allowable loss | £4,000 |  |

**Notes**
(a) Re-basing does not apply as its effect would be to increase a loss.

(b) Indexation is not available in either calculation as it cannot increase a loss.

(c) If a universal re-basing election had been made (under *Sec 35(5)*), the allowable loss would have been £7,000, but the election must extend to all assets.

## 204.2 Assets held on 31 March 1982

204.2 **DEFERRED CHARGES ON GAINS BEFORE 31 MARCH 1982** [*TCGA 1992, s 36, 4 Sch*]

Kirk purchased 3,000 unquoted ordinary shares in W Limited for £18,000 on 1 January 1980 and later gave them to his son, Michael, claiming hold-over relief under *FA 1980, s 79*. Michael sells the shares for £50,000 (net) on 10 June 1999. The shares had a value of £22,000 at 31 March 1982.

Assuming the gift to have taken place on

  (i)   1 February 1982 (market value of shares £21,000),
  (ii)  30 April 1988 (market value £39,000), and
  (iii) 1 June 1985 (market value £30,000),

the capital gains position is as set out below. The relevant indexation factors are

| | |
|---|---|
| March 1982 to June 1985 | 0.202 |
| March 1982 to April 1988 | 0.332 |
| March 1982 to April 1998 (note (*f*)) | 1.047 |
| June 1985 to April 1998 (note (*f*)) | 0.704 |
| April 1988 to April 1998 (note (*f*)) | 0.537 |

### (i) Gift on 1 February 1982

| | |
|---|---|
| Kirk's chargeable gain (deferred) (£21,000 − £18,000) | £3,000 |
| Michael's acquisition cost (£21,000 − £3,000) | £18,000 |

Michael's chargeable gain is

| | £ | £ |
|---|---:|---:|
| Proceeds 10.6.99 | 50,000 | 50,000 |
| Cost (as above) | 18,000 | |
| Market value 31.3.82 | | 22,000 |
| Unindexed gain | 32,000 | 28,000 |
| Indexation allowance £22,000 × 1.047 | 23,034 | 23,034 |
| Gain after indexation | £8,966 | £4,966 |
| | | |
| Chargeable gain 1999/2000 | | £4,966 |

The deferred gain of £3,000 effectively falls out of charge as Michael held the shares at 31.3.82 and thus receives the benefit of re-basing to 1982.

### (ii) Gift on 30 April 1988

Kirk's chargeable gain is

| | £ | £ |
|---|---:|---:|
| Disposal value | 39,000 | 39,000 |
| Cost | 18,000 | |
| Market value 31.3.82 | | 22,000 |
| Unindexed gain | 21,000 | 17,000 |
| Indexation allowance £22,000 × 0.332 | 7,304 | 7,304 |
| Gain after indexation | £13,696 | £9,696 |
| | | |
| Chargeable gain (deferred) | | £9,696 |

## Assets held on 31 March 1982    204.2

Michael's chargeable gain is

|  | £ | £ |
|---|---:|---:|
| Proceeds 10.6.99 |  | 50,000 |
| Cost | 39,000 |  |
| *Deduct* deferred gain | 9,696 |  |
|  | 29,304 |  |
| Indexation allowance £29,304 × 0.537 | 15,736 | 45,040 |
| Chargeable gain 1999/2000 |  | £4,960 |

Michael cannot re-base to 1982 as he did not hold the shares at 31.3.82. However, as the deferred gain was itself computed by reference to the 31.3.82 value, he has effectively received full relief for the uplift in value between 1.1.80 and 31.3.82. The small difference between his gain of £4,960 and that of £4,966 in (i) above is due to the rounding of indexation factors to three decimal places.

### (iii) Gift on 1 June 1985

Kirk's chargeable gain is

|  | £ | £ |
|---|---:|---:|
| Disposal value |  | 30,000 |
| Cost | 18,000 |  |
| Indexation allowance £22,000 × 0.202 | 4,444 | 22,444 |
| Chargeable gain (deferred) |  | £7,556 |

It is assumed that a claim would have been made to base indexation on the 31.3.82 value, this being greater than cost.

Michael's chargeable gain is

|  | £ | £ |
|---|---:|---:|
| Proceeds 10.6.99 |  | 50,000 |
| Cost | 30,000 |  |
| *Deduct* one-half of deferred gain £7,556 × ½ | 3,778 |  |
|  | 26,222 |  |
| Indexation allowance £26,222 × 0.704 | 18,460 | 44,682 |
| Chargeable gain 1999/2000 |  | £5,318 |

Michael cannot benefit from re-basing to 1982 as he did not hold the shares at 31.3.82, nor is the deferred gain itself calculated by reference to the re-basing rules as the disposal (i.e. the gift) took place before 6.4.88. Under *TCGA 1992, s 36, 4 Sch 1(a), 2*, the deduction in respect of a deferred gain is halved where the deferral took place after 31.3.82 and before 6.4.88 and was, wholly or partly, in respect of a chargeable gain accruing on an asset held at 31.3.82, thus giving some relief, albeit on an arbitrary basis.

#### Notes
(a)   A claim for the deduction to be halved must be made by the first anniversary of 31 January following the year of assessment in which the ultimate disposal takes place. [*TCGA 1992, 4 Sch 9; FA 1996, 21 Sch 43*].

(b)   These provisions apply not only to hold-over relief on gifts, under *FA 1980, s 79*, but to a number of situations in which gains are held over or rolled over, as listed in *TCGA 1992, 4 Sch 2(5)*, of which the most common is rollover relief on

## 204.2 Assets held on 31 March 1982

replacement of business assets under *TCGA 1992, s 152*. [*TCGA 1992, 4 Sch 1(a), 2*].

(c) There are special rules where the disposal giving rise to the deferral is preceded by a no gain/no loss disposal (as defined by *TCGA 1992, s 35(3)(d)*) and where the ultimate disposal is preceded by a no gain/no loss disposal. [*TCGA 1992, 4 Sch 5–7*].

(d) See also 209 HOLD-OVER RELIEFS and 222 ROLLOVER RELIEF for the general application of these reliefs.

(e) General hold-over relief under *FA 1980, s 79* is not available for gifts after 13 March 1989.

(f) Other than for the purposes of corporation tax on chargeable gains, indexation allowance is frozen at its April 1998 level. Therefore, the indexation factor for April 1998 is used in respect of disposals in a later month (and expenditure incurred in April 1998 or later does not attract indexation allowance at all). See 210 INDEXATION.

(g) In all cases, the 1999/2000 chargeable gain is subject to any available TAPER RELIEF (226).

# 205 Companies

**Cross-references.** See also CT 104 CAPITAL GAINS.

## 205.1 CAPITAL LOSSES

P Ltd, which makes up accounts to 30 June annually, changes its accounting date to 31 December. It makes up 18-month accounts to 31 December 1999, and its chargeable gains and allowable losses are as follows

| | Gains/(losses) £ |
|---|---:|
| 31.7.98 | 4,600 |
| 19.10.98 | 11,500 |
| 1.12.98 | 3,500 |
| 28.3.99 | (8,300) |
| 21.7.99 | 8,500 |
| 1.9.99 | (25,000) |
| 20.12.99 | 7,000 |

**The period of account is split into two accounting periods**

| | |
|---|---:|
| **1.7.98 – 30.6.99** | |
| Net chargeable gain | £11,300 |
| **1.7.99 – 31.12.99** | |
| Net allowable loss | £9,500 |

**Notes**

(a) The loss must be carried forward and cannot be set off against the £11,300 net gain.

(b) For a further example, see CT 104.1 CAPITAL GAINS.

## 205.2 Companies

### 205.2 SHARES — ACQUISITIONS AND DISPOSALS WITHIN SHORT PERIOD [*TCGA 1992, s 106*]

S Ltd has the following transactions in shares in Q plc, a quoted company with share capital of £1m divided into 25p ordinary shares.

|  | Date | Number of shares | Price £ |
|---|---|---|---|
| Purchase | 1.6.96 | 100,000 | 62,000 |
| Purchase | 1.8.99 | 50,000 | 49,000 |
| Sale | 15.8.99 | 80,000 | 60,000 |
| Purchase | 31.8.99 | 50,000 | 35,000 |

**The position is as follows**

The shares sold on 15.8.99 are identified with the two purchases on 1.8.99 and 31.8.99.

£

**(i) Purchase on 1.8.99**

| | | |
|---|---|---|
| Proceeds $\dfrac{50,000}{80,000} \times £60,000$ | | 37,500 |
| Cost | | 49,000 |
| Allowable loss | | £11,500 |

**(ii) Purchase on 31.8.99**

| | | |
|---|---|---|
| Proceeds $\dfrac{30,000}{80,000} \times £60,000$ | | 22,500 |
| Cost $\dfrac{30,000}{50,000} \times £35,000$ | | 21,000 |
| Chargeable gain | | £1,500 |

**Allowable loss on transaction** £10,000

### Notes

(*a*) Where a company disposes of shares (including securities other than gilt-edged securities) and acquires similar shares within one month before or after the disposal through a stock exchange or within six months in other circumstances, the shares acquired and disposed of are matched. For these rules to apply, the number of shares held at some time in the one month (or six months) before the disposal must be not less than 2% of the number issued. Shares acquired within one month (or six months) before or after the disposal are called 'available shares'.

(*b*) Subject to *TCGA 1992, s 105* (matching of same day acquisitions and disposals), disposals are identified first from 'available shares', taking acquisitions before the disposal (latest first) before acquisitions after the disposal (earliest first). Once all 'available shares' have been matched with the disposal, the identification of any remaining shares disposed of follows the ordinary rules.

# 206 Disposal

## 206.1 ALLOWABLE AND NON-ALLOWABLE EXPENDITURE

**(A) Allowable expenditure** [*TCGA 1992, s 38*]

In 1999/2000 T sold a house which he had owned since 1987 and which was let throughout the period of ownership (other than as furnished holiday accommodation). The house cost £34,000, with legal costs of £900, in June 1987. T spent £2,000 on initial dilapidations in July 1987. In November 1997, he added an extension at a cost of £5,500 for which he received a local authority grant of £2,500 on completion. Legal costs of £500 were incurred on obtaining vacant possession at the end of the final tenancy in May 1999. The sale proceeds were £70,000 before deducting incidental costs (including valuation fees) of £1,200.

| Indexation factors | | | |
|---|---|---|---|
| June 1987 to April 1998 (note (*b*)) | | 0.596 | |
| July 1987 to April 1998 | | 0.597 | |
| November 1997 to April 1998 | | 0.019 | |

|  | £ | £ | £ |
|---|---|---|---|
| Sale proceeds | | 70,000 | |
| *Deduct* costs of sale | | 1,200 | 68,800 |
| | | | |
| Cost of house | | 34,000 | |
| *Add* incidental costs of purchase | | 900 | |
| | | 34,900 | |
| Improvement costs: | | | |
|   initial dilapidations    note (*a*) | 2,000 | | |
|   extension, less grant | 3,000 | 5,000 | |
| | | | |
| Cost of obtaining vacant possession (enhancement cost) | | 500 | 40,400 |
| | | | |
| Unindexed gain | | 28,400 | |
| Indexation allowance: | | | |
| £34,900 × 0.596 | 20,800 | | |
| £2,000 × 0.597 | 1,194 | | |
| £3,000 × 0.019 | 57 | 22,051 | |
| | | | |
| Chargeable gain | | £6,349 | |

**Notes**

(*a*) It is assumed that the cost of the initial dilapidations would have been disallowed for Schedule A purposes under the rule in *Law Shipping Co Ltd v CIR, CS 1923, 12 TC 621.* If, however, any of the expenditure had been so allowed, a deduction would to that extent be precluded as an allowable deduction for CGT purposes by TCGA 1992, s 39.

(*b*) Other than for the purposes of corporation tax on chargeable gains, indexation allowance is frozen at its April 1998 level. Therefore, the indexation factor for April 1998 is used in respect of disposals in a later month (and expenditure incurred in April 1998 or later does not attract indexation allowance at all). See 210 INDEXATION.

## 206.2 Disposal

(c) No taper relief is due as the asset (being a non-business asset) has not been held for the requisite three-year period after 5 April 1998. [*TCGA 1992, s 2A(5); FA 1998, s 121(1)*].

**(B) Non-allowable expenditure — capital allowances** [*TCGA 1992, s 41*]
S Ltd acquired land in March 1994 for £90,000 on which it constructed a factory for use in its manufacturing trade. The cost of construction was £45,000 incurred in June 1994. In June 1999, the company sold the freehold factory for £140,000, of which £100,000 related to the land and £40,000 to the building. Industrial buildings allowances of £9,000 had been given and there was a balancing charge of £4,000. The indexation factor for the period March 1994 to June 1999 is 0.162.

|  | Land | Building | |
|---|---|---|---|
|  | £ | £ | £ |
| Disposal consideration | 100,000 |  | 40,000 |
| Allowable cost | 90,000 | 45,000 |  |
| *Deduct* net allowances given |  | 5,000 | 40,000 |
| Unindexed gain | 10,000 |  | Nil |
| Indexation allowance £90,000 × 0.162 = £14,580, but restricted to | 10,000 |  |  |
| Chargeable gain/(allowable loss) | Nil |  | Nil |

### 206.2 PART DISPOSALS [*TCGA 1992, s 42*]

Note. See also 213.1 LAND for small part disposals of land.

**(A)**
T purchased a 300 acre estate in March 1985 for £1m plus legal and other costs of £50,000. In January 1988 he spent £47,000 on improvements to the main house on the estate (not his main residence), which he sells in September 1999 for £660,000. The costs of sale are £40,000. The value of the remaining land is £2.34m. The indexation factor from March 1985 to April 1998 is 0.752, and that for January 1988 to April 1998 is 0.574 (see note (*b*)).

|  | £ | £ |
|---|---|---|
| Sale proceeds |  | 660,000 |
| *Deduct* incidental costs |  | 40,000 |
|  |  | 620,000 |
| Cost £1,050,000 × $\frac{660,000}{660,000 + 2,340,000}$ | 231,000 |  |
| Improvement costs | 47,000 | 278,000 |
| Unindexed gain |  | 342,000 |
| Indexation allowance: |  |  |
| £231,000 × 0.752 | 173,712 |  |
| £47,000 × 0.574 | 26,978 | 200,690 |
| Chargeable gain |  | £141,310 |

## Notes

(a) The improvements expenditure is not apportioned as it relates entirely to the part of the estate being sold. [*TCGA 1992, s 42(4)*].

(b) Other than for the purposes of corporation tax on chargeable gains, indexation allowance is frozen at its April 1998 level. Therefore, the indexation factor for April 1998 is used in respect of disposals in a later month (and expenditure incurred in April 1998 or later does not attract indexation allowance at all). See 210 INDEXATION.

### (B)

U inherited some land at a probate value of £500,000 in November 1981. Its market value at 31 March 1982 was £540,000. In November 1987, he sold part of the land for £240,000, the remaining land then being worth £480,000. He sells the remaining land in April 1999 for £600,000 and elects under *TCGA 1992, s 35(5)* for all his assets held at 31 March 1982 to be treated as sold and re-acquired by him at their market value on that date.

**The gain, subject to indexation, on the part disposal in November 1987 is**

|  | £ |
|---|---|
| Proceeds | 240,000 |
| Cost £500,000 × $\dfrac{240,000}{240,000 + 480,000}$ | 166,667 |
| Gain subject to indexation | £73,333 |

**The gain, subject to indexation, on the disposal in April 1999 is**

|  | £ |
|---|---|
| Proceeds | 600,000 |
| Market value 31.3.82 | |
| £540,000 × $\dfrac{480,000}{240,000 + 480,000}$ | 360,000 |
| Gain subject to indexation to April 1998 | £240,000 |

### Note

(a) Where re-basing applies and there has been a part disposal after 31 March 1982 and before 6 April 1988, the proportion of 31 March 1982 value to be brought into account on the ultimate disposal is the same as the proportion of cost unallowed on the part disposal, as if the re-basing provisions had applied to the part disposal. [*TCGA 1992, 3 Sch 4(1)*].

## 206.2 Disposal

**(C)**
V bought the film rights of a novel for £50,000 in May 1995. A one-third share of the rights was sold to W Ltd in March 1996 for £20,000, when the rights retained had a value of £45,000. In December 1999, V's rights were sold to a film company for £100,000 plus a right to royalties, such right being estimated to be worth £150,000. The indexation factor for the periods May 1995 to March 1996 and May 1995 to April 1998 (see note (*b*)) are 0.013 and 0.087 respectively.

| **March 1996** | £ |
|---|---:|
| Sale proceeds | 20,000 |
| Cost £50,000 × $\dfrac{20,000}{20,000 + 45,000}$ | 15,385 |
| Unindexed gain | 4,615 |
| Indexation allowance £15,385 × 0.013 | 200 |
| Chargeable gain 1995/96 | £4,415 |

| **December 1999** | £ |
|---|---:|
| Sale proceeds (£100,000 + £150,000) | 250,000 |
| Cost (£50,000 − £15,385) | 34,615 |
| Unindexed gain | 215,385 |
| Indexation allowance £34,615 × 0.087 | 3,012 |
| Chargeable gain (subject to any available TAPER RELIEF (226)) | £212,373 |

**Notes**

(*a*)  The right to royalties is itself an asset and could be the subject of a future disposal by V. See 206.3(B) below and, where applicable, 227 WASTING ASSETS.

(*b*)  Other than for the purposes of corporation tax on chargeable gains, indexation allowance is frozen at its April 1998 level. Therefore, the indexation factor for April 1998 is used in respect of disposals in a later month (and expenditure incurred in April 1998 or later does not attract indexation allowance at all). See 210 INDEXATION.

**(D)**
C inherited land valued at £72,000 in May 1985. He granted rights of way over the land to a neighbouring landowner in March 1990, in consideration for a parcel of land adjacent to his, valued at £21,000. The value of the original land, subject to the right of way, was then £147,000. In March 2000, C sold the whole of the land for £170,000.

| Indexation factors | | |
|---|---|---|
| May 1985 to March 1990 | | 0.275 |
| May 1985 to April 1998 (note (c)) | | 0.708 |
| March 1990 to April 1998 (note (c)) | | 0.339 |

**Part disposal in March 1990**  £
Disposal consideration                                21,000
Allowable expenditure

$$\frac{21,000}{21,000 + 147,000} \times £72,000 \qquad\qquad 9,000$$

Unindexed gain                                        12,000
Indexation allowance £9,000 × 0.275                    2,475

Chargeable gain                                       £9,525

**Disposal in March 2000**                              £
Disposal consideration                               170,000
*Deduct* Original land £(72,000 − 9,000)   63,000
         Addition                          21,000    84,000

Unindexed gain                                        86,000
Indexation allowance
(a)  Original land £63,000 × 0.708        44,604
(b)  Addition £21,000 × 0.339              7,119
                                                      51,723

Chargeable gain                                      £34,277

**Notes**

(a) It is assumed that the additional land is merged with the existing land to give a single asset.

(b) A claim under what is now *TCGA 1992, s 242* (small part disposals of land — see 213.1 LAND) could not be made in respect of the March 1990 part disposal as the consideration exceeded £20,000.

(c) Other than for the purposes of corporation tax on chargeable gains, indexation allowance is frozen at its April 1998 level. Therefore, the indexation factor for April 1998 is used in respect of disposals in a later month (and expenditure incurred in April 1998 or later does not attract indexation allowance at all). See 210 INDEXATION.

## 206.3 Disposal

### 206.3 CAPITAL SUMS DERIVED FROM ASSETS [*TCGA 1992, s 22(1)*]

**(A) General**

A Ltd holds the remainder of a 99-year lease of land, under which it has mineral rights. The lease, which commenced in 1983, was acquired in April 1992 by assignment for £80,000. Following a proposal to extract minerals, the freeholder pays A Ltd £100,000 in June 1999 in consideration of relinquishing the mineral rights, in order to prevent such development. The value of the lease after the alteration is £150,000.

|  | £ |
|---|---:|
| Disposal proceeds | 100,000 |
| Allowable cost $\dfrac{100{,}000}{100{,}000 + 150{,}000} \times £80{,}000$ | 32,000 |
| Gain subject to indexation | £68,000 |

**(B) Deferred consideration**

Z owns 2,000 £1 ordinary shares in B Ltd, for which he subscribed at par in August 1991. On 31 March 1996, he and the other shareholders in B Ltd sold their shares to another company for £10 per share plus a further unquantified cash amount calculated by means of a formula relating to the future profits of B Ltd. The value in March 1996 of the deferred consideration was estimated at £2 per share. On 30 April 1999, Z receives a further £4.20 per share under the sale agreement. The indexation factor for the period August 1991 to March 1996 is 0.130, and for the period March 1996 to April 1998 (note (*c*)) is 0.073.

**1995/96**

|  | £ | £ |
|---|---:|---:|
| Disposal proceeds 2,000 at £10 | 20,000 |  |
| Value of rights 2,000 at £2 | 4,000 | 24,000 |
| Cost of acquisition |  | 2,000 |
| Unindexed gain |  | 22,000 |
| Indexation allowance £2,000 × 0.130 |  | 260 |
| Chargeable gain |  | £21,740 |

**1999/2000**

|  | £ |
|---|---:|
| Disposal of rights to deferred consideration |  |
| Proceeds 2,000 × £4.20 | 8,400 |
| Deemed cost of acquiring rights | 4,000 |
| Unindexed gain | 4,400 |
| Indexation allowance |  |
| £4,000 × 0.073 | 292 |
| Chargeable gain | £4,108 |

**Notes**

(*a*) A right to unquantified and contingent future consideration on the disposal of an asset is itself an asset, and the future consideration when received is a capital sum derived from that asset (*Marren v Ingles* HL 1980, 54 TC 76 and *Marson v Marriage* Ch D 1979, 54 TC 59).

# Disposal 206.3

(b) See 224.4(C) SHARES AND SECURITIES for position where deferred consideration is to be satisfied in shares and/or debentures in the acquiring company.

(c) Other than for the purposes of corporation tax on chargeable gains, indexation allowance is frozen at its April 1998 level. See 210 INDEXATION.

**(C)**
Suppose that in the previous example, the deferred consideration was valued at £4.20 per share in March 1996, but only £2 per share was received on 30 April 1999.

**1995/96**

|  | £ | £ |
|---|---:|---:|
| Disposal proceeds | 20,000 |  |
| Value of rights | 8,400 | 28,400 |
| Cost of acquisition |  | 2,000 |
| Unindexed gain |  | 26,400 |
| Indexation allowance £2,000 × 0.130 |  | 260 |
| Chargeable gain |  | £26,140 |

**1999/2000**

| | |
|---|---:|
| Disposal of rights 2,000 × £2 | 4,000 |
| Deemed acquisition cost | 8,400 |
| Allowable loss | £4,400 |

**Note**
(a) There is no provision for reopening the 1995/96 assessment or setting off the 1999/2000 loss against the 1995/96 gain.

## 206.4 Disposal

### 206.4 RECEIPT OF COMPENSATION [*TCGA 1992, ss 22, 23*]

**(A)**
C owns a freehold warehouse which is badly damaged by fire as a result of inflammable goods having been inadequately packaged. The value of the warehouse after the fire is £90,000, and it cost £120,000 in 1989. The owner of the goods is held liable for the damage and pays C £60,000 compensation in October 1999.

|  | £ |
|---|---|
| Disposal proceeds | 60,000 |
| Allowable cost $\dfrac{60,000}{60,000 + 90,000} \times £120,000$ | 48,000 |
| Gain subject to indexation to April 1998 and any available taper relief | £12,000 |

**(B) Restoration using insurance moneys**
A diamond necklace owned by D cost £100,000 in 1991. D is involved in a motor accident in which the necklace is damaged. Its value is reduced to £80,000. D receives £40,000 under an insurance policy in May 1999 and spends £45,000 on having the necklace restored.

**(i) No claim under *TCGA 1992, s 23***

|  | £ |
|---|---|
| Disposal proceeds | 40,000 |
| Allowable cost $\dfrac{40,000}{40,000 + 80,000} \times £100,000$ | 33,333 |
| Gain subject to indexation to April 1998 | £6,667 |
| Allowable cost in relation to subsequent disposal £100,000 − £33,333 + £45,000 | £111,667 |

**(ii) Claim under *TCGA 1992, s 23***
No chargeable gain arises

|  | |
|---|---|
| Allowable cost originally | 100,000 |
| *Deduct* amount received on claim | 40,000 |
|  | 60,000 |
| *Add* expenditure on restoration | 45,000 |
| Allowable cost in relation to subsequent disposal | £105,000 |

## (C) Part application of capital sum received

E is the owner of a large estate consisting mainly of parkland which he acquired for £150,000 in August 1987. He grants a one-year licence in August 1999 to an exploration company to prospect for minerals, in consideration for a capital sum of £50,000. The exploration proves unsuccessful and on expiry of the licence E spends £20,000 on restoration of the drilling sites to their former state. The market value of the estate after granting the licence is £350,000, and it is £400,000 after restoration.

### (i) No claim under *TCGA 1992, s 23(3)*

| | £ |
|---|---|
| Disposal proceeds | 50,000 |
| *Deduct* allowable cost $\dfrac{50,000}{50,000 + 350,000} \times £150,000$ | 18,750 |
| Gain subject to indexation | £31,250 |
| Allowable expenditure remaining £150,000 − £18,750 + £20,000 | £151,250 |

### (ii) Claim made under *TCGA 1992, s 23(3)*

| | £ |
|---|---|
| Deemed disposal proceeds (£50,000 − £20,000) | 30,000 |
| *Deduct* | |
| Allowable cost $\dfrac{30,000}{30,000 + 400,000} \times £(150,000 + 20,000)$ | 11,860 |
| Gain subject to indexation | £18,140 |
| Allowable expenditure remaining £150,000 − £20,000 − £11,860 + £20,000 | £138,140 |

## (D) Capital sum exceeding allowable expenditure

F inherited a painting in 1980 when it was valued at £2,000. Its value at 31 March 1982 was £3,000. In March 1987, by which time its value had increased considerably, the painting suffered damage whilst on loan to an art gallery and F received £10,000 compensation. The value of the painting was then £30,000. It then cost F £9,800 to have the painting restored. In June 1999, he sells the painting for £50,000.

### (i) No election under *TCGA 1992, s 23(2)*

| | £ |
|---|---|
| Disposal proceeds March 1987 | 10,000 |
| Allowable cost $\dfrac{10,000}{10,000 + 30,000} \times £2,000$ | 500 |
| Unindexed gain 1986/87 | £9,500 |
| Allowable cost in relation to subsequent disposal £2,000 − £500 + £9,800 | £11,300 |

## 206.4 Disposal

|  | £ | £ |
|---|---|---|
| Disposal proceeds June 1999 | 50,000 | 50,000 |
| Allowable cost without re-basing | 11,300 | |
| Allowable cost with re-basing | | |
| $£3,000 \times \dfrac{30,000}{10,000 + 30,000} = £2,250 + £9,800$ | | 12,050 |
| Gain subject to indexation 1999/2000 | £38,700 | £37,950 |

It is clear that re-basing will apply and the chargeable gain will be £37,950 less indexation allowance to April 1998 based on £12,050.

### (ii) Election under *TCGA 1992, s 23(2)*

|  | £ |
|---|---|
| Disposal proceeds March 1987 | 10,000 |
| *Less* allowable expenditure | 2,000 |
| Unindexed gain 1986/87 | £8,000 |
| Allowable cost in relation to subsequent disposal £2,000 – £2,000 + £9,800 | £9,800 |

|  | £ | £ |
|---|---|---|
| Disposal proceeds June 1999 | 50,000 | 50,000 |
| Allowable cost without re-basing | 9,800 | |
| Allowable cost with re-basing   note (*b*) | | |
| £3,000 – £2,000 + £9,800 | | 10,800 |
| Gain subject to indexation 1999/2000 | £40,200 | £39,200 |

Again, re-basing will clearly apply and the chargeable gain will be £39,200 less indexation allowance to April 1998 based on £10,800.

**Notes**

(*a*) Although not illustrated in this example, indexation allowance must be deducted before comparing the positions with and without re-basing in order to ascertain whether or not re-basing applies.

(*b*) Where there is a disposal after 5 April 1989 to which re-basing applies and, if re-basing had not applied, the allowable expenditure would have fallen to be reduced under *TCGA 1992, s 23(2)* by reference to a capital sum received after 31 March 1982 but before 6 April 1988, the 31 March 1982 value is reduced by the amount previously allowed against the capital sum. [*TCGA 1992, 3 Sch 4(2)*].

**(E) Indexation allowance and taper relief** [*TCGA 1992, ss 2A, 53(1)(1A)(3), 57; FA 1998, ss 121, 122(1)(6)(7)*]

A owns a freehold factory which cost £100,000 in June 1987. Because of mining operations nearby, part of the factory is severely damaged by subsidence and has to be demolished and rebuilt. The value of the factory after the damage is £150,000. The risk is not covered under A's insurance policy but the mining company agrees to pay compensation of £50,000 in full settlement, received in February 1998. The cost of demolition and rebuilding is £60,000, incurred in May 1998. The factory is sold in March 2000 for £300,000. The factory is a business asset for taper relief purposes.

| Indexation factors | June 1987 to February 1998 | 0.573 |
| --- | --- | --- |
| | June 1987 to April 1998 (note (*b*)) | 0.596 |
| | February 1998 to April 1998 (note (*b*)) | 0.014 |

### (i) No claim under *TCGA 1992, s 23(1)*

(*a*) Part disposal February 1998 £
    Disposal proceeds    50,000

*Deduct* allowable cost $\dfrac{50,000}{50,000 + 150,000} \times £100,000$    25,000

| | |
| --- | --- |
| Unindexed gain | 25,000 |
| Indexation allowance £25,000 × 0.573 | 14,325 |
| Chargeable gain | £10,675 |

(*b*) Disposal March 2000
| | |
| --- | --- |
| Disposal proceeds | 300,000 |
| *Deduct* allowable cost £(100,000 − 25,000) + £60,000 | 135,000 |
| Unindexed gain | 165,000 |

Indexation allowance
| | | |
| --- | --- | --- |
| Original cost £(100,000 − 25,000) × 0.596 | 44,700 | |
| Rebuilding cost (note (*b*)) | — | 44,700 |
| Chargeable gain subject to taper relief | | £120,300 |
| Tapered gain (85%) | | £102,255 |

### (ii) Claim under *TCGA 1992, s 23(1)*

(*a*) No chargeable gain in February 1998    £
| | |
| --- | --- |
| Allowable cost | 100,000 |
| Rebuilding cost | 60,000 |
| | 160,000 |
| *Deduct* receipt rolled over | 50,000 |
| Revised allowable cost | £110,000 |

(*b*) Disposal March 2000
| | |
| --- | --- |
| Disposal proceeds | 300,000 |
| *Deduct* allowable cost | 110,000 |
| Unindexed gain | 190,000 |

Indexation allowance
| | | |
| --- | --- | --- |
| Original cost £100,000 × 0.596 | 59,600 | |
| Rebuilding cost (note (*b*)) | — | |
| | 59,600 | |
| *Deduct* | | |
| Receipt rolled over £50,000 × 0.014 | (700) | 58,900 |
| Chargeable gain subject to taper relief | | £131,100 |
| Tapered gain (85%) | | £111,435 |

## 206.4 Disposal

**Notes**

(*a*) Taper relief is at 15% of the otherwise chargeable gain, the factory being deemed to have been held for two years after 5 April 1998 by virtue of its having been acquired before 17 March 1998. [*TCGA 1992, s 2A(5)(8)(9); FA 1998, s 121(1)(4)*]. In practice, any losses on other 1999/2000 disposals must be taken into account before taper relief is applied to the gain (see 226.1(B) TAPER RELIEF).

(*b*) Note that, as well as deferring what would have been the gain on the part disposal, the effect of the claim under *TCGA 1992, s 23(1)* is to increase the quantum of taper relief available on the ultimate disposal.

(*c*) Other than for the purposes of corporation tax on chargeable gains, indexation allowance is frozen at its April 1998 level. Therefore, the indexation factor for April 1998 is used in respect of disposals in a later month, and expenditure incurred in April 1998 or later does not attract indexation allowance at all. See 210 INDEXATION.

**Disposal 206.5**

206.5 **OPTIONS** [*TCGA 1992, ss 44, 46, 144, 145; FA 1998, s 122(5)–(7)*]

**Cross-reference.** See also 227.2 WASTING ASSETS.

On 1 February 1996 F granted an option to G for £10,000 to acquire freehold land bought by F for £50,000 in September 1992. The option is for a period of 5 years, and the option price is £100,000 plus 1% thereof for each month since the option was granted. On 1 February 1998, G sold the option to H for £20,000. On 30 June 1999, H exercises the option and pays F £141,000 for the land. Neither G nor H intended to use the land for the purposes of a trade.

| | | |
|---|---|---|
| Indexation factors | September 1992 to April 1998 (note (*b*)) | 0.166 |
| | February 1996 to February 1998 | 0.062 |

**1996 Grant of option by F**

| | £ |
|---|---|
| Disposal proceeds | 10,000 |
| Allowable cost | — |
| Chargeable gain | £10,000 |

**1998 Disposal of option by G**

| | |
|---|---|
| Disposal proceeds | 20,000 |
| Allowable cost $\dfrac{5-2}{5} \times £10,000$ | 6,000 |
| Unindexed gain | 14,000 |
| Indexation allowance £6,000 × 0.062 | 372 |
| Chargeable gain | £13,628 |

**1999 Exercise of option**

| | |
|---|---|
| (i) Earlier assessment on F vacated | |
| (ii) Aggregate disposal proceeds (£10,000 + £141,000) | 151,000 |
| Allowable cost of land | 50,000 |
| Unindexed gain | 101,000 |
| Indexation allowance £50,000 × 0.166 | 8,300 |
| Chargeable gain (on F) | £92,700 |

**H's allowable expenditure is**

| | |
|---|---|
| Cost of option (indexation due from February 1998) | 20,000 |
| Cost of land (month of acquisition June 1999, so no indexation due) | 141,000 |
| | £161,000 |

**Notes**

(*a*) The wasting asset rules (see 227 WASTING ASSETS) apply on the disposal of the option by G (though certain options are exempted from these rules — see *TCGA 1992, s 144*). As these rules can only apply on a disposal, they cannot apply on the

## 206.5 Disposal

exercise of the option by H (as the exercise of an option is not treated as a disposal), so his acquisition cost remains intact.

(b) Other than for the purposes of corporation tax on chargeable gains, indexation allowance is frozen at its April 1998 level. Therefore, the indexation factor for April 1998 is used in respect of disposals in a later month, and expenditure incurred in April 1998 or later does not attract indexation allowance at all. See 210 INDEXATION.

(c) For the purposes of computing any available TAPER RELIEF (226) on a future disposal, H's acquisition of the asset is deemed to have occurred on 30 June 1999, i.e. the date he exercised the option and not the date he acquired it. [*TCGA 1992, A1 Sch 13(3); FA 1998, s 121, 20 Sch*].

# 207 Enterprise Investment Scheme

**Cross-reference.** See also IT 5.2 ENTERPRISE INVESTMENT SCHEME.

## 207.1 DISPOSAL OF EIS SHARES MORE THAN FIVE YEARS AFTER ACQUISITION [*TCGA 1992, s 150A(2)(3); FA 1994, 15 Sch 28, 30; FA 1995, 13 Sch 2(1)(3); FA 1998, 13 Sch 24(1)*]

On 8 November 1999 P subscribes £450,000 for 300,000 shares in the EIS company, S Ltd, and obtains an EIS income tax deduction of £30,000 (£150,000 × 20%) for 1999/2000. On 3 April 2005 he sells the entire holding for £810,000. The shares are non-business assets for the purposes of taper relief.

**The chargeable gain arising is calculated as follows**

| | £ |
|---|---:|
| Disposal proceeds | 810,000 |
| Cost | 450,000 |
| Gain | 360,000 |
| *Less TCGA 1992, s 150A(2)(3)* exemption | |
| £360,000 × $\frac{30,000}{90,000}$ note (*b*) | 120,000 |
| Chargeable gain | 240,000 |
| *Less* taper relief @ 15% (note (*d*)) | 36,000 |
| Taxable gain | £204,000 |

### Notes

(*a*) Gains arising on the sale more than five years after issue of shares qualifying for EIS income tax relief are not chargeable gains unless the EIS relief is withdrawn before disposal.

(*b*) Where the income tax relief is not given on the full EIS subscription (otherwise than because of insufficient income), capital gains tax relief is given on a proportion of the gain on the disposal or part disposal.

The gain is reduced by the multiple A/B where

A = the actual income tax reduction and
B = the tax at the lower rate for the year of relief on the amount subscribed for the issue.

A = £150,000 × 20% = £30,000
B = £450,000 × 20% = £90,000

(*c*) Expenditure incurred after 31 March 1998 other than by companies does not attract indexation allowance. [*TCGA 1992, ss 53(1A), 54(1)(1A); FA 1998, s 121(1)–(3)*].

(*d*) In practice, any losses on other 2004/05 disposals must be taken into account before taper relief is applied to the gain (see 226.1(B) TAPER RELIEF).

## 207.2 Enterprise Investment Scheme

207.2 **LOSS ON DISPOSAL OF EIS SHARES** [*TCGA 1992, s 150A(1)(2A); FA 1994, 15 Sch 28, 30; FA 1995, 13 Sch 2(1)(2); FA 1998, 13 Sch 24(1)*]

### (A) Disposal more than five years after acquisition
Assuming the facts otherwise remain the same as in 207.1 above but that the shares are sold for £300,000 on 3 April 2005.

**The allowable loss arising is calculated as follows**

|  | £ | £ |
|---|---|---|
| Disposal proceeds |  | 300,000 |
| *Less* Cost | 450,000 |  |
| *Less* Income tax relief given (and not withdrawn) | 30,000 | 420,000 |
| Allowable loss |  | £120,000 |

**Note**
(*a*)  Any loss arising is reduced by deducting the amount of the EIS relief (given and not withdrawn) from the acquisition cost.

### (B) Disposal within five years of acquisition
The facts are otherwise as in (A) above except that the shares are sold in an arm's length bargain on 3 April 2001, i.e. within five years after their issue.

**Income tax relief given for 1999/2000 is withdrawn as follows**

Relief attributable (£150,000 @ 20%)          £30,000 (1)

$$\text{Consideration } £300,000 \times \frac{30,000 \ (£150,000 \ @ \ 20\%)}{90,000 \ (£450,000 \ @ \ 20\%)} @ \ 20\% \quad £20,000 \ (2)$$

The amount at (1) is greater than that at (2), so income tax relief of £20,000 is withdrawn. [*ICTA 1988, s 299(1)–(4); FA 1994, 15 Sch 12; FA 1998, s 74, 13 Sch 12(1)–(3)(8)*].

The relief not withdrawn is therefore £(30,000 − 20,000) =      £10,000

**The allowable loss arising is calculated as follows**

|  | £ | £ |
|---|---|---|
| Disposal proceeds |  | 300,000 |
| *Less* Cost | 450,000 |  |
| *Less* Income tax relief not withdrawn | 10,000 | 440,000 |
| Allowable loss |  | £140,000 |

**Notes**
(*a*)  For the purposes of computing an allowable loss, the consideration is reduced by the relief attributable to the shares. [*TCGA 1992, s 150A(1)*]. The relief attributable is that remaining following any withdrawal of relief.

(*b*)  A withdrawal of income tax relief arises on a disposal of EIS shares within the relevant period under *ICTA 1988, s 312(1A)(a)*, i.e. within five years after their issue. [*ICTA 1988, s 299(1)*].

## Enterprise Investment Scheme 207.3

207.3 **EIS DEFERRAL RELIEF AFTER 5 APRIL 1998** [*TCGA 1992, 5B, 5BA Schs; FA 1995, 13 Sch 4(3)(4); FA 1998, s 74, 13 Sch 26–36; FA 1999, ss 72, 73, 7, 8 Schs*]

**(A)**

On 1 June 1999, X realises a gain of £300,000 (after indexation but before taper relief) on the disposal of an asset. He had owned the asset since 1992 and it was a business asset for taper relief purposes. X makes no other disposals in 1999/2000 and does not qualify for retirement relief. On 1 February 2001, X acquires by subscription 65% of the issued ordinary share capital of ABC Ltd at a total subscription price of £247,000. This is a qualifying investment for the purposes of EIS deferral relief, and the ABC shares are also a business asset for taper relief purposes. X makes a claim to defer the maximum £247,000 of the June 1999 gain against the qualifying investment.

On 1 July 2007, X sells 40% of his holding in ABC Ltd for £198,800. He makes no other disposals in 2007/08.

**X's CGT position for 1999/2000 is as follows**

|  | £ |
|---|---:|
| Indexed gain | 300,000 |
| *Less* EIS deferral relief | 247,000 |
|  | 53,000 |
| *Less* taper relief £53,000 @ 15% | 7,950 |
|  | 45,050 |
| *Less* annual exemption | 7,100 |
| Taxable gain | £37,950 |

**X's CGT position for 2007/08 is as follows**

|  | £ |
|---|---:|
| *Gain on ABC Ltd shares* |  |
| Disposal proceeds | 198,800 |
| *Less* cost (£247,000 @ 40%) | 98,800 |
|  | 100,000 |
| *Less* taper relief £100,000 @ 45% | 45,000 |
| Chargeable gain | £55,000 |
| *Deferred gain brought into charge* |  |
| Total gain deferred | £247,000 |

|  | £ |
|---|---:|
| Clawback restricted to expenditure to which disposal relates | 98,800 |
| *Less* taper relief £98,800 @ 15% | 14,820 |
| Gain | £83,980 |
| Taxable gains 2007/08 (subject to annual exemption) (£55,000 + £83,980) | £138,980 |
| Gain remaining deferred until any future chargeable event (£247,000 − £98,800) | £148,200 |

## 207.3 Enterprise Investment Scheme

**Notes**

(a) No part of X's subscription for ABC Ltd shares can qualify for EIS income tax relief. X is connected with the company by virtue of his shareholding being greater than 30%. (In practice, the holdings of his associates, e.g. wife and children, must also be taken into account in applying the 30% limit.) [ICTA 1988, ss 291(1), 291B, 312(1); FA 1998, s 74, 13 Sch 6(1)].

(b) As the ABC Ltd shares do not qualify for income tax relief, there is no CGT exemption for the gain arising on disposal even though the shares were held for the requisite five-year period.

(c) Taper relief is given by reference to the number of complete years an asset has been held after 5 April 1998. An extra one year is added to the holding period of an asset acquired before 17 March 1998. See 226 TAPER RELIEF. Taper relief on the deferred gain becoming chargeable is given by reference to the time and circumstances of the original disposal, not the disposal of the EIS shares giving rise to the chargeable event, but see (B) below re cases of serial reinvestment. [TCGA 1992, A1 Sch 16; FA 1998, s 121, 20 Sch].

(d) Expenditure incurred after 31 March 1998 other than by companies does not attract indexation allowance. [TCGA 1992, ss 53(1A), 54(1)(1A); FA 1998, s 121(1)–(3)].

**(B)**

On 1 June 1999, Anna realises a gain of £300,000 (after indexation but before taper relief) on the disposal of a complete holding of shares in ABC Ltd (an EIS company) for which she had subscribed on 1 June 1998 and in respect of which she had deferred a gain of £10,000 which would otherwise have accrued in 1997/98 on a disposal of quoted shares. The ABC Ltd shares were a business asset for taper relief purposes. Anna makes no other disposals in 1999/2000. On 1 December 2000, she subscribes £260,000 for new ordinary shares in a new company, EIS Ltd. The investment is a qualifying investment for the purposes of EIS deferral relief, but the shares are a non-business asset for the purposes of taper relief. Anna makes a claim to defer the maximum £260,000 of the June 1999 gain against her investment in EIS Ltd.

On 1 June 2006, Anna sells her holding of EIS Ltd shares for £540,000. She makes no other disposals in 2006/07.

**Anna's CGT position for 1999/2000 is as follows**

|  | £ |
|---|---|
| Gain on ABC Ltd shares | 300,000 |
| Less deferred under EIS provisions | 260,000 |
|  | 40,000 |
| Less taper relief £40,000 @ 7.5% (Qualifying holding period 1.6.98–1.6.99 = 1 year) | 3,000 |
|  | 37,000 |
| Previously deferred gain now chargeable | 10,000 |
|  | 47,000 |
| Less annual exemption | 7,100 |
| Taxable gain 1999/2000 | £39,000 |

**Anna's CGT position for 2006/07 is as follows**

| | £ |
|---|---|
| *Gain on EIS Ltd shares* | |
| Disposal proceeds | 540,000 |
| *Less* cost | 260,000 |
| | 280,000 |
| *Less* taper relief £280,000 @ 15% (Qualifying holding period 1.12.2000 – 1.6.06 = 5 years) | 42,000 |
| Gain | £238,000 |

| | £ |
|---|---|
| *Deferred gain brought into charge* | |
| Gain deferred | 260,000 |
| *Less* taper relief* | 62,000 |
| Gain | £198,000 |

*Period of ownership/Qualifying holding period:

| | |
|---|---|
| 1.6.98–1.6.99 (business asset) | 1 year |
| 1.12.2000–1.6.06 (non-business asset) | 5.5 years |
| Total | 6.5 years |

Number of whole years in qualifying holding period = 6
£260,000 × 1/6.5 = £40,000 (qualifies for 6 years' business asset taper relief)
£210,000 × 5.5/6.5 = £220,000 (qualifies for 6 years' non-business asset taper relief)

| | £ |
|---|---|
| £40,000 × 45% = | 18,000 |
| £220,000 × 20% = | 44,000 |
| Total taper relief | £62,000 |

| | |
|---|---|
| Taxable gains 2006/07 (subject to annual exemption) (£238,000 + £198,000) | £436,000 |

**Notes**

(a) A special taper relief rule applies in cases of serial EIS investment. It applies in consequence of the disposal after 5 April 1999 of a holding of EIS shares (the initial investment) (which were issued after 5 April 1998 and to which either CGT deferral relief or income tax relief (or both) is attributable) where the whole or part of the gain otherwise accruing is deferred by reinvestment in further EIS shares (the second investment). Upon a disposal of the second investment, with the result that the deferred gain on the initial investment is revived, taper relief is calculated in respect of the revived gain as if the holding periods of the two investments were combined. [*TCGA 1992, s 150D, 5BA Sch; FA 1999, s 72, 7 Sch*]. See generally 226 TAPER RELIEF.

(b) Where the revived gain is itself deferred by means of a third EIS investment (not illustrated in this example), the holding periods of all three investments are combined for taper relief purposes, and so on as regards fourth and subsequent investments.

## 208.1 Exemptions and Reliefs

# 208 Exemptions and Reliefs

**Cross-references.** See also 219 PRIVATE RESIDENCES, 220 QUALIFYING CORPORATE BONDS and 227 WASTING ASSETS.

## 208.1 CHATTELS

### (A) Marginal relief [*TCGA 1992, s 262(2)*]

On 1 April 1987, Y acquired by inheritance a painting valued for probate at £900. He sold it for £7,200 on 30 October 1999, incurring costs of £150. The indexation factor for the period April 1987 to April 1998 (note (*a*)) is 0.597.

|  | £ | £ |
|---|---:|---:|
| Disposal proceeds | 7,200 | |
| Incidental costs | 150 | 7,050 |
| Acquisition cost | | 900 |
| Unindexed gain | | 6,150 |
| Indexation allowance £900 × 0.597 | | 537 |
| Chargeable gain | | £5,613 |
| Marginal relief | | |
| Chargeable gain limited to $\frac{5}{3}$ × (£7,200 − £6,000) | | £2,000 |

**Note**

(*a*) Other than for the purposes of corporation tax on chargeable gains, indexation allowance is frozen at its April 1998 level. Therefore, the indexation factor for April 1998 is used in respect of disposals in a later month (and expenditure incurred in April 1998 or later does not attract indexation allowance at all). See 210 INDEXATION.

### (B) Loss relief [*TCGA 1992, s 262(3)*]

Z bought a piece of antique jewellery for £7,000 in February 1988. In January 2000, he is forced to sell it, but at auction it realises only £1,500 and Z incurs costs of £100.

|  | £ | £ |
|---|---:|---:|
| Deemed disposal consideration | | 6,000 |
| Cost of disposal | 100 | |
| Cost of acquisition | 7,000 | 7,100 |
| Allowable loss | | £1,100 |

**Note**

(*a*) Where the disposal consideration for tangible moveable property is less than £6,000 and there would otherwise be a loss, the consideration is deemed to be £6,000.

# Exemptions and Reliefs 208.1

**(C) Partial disposal of assets forming sets** [*TCGA 1992, s 262(4)*]
AB purchased a set of six 18th century dining chairs in 1979 for £1,200. After incurring restoration costs of £300 in 1981, he sold two of them in May 1996 to an unconnected person for £2,900. In October 1999, he sold the other four to the same buyer for £4,900. The value of the complete set at 31 March 1982 was £1,800.

| | |
|---|---|
| Indexation factors   March 1982 to May 1996 | 0.925 |
|                      March 1982 to April 1998 (note (*c*)) | 1.047 |

The two disposals are treated as one for the purposes of the chattel exemption and marginal relief, the consideration for which is £7,800. Marginal relief on this basis would give a total chargeable gain of £3,000 ([£7,800 – £6,000] × $\frac{5}{3}$) which is to be compared with the following:

| **May 1996** | £ | £ | £ |
|---|---|---|---|
| Disposal proceeds | | 2,900 | 2,900 |
| Acquisition cost | 1,200 | | |
| Enhancement cost | 300 | | |
| | 1,500 | | |
| Cost of two chairs sold £1,500 × $\frac{2}{6}$ | | 500 | |
| Market value 31.3.82 £1,800 × $\frac{2}{6}$ | | | 600 |
| Unindexed gain | | 2,400 | 2,300 |
| Indexation allowance £600 × 0.925 | | 555 | 555 |
| Gain after indexation | | £1,845 | £1,745 |
| Chargeable gain | | | £1,745 |

| **October 1999** | £ | £ |
|---|---|---|
| Disposal proceeds | 4,900 | 4,900 |
| Allowable cost £1,500 × $\frac{4}{6}$ | 1,000 | |
| Market value 31.3.82 £1,800 × $\frac{4}{6}$ | | 1,200 |
| Unindexed gain | 3,900 | 3,700 |
| Indexation allowance £1,200 × 1.047 | 1,256 | 1,256 |
| Gain after indexation | £2,644 | £2,444 |
| Chargeable gain | | £2,444 |
| | | |
| Total chargeable gains (£1,745 + £2,444) | | £4,189 |

The total gain of £4,189 compares with a gain of £3,000 using marginal relief. Marginal relief is therefore effective and the total chargeable gain is £3,000.

The gain is apportioned to tax years as follows (note (*b*))

1996/97 £3,000 × $\dfrac{2,900}{7,800}$ =   £1,115

1999/2000 £3,000 × $\dfrac{4,900}{7,800}$ =   £1,885

## 208.1 Exemptions and Reliefs

**Notes**

(*a*) Prior to the second disposal, the first disposal would have been exempt, the proceeds being within the £6,000 chattel exemption.

(*b*) The gain as reduced by marginal relief is apportioned between tax years in the same ratio as the proportion of total sale proceeds applicable to each year (Revenue Capital Gains Manual, CG 76637).

(*c*) Other than for the purposes of corporation tax on chargeable gains, indexation allowance is frozen at its April 1998 level. Therefore, the indexation factor for April 1998 is used in respect of disposals in a later month (and expenditure incurred in April 1998 or later does not attract indexation allowance at all). See 210 INDEXATION.

(*d*) See also 202.4 ANTI-AVOIDANCE.

# 209  Hold-Over Reliefs

## 209.1 RELIEF FOR GIFTS [*TCGA 1992, s 260*]

### (A) Chargeable lifetime transfers

B owns a house which he has not occupied as a private residence. He purchased the house for £9,200 inclusive of costs in 1977 and in January 2000 he gives it to a discretionary trust of which he is the settlor. The market value of the house is agreed to be £60,000 at the date of transfer, and B incurs transfer costs of £1,000. The indexation factor for the period March 1982 to April 1998 (note (*c*)) is 1.047. The house had a value of £21,000 at 31 March 1982.

|  | £ | £ |
|---|---:|---:|
| Disposal consideration | 60,000 | 60,000 |
| *Deduct* Costs of disposal | 1,000 | 1,000 |
|  | 59,000 | 59,000 |
| Cost | 9,200 |  |
| Market value 31.3.82 |  | 21,000 |
| Unindexed gain | 49,800 | 38,000 |
| Indexation allowance £21,000 × 1.047 | 21,987 | 21,987 |
| Gain after indexation | £27,813 | £16,013 |
| Chargeable gain |  | £16,013 |

If B elects under *Sec 260*, his chargeable gain is reduced to nil, and the trustees' acquisition cost of the house is treated as £43,987 (£60,000 − £16,013).

**Notes**

(*a*)   Relief under *Sec 260* is restricted, generally, to transfers which are, or would but for annual exemptions be, chargeable lifetime transfers for inheritance tax purposes.

(*b*)   There are special rules where deferral took place after 31 March 1982 but before 6 April 1988, for which see 204.2 ASSETS HELD ON 31 MARCH 1982.

(*c*)   Other than for the purposes of corporation tax on chargeable gains, indexation allowance is frozen at its April 1998 level. Therefore, the indexation factor for April 1998 is used in respect of disposals in a later month (and expenditure incurred in April 1998 or later does not attract indexation allowance at all). See 210 INDEXATION.

(*d*)   A held-over gain cannot attract taper relief. On a future disposal by the donee, any gain will be tapered by reference only to the donee's period of ownership.

(*e*)   Separate rules apply to transfers of assets between MARRIED PERSONS (215).

## 209.1 Hold-Over Reliefs

**(B) Disposal consideration** [*TCGA 1992, s 260(5)*]
The facts are as in (A) above except that B sells the house to the trustees for £30,000.

|  | £ | £ |
|---|---:|---:|
| Chargeable gain (as above)    note (*a*) |  | 16,013 |
| *Deduct* |  |  |
| Actual consideration passing | 30,000 |  |
| B's allowable costs    note (*b*) | (21,000) |  |
|  |  | 9,000 |
| Held-over gain |  | £7,013 |
| (i) B's chargeable gain is reduced to £16,013 − £7,013 |  | £9,000 |
| (ii) The trustees' allowable cost is reduced to £60,000 − £7,013 |  | £52,987 |

**Notes**
(*a*) The disposal consideration is taken as the open market value of the house at the date of disposal because B and the trustees are connected persons. Thus, the computation of the gain is as in (A) above.

(*b*) B's allowable costs are those allowable under *TCGA 1992, s 38*, which does not include indexation allowance.

**(C) Relief for IHT** [*TCGA 1992, s 260(7)*]
The facts are as in (A) above. Before transferring the house, B had made substantial chargeable transfers. Inheritance tax of £12,000 is payable on the transfer. The trustees sell the house in December 2000 for £55,000.

|  | £ | £ |
|---|---:|---:|
| Disposal proceeds |  | 55,000 |
| Acquisition cost | 60,000 |  |
| *Deduct* held-over gain | 16,013 |  |
|  |  | 43,987 |
| Gain |  | 11,013 |
| IHT attributable to earlier transfer (restricted) |  | 11,013 |
| Chargeable gain |  | Nil |

**Notes**
(*a*) The IHT deduction is limited to the amount of the gain and cannot create or increase a loss. [*TCGA 1992, s 260(7)*].

(*b*) A similar inheritance tax relief operates where the original gain was held over under *FA 1980, s 79*. [*TCGA 1992, s 67*].

(*c*) Expenditure incurred (or deemed to be incurred) in April 1998 or later (other than by companies) does not attract indexation allowance. [*TCGA 1992, ss 53(1A), 54(1A); FA 1998, s 122(1)–(3)*].

## Hold-Over Reliefs 209.2

209.2 **RELIEF FOR GIFT OF BUSINESS ASSETS** [*TCGA 1992, s 165, 7 Sch; FA 1993, 7 Sch 1; FA 1996, s 176*]

**(A)**

S has carried on his antique dealing business for 10 years. The assets of the business are valued as follows

|  | £ |
|---|---|
| Freehold shop and office | 285,000 |
| Goodwill | 90,000 |
| Stocks | 50,000 |
| Debtors | 9,500 |
| Cash | 4,500 |

Before the business began, S let the shop premises for one year. In October 1999, S transfers the business as a going concern to a company which he has formed with share capital of £1,000, held wholly by him. The transfer consideration is £1. At the time of the transfer S is 51. The gain arising in respect of the freehold is £209,000 and on goodwill it is £56,000 (both after deducting indexation allowance to April 1998).

|  | £ | £ |
|---|---|---|
| **Gains eligible for retirement relief** |  |  |
| (£209,000 + £56,000) |  | 265,000 |
| Relief £200,000 × 100% | 200,000 |  |
| £65,000 × 50% | 32,500 | 232,500 |
| Chargeable gain |  | £32,500 |

**If S and the company jointly claim relief** under *TCGA 1992, s 165*, part of the chargeable gain may be rolled over, as follows

|  | Freehold | Goodwill |  |
|---|---|---|---|
|  | £ | £ | £ |
| Total gain | 209,000 | 56,000 |  |
| Reduction for non-trade use [*TCGA 1992, 7 Sch 5*] ($\frac{1}{11}$) | 19,000 |  |  |
|  | £190,000 | £56,000 |  |
| Held-over gain before adjustment |  |  | 246,000 |
| Chargeable gain after retirement relief [*TCGA 1992, 7 Sch 8*] |  |  | 32,500 |
| Excess |  |  | £213,500 |
| Held-over gain (£246,000 − £213,500) |  |  | £32,500 |
| Chargeable gain |  |  | Nil |

**Notes**

(*a*) There is no statutory formula for apportioning the held-over gain after retirement relief between different assets. The following is one possible method of computing the revised base costs in the hands of the company.

## 209.2 Hold-Over Reliefs

Freehold

Gain held over $\dfrac{209{,}000}{265{,}000} \times £32{,}500$ £25,632

Revised base cost (£285,000 − £25,632) £259,368

Goodwill

Gain held over $\dfrac{209{,}000}{265{,}000} \times £32{,}500$ £6,868

Revised base cost (£90,000 − £6,868) £83,132

(b) If S had transferred the business to the company in consideration for the issue of shares, *TCGA 1992, s 162* (see 209.3 below) would have applied, but business assets relief under *Sec 165* would not. Retirement relief would still have applied in priority, so that the chargeable gain would have been £32,500. This gain would then have been rolled over against the base cost of the shares acquired by S.

(c) See 204.2 ASSETS HELD ON 31 MARCH 1982 for the relief given under *TCGA 1992, 4 Sch* where gains were held over after 31 March 1982 and before 6 April 1988 and a disposal occurs after 5 April 1988. This relief applies, inter alia, to gains held over under the business gifts relief rules illustrated above.

**(B)**
K holds 10,000 shares in her personal trading company, LO Ltd, which she acquired by inheritance in April 1997 at a probate value of £200,000. On 30 April 1999, she gifts 4,000 shares to her daughter. Their market value is £140,000 and the market value of K's remaining 6,000 shares is £210,000. K is 50 years of age at the time of the gift. K and her daughter jointly claim hold-over relief under *TCGA 1992, s 165*. At the date of disposal, the market values of the company's assets are as follows.

|  | Assets | Chargeable assets | |
|---|---|---|---|
|  |  | Business | Non-business |
|  | £ | £ | £ |
| Business premises | 200,000 | 200,000 |  |
| Goodwill | 50,000 | 50,000 |  |
| Trading stock | 30,000 |  |  |
| Debtors | 10,000 |  |  |
| Cash | 10,000 |  |  |
| Investments | 50,000 |  | 50,000 |
| Fixtures (all valued at less than £6,000) | 20,000 |  |  |
|  |  | £250,000 | £50,000 |

The indexation factor for the period April 1997 to April 1998 (note (*e*)) is 0.040.

### Hold-Over Reliefs 209.2

The gain on the gift of shares is calculated as follows.

|  | £ |
|---|---|
| Deemed consideration | 140,000 |
| Cost £200,000 × $\dfrac{140,000}{140,000 + 210,000}$ | 80,000 |
| Unindexed gain | 60,000 |
| Indexation allowance £80,000 × 0.040 | 3,200 |
| Gain after indexation | £56,800 |

The gain eligible for retirement relief is as follows.

$$\frac{\text{Chargeable business assets}}{\text{Chargeable assets}} = \frac{250,000}{300,000} \times £56,800 \qquad £47,333$$

The maximum amount qualifying for retirement relief at 100% is calculated by reference to a two-year qualifying period and is thus £200,000 × 20% = £40,000. The balance of £7,333 qualifies at 50%. Thus, retirement relief of £43,667 is available, leaving a chargeable gain of £13,133 (£56,800 − £43,667).

The gain available for hold-over relief (disregarding retirement relief) is calculated as follows.

$$£56,800 \times \frac{250,000}{300,000} \quad [\textit{TCGA 1992, 7 Sch 7}] \qquad £47,333$$

However, the held-over gain is not to exceed the 'relevant proportion' of the *chargeable* gain disregarding hold-over relief under *Sec 165*. [*TCGA 1992, 7 Sch 8(3)*]. The maximum available for hold-over is thus

$$£13,133 \times \frac{250,000}{300,000} \qquad £10,944$$

The final position is thus as follows.

|  | £ | £ |
|---|---|---|
| Total gain after indexation |  | 56,800 |
| Eligible for retirement relief | 43,667 |  |
| Eligible for hold-over relief | 10,944 | 54,611 |
| Chargeable gain 1999/2000 (subject to TAPER RELIEF (226)) |  | £2,189 |

The base cost of the 4,000 shares in the hands of K's daughter is £129,056 (market value of £140,000 less held-over gain of £10,944).

## 209.2 Hold-Over Reliefs

**Notes**

(*a*) This example illustrates the provisions of *TCGA 1992, 7 Sch 7* (restriction of held-over gain under *Sec 165* on disposal of shares where some of the company's chargeable assets are not chargeable business assets) and those of *TCGA 1992, 7 Sch 8(3)* (interaction of hold-over relief and retirement relief).

(*b*) If the appropriate proportion (i.e. chargeable business assets over chargeable assets) of the gain had been fully covered by retirement relief, hold-over relief would have been precluded by *TCGA 1992, s 165(3)(b)*.

(*c*) See also 221.2 RETIREMENT RELIEF for the calculation of gains qualifying for relief.

(*d*) This example is based on a strict interpretation of *TCGA 1992, 7 Sch 8(3)*. An alternative view is that the gain left in charge should not be less than £9,467 (£56,800 − £47,333), with hold-over relief being restricted accordingly.

(*e*) Other than for the purposes of corporation tax on chargeable gains, indexation allowance is frozen at its April 1998 level. See 210 INDEXATION.

## 209.3 TRANSFER OF BUSINESS TO A COMPANY [*TCGA 1992, s 162*]

W carries on an antiquarian bookselling business. He decides to form an unquoted company, P Ltd, to carry on the business. He then transfers, in August 1999, the whole of the business undertaking, assets and liabilities to P Ltd, in consideration for the issue of shares, plus an amount left outstanding on interest-free loan. The business assets and liabilities transferred are valued as follows

|  |  | Value | Chargeable gain (after indexation to April 1998) |
|---|---|---|---|
|  | £ | £ | £ |
| Freehold shop premises |  | 80,000 | 52,000 |
| Goodwill |  | 36,000 | 26,000 |
| Fixtures and fittings |  | 4,000 | — |
| Trading stock |  | 52,000 | — |
| Debtors |  | 28,000 | — |
|  |  | 200,000 |  |
| Mortgage on shop | 50,000 |  |  |
| Trade creditors | 20,000 | 70,000 | — |
|  |  | £130,000 | £78,000 |

The company issues 100,000 £1 ordinary shares, valued at par, to W in August 1999, and the amount left outstanding is £30,000. In March 2000, W sells 20,000 of his shares for £45,000 to X. W's remaining shareholding is then worth £155,000.

### (i) Amount of chargeable gain rolled over on transfer of the business

$$\frac{100,000}{130,000} \times £78,000 \qquad £60,000$$

Of the chargeable gain, £18,000 (£78,000 − £60,000) remains taxable, subject to taper relief.

The allowable cost of W's shares is £40,000 (£100,000 − £60,000).

### (ii) On the sale of shares to X, W realises a chargeable gain

|  | £ | £ |
|---|---|---|
| Disposal consideration |  | 45,000 |
| Allowable cost £40,000 × $\frac{45,000}{45,000 + 155,000}$ |  | 9,000 |
| Chargeable gain (no taper relief as shares held less than 12 months) |  | £36,000 |

**Notes**

(*a*) Relief under *Sec 162* is given automatically and without the need for a claim.

(*b*) See 204.2 ASSETS HELD ON 31 MARCH 1982 for the relief given under *TCGA 1992, 4 Sch* where gains were held over after 31 March 1982 and before 6 April 1988 and a disposal occurs after 5 April 1988. This relief applies, inter alia, to gains held over under the rules illustrated above.

(*c*) Expenditure incurred (or deemed to be incurred) in April 1998 or later (other than by companies) does not attract indexation allowance. [*TCGA 1992, ss 53(1A), 54(1A); FA 1998, s 122(1)–(3)*].

## 210.1 Indexation

# 210 Indexation

**Cross-references.** See 224.9 SHARES AND SECURITIES for indexation on a building society share account where cash bonus received on takeover or conversion, 225 SHARES AND SECURITIES — IDENTIFICATION RULES.

210.1 **INDEXATION ALLOWANCE — GENERAL RULES** [*TCGA 1992, ss 53–56; FA 1994, s 93(1)–(5)(11); FA 1998, s 122(1)–(3)(6)(7)*]

### (A) Calculation of indexation factor — companies

M Ltd bought a freehold factory in December 1983 for £500,000. Further buildings are erected at a cost of £200,000 in May 1990. In June 1999 the factory is sold for £2m. The retail price index (RPI) was re-based in January 1987 from 394.5 to 100 and the relevant values are as follows

| December | 1983 | 342.8 |
|---|---|---|
| May | 1990 | 126.2 |
| June | 1999 | 165.6 |

|  | £ | £ |
|---|---|---|
| Disposal consideration | | 2,000,000 |
| *Deduct* Cost of factory and site | 500,000 | |
| Cost of additions | 200,000 | 700,000 |
| Unindexed gain | | 1,300,000 |

Indexation allowance
(i)     Factory and site
       Indexation factor

$$\left(\frac{394.5 \times 165.6}{342.8}\right) - 100 = 90.6\%$$

       Indexed rise
       £500,000 × 0.906                         453,000

(ii)     Additions
       Indexation factor

$$\frac{165.6 - 126.2}{126.2} = 0.312$$

       Indexed rise
       £200,000 × 0.312              62,400         515,400

Gain chargeable to corporation tax                  £784,600

**Note**
(*a*)    Alternatively the indexation factor on the pre-January 1987 expenditure can be calculated using the revised RPI figures so that, for example,

      December 1983            =    86.89
      June 1999                   =    165.6

$$\text{Indexation from December 1983 to June 1999} = \frac{165.6 - 86.89}{86.89} = 0.906$$

# Indexation 210.1

**(B) Calculation of indexation factor — individuals etc.**
All the facts are as in (A) above except that M is an individual rather than a company. Additional information: the value of the RPI for April 1998 (see note (*a*)) was 162.6, and the factory is a business asset for taper relief purposes.

|  | £ | £ |
|---|---|---|
| Disposal consideration |  | 2,000,000 |
| *Deduct* Expenditure (December 1983) | 500,000 |  |
| Expenditure (May 1990) | 200,000 | 700,000 |
| Unindexed gain |  | 1,300,000 |
| Indexation allowance |  |  |

(i) Expenditure (December 1983)
Indexation factor

$$\frac{162.6 - 86.89}{86.89} = 0.871$$

Indexed rise
£500,000 × 0.871   435,500

(ii) Expenditure (May 1990)
Indexation factor

$$\frac{162.6 - 126.2}{126.2} = 0.288$$

| | | |
|---|---|---|
| Indexed rise £200,000 × 0.288 | 57,600 | 493,100 |
| Gain | | 806,900 |
| *Deduct* Taper relief (£806,900 × 15%) | | 121,035 |
| Chargeable gain | | £685,865 |

**Notes**

(*a*) For individuals, trustees and personal representatives (but not for companies), indexation allowance is frozen at its April 1998 level. Therefore, the indexation factor for April 1998 is used in respect of disposals in a later month (and expenditure incurred in April 1998 or later does not attract indexation allowance at all). [*TCGA 1992, ss 53(1A), 54(1A); FA 1998, s 122(1)–(3)*].

(*b*) Taper relief is given by reference to the number of complete years an asset has been held after 5 April 1998. As in this example, an extra one year is added to the holding period of an asset acquired before 17 March 1998. See 226 TAPER RELIEF. Taper relief is applied to the otherwise chargeable gain (*after* indexation to April 1998).

(*c*) In practice, any losses on other 1999/2000 disposals must be taken into account before taper relief is applied to the gain (see 226.1(B) TAPER RELIEF).

## 210.1 Indexation

**(C) Disposal of asset held on 31 March 1982**
X acquired an antique for £6,000 in August 1979. He sold it for £17,000 in December 1999. The agreed market value of the clock at 31 March 1982 is £7,500. The indexation factor for March 1982 to April 1998 (see note (*a*) to (B) above) is 1.047.

|  | £ | £ |
|---|---:|---:|
| Disposal consideration | 17,000 | 17,000 |
| *Deduct* Cost | 6,000 | |
| Market value 31.3.82 | | 7,500 |
| Unindexed gain | 11,000 | 9,500 |
| Indexation allowance £7,500 × 1.047 | 7,853 | 7,853 |
| Gain after indexation | £3,147 | £1,647 |
| Chargeable gain | | £1,647 |

**Notes**
(*a*) In both the calculation using cost and that using 31 March 1982 value, indexation is automatically based on 31 March 1982 value. If, however, a greater allowance would have been produced by basing indexation on cost, that would automatically have applied instead. If, however, an irrevocable election were to be made under *TCGA 1992, s 35(5)* for all assets to be treated as sold and re-acquired at 31 March 1982, indexation must then be based on 31 March 1982 value whether it is beneficial or not. [*TCGA 1992, s 55(1)(2)*].

(*b*) See also 204.1 ASSETS HELD ON 31 MARCH 1982.

**(D) Losses — indexation allowance restriction** [*TCGA 1992, s 53(1)(b)(2A); FA 1994, s 93(1)–(3)(11)*]
In June 1990, M had purchased two paintings, each for £25,000. In September 1998, he sells the paintings for £30,000 (A) and £23,000 (B) respectively. Incidental costs of purchase and sale are ignored for the purposes of this example. The indexation factor for the period June 1990 to April 1998 (see note (*a*) to (B) above) is 0.283.

**The gains/losses on the sales are as follows**

|  | (A) £ | (B) £ |
|---|---:|---:|
| Proceeds | 30,000 | 23,000 |
| Cost | 25,000 | 25,000 |
| Unindexed gain/(loss) | 5,000 | (2,000) |
| Indexation allowance £25,000 × 0.283 = £7,075 but restricted to | (5,000) | Nil |
| Chargeable gain/(allowable loss) | Nil | £(2,000) |

**Note**
(*a*) For disposals after 29 November 1993, indexation allowance can reduce an unindexed gain to nil but cannot create or increase a loss. A restricted transitional relief was available for disposals after 29 November 1993 and before 6 April 1995; this was illustrated in earlier editions of this book. [*FA 1994, s 93(11), 12 Sch*].

## 210.2 NO GAIN/NO LOSS TRANSFERS

**(A) Inter-spouse transfers — asset acquired by first spouse before 1 April 1982 — no indexation allowance restriction on ultimate disposal** [*TCGA 1992, ss 55(5)(6), 56(2), 58; FA 1994, s 93(5)(11)*]

Mr N inherited a country cottage in 1977 at a probate value of £12,000. Its market value at 31 March 1982 was £30,000. In July 1988, Mr N incurred enhancement expenditure of £5,000 on the cottage. In May 1990, he gave the cottage to his wife. In November 1999, Mrs N sells it for £85,000. At no time was the cottage the main residence of either spouse. The relevant indexation factors are as follows:

| | |
|---|---|
| March 1982 to May 1990 | 0.589 |
| July 1988 to May 1990 | 0.183 |
| March 1982 to April 1998 (note (*d*)) | 1.047 |
| July 1988 to April 1998 (note (*d*)) | 0.524 |

**(i) Disposal in May 1990**

Consideration deemed to be such that neither gain nor loss arises.

| | £ | £ |
|---|---:|---:|
| Cost of cottage to Mr N | | 12,000 |
| Enhancement expenditure | | 5,000 |
| | | 17,000 |
| Indexation allowance: | | |
| £30,000 × 0.589 | 17,670 | |
| £5,000 × 0.183 | 915 | 18,585 |
| Cost of cottage to Mrs N | | £35,585 |

**(ii) Disposal in November 1999**

| | £ | £ | £ |
|---|---:|---:|---:|
| Sale proceeds | | 85,000 | 85,000 |
| Cost | 35,585 | | |
| *Deduct* indexation allowance previously given | 18,585 | | |
| | 17,000 | | |
| *Deduct* enhancement expenditure | 5,000 | (12,000) | |
| Market value 31.3.82 | | | (30,000) |
| Enhancement expenditure (July 1988) | | (5,000) | (5,000) |
| Unindexed gain | | 68,000 | 50,000 |
| Indexation allowance: | | | |
| £30,000 × 1.047 | | (31,410) | (31,410) |
| £5,000 × 0.524 | | (2,620) | (2,620) |
| Gain after indexation | | £33,970 | £15,970 |
| Chargeable gain | | | £15,970 |

**Notes**

(*a*) Having acquired the asset by means of a no gain/no loss disposal, under *CGTA 1979, s 44* (now *TCGA 1992, s 58*), from her husband, who held it at 31 March 1982, Mrs N is deemed to have held the asset at 31 March 1982 for the purpose of the re-basing provisions, and also the provisions under which indexation allowance is computed using value at 31 March 1982. [*TCGA 1992, s 55(5)(6), 3 Sch 1*].

## 210.2 Indexation

(b) Where for re-basing/indexation purposes a person is deemed to have held an asset at 31 March 1982, that person can also be treated as having incurred enhancement expenditure which was in fact incurred after that date by a previous holder of the asset. (Revenue Tax Bulletin August 1992 p 32).

(c) Re-basing does not apply to the no gain/no loss disposal. [*TCGA 1992, s 35(3)(d)(i)*].

(d) Other than for the purposes of corporation tax on chargeable gains, indexation allowance is frozen at its April 1998 level. Therefore, the indexation factor for April 1998 is used in respect of disposals in a later month (and expenditure incurred in April 1998 or later does not attract indexation allowance at all). See 210.1(B) above.

(e) See also (B)–(D) below and 215 MARRIED PERSONS.

**(B) Inter-spouse transfers — asset acquired by first spouse after 31 March 1982 — gain on ultimate disposal** [*TCGA 1992, s 56(2)*]
The facts are as in (A) above except that Mr N inherited the cottage in April 1982 at a probate value of £30,000. The relevant indexation factors are:

| | |
|---|---|
| April 1982 to May 1990 | 0.557 |
| July 1988 to May 1990 | 0.183 |
| May 1990 to April 1998 | 0.288 |

**(i) Disposal in May 1990**
Consideration deemed to be such that neither gain nor loss arises.

| | £ | £ |
|---|---:|---:|
| Cost of cottage to Mr N | | 30,000 |
| Enhancement expenditure | | 5,000 |
| | | 35,000 |
| Indexation allowance: | | |
| £30,000 × 0.557 | 16,710 | |
| £5,000 × 0.183 | 915 | 17,625 |
| Cost of cottage to Mrs N | | £52,625 |

**(ii) Disposal in November 1999**

| | £ |
|---|---:|
| Sale proceeds | 85,000 |
| Cost (as above) | 52,625 |
| Unindexed gain | 32,375 |
| Indexation allowance £52,625 × 0.288 | 15,156 |
| Chargeable gain | £17,219 |

**Note**
(a) For further examples on inter-spouse transfers, see (A) above and 215 MARRIED PERSONS. The principles in (C) and (D) below also apply to inter-spouse transfers (except that, for inter-spouse transfers, indexation allowance cannot be computed beyond April 1998 — see note (d) to (A) above).

## Indexation 210.2

**(C) Intra-group transfers — asset acquired by group before 1 April 1982 — indexation allowance restricted on ultimate disposal** [*TCGA 1992, ss 55(5)–(9), 56(2), 171; FA 1994, s 93(4)*]

J Ltd and K Ltd are 75% subsidiaries of H Ltd. J Ltd acquired a property in 1980 for £20,000. Its market value at 31 March 1982 was £25,000. In May 1990, J Ltd transferred the property to K Ltd. In June 1999, K Ltd sells the property outside the group. The sale proceeds are (1) £18,000 or (2) £29,000. The relevant indexation factors are as follows:

| | |
|---|---|
| March 1982 to May 1990 | 0.589 |
| March 1982 to June 1999 | 1.085 |

**(i) Disposal in May 1990**
Consideration deemed to be such that neither gain nor loss arises.

| | £ |
|---|---|
| Cost of asset to J Ltd | 20,000 |
| Indexation allowance £25,000 × 0.589 | 14,725 |
| Cost of asset to K Ltd | £34,725 |

**(ii) Disposal in June 1999**

*(1) Proceeds £18,000*

| | £ | £ | £ |
|---|---|---|---|
| Proceeds | | 18,000 | 18,000 |
| Cost | 34,725 | | |
| *Deduct* Indexation allowance previously given | 14,725 | | |
| | | (20,000) | |
| Market value 31.3.82 | | | (25,000) |
| | | (2,000) | (7,000) |
| *Add* Rolled-up indexation | | (14,725) | (14,725) |
| Loss after rolled-up indexation | | £(16,725) | £(21,725) |
| | | | |
| Allowable loss | | £16,725 | |

## 210.2 Indexation

*(2) Proceeds £29,000*

|  | £ | £ | £ |
|---|---:|---:|---:|
| Proceeds |  | 29,000 | 29,000 |
| Cost | 34,725 |  |  |
| *Deduct* Indexation allowance previously given | 14,725 |  |  |
|  |  | (20,000) |  |
| Market value 31.3.82 |  |  | (25,000) |
| Unindexed gain |  | 9,000 | 4,000 |
| Indexation allowance: £25,000 × 1.085 = £27,125 but restricted to |  | (9,000) | (4,000) |
|  |  | Nil | Nil |
| Excess of rolled-up indexation (£14,725) over indexation allowance given above |  | (5,725) | (10,725) |
| Loss after rolled-up indexation |  | £(5,725) | £(10,725) |
| Allowable loss |  | £5,725 |  |

**Notes**

(a) The calculation first follows that in (A) above. [*TCGA 1992, s 55(5)(6)*]. As the ultimate disposal is after 29 November 1993 and indexation allowance is either unavailable as in (1) above or restricted as in (2) above, special provisions enable the person making the disposal to obtain the benefit of any indexation allowance already accrued on no gain/no loss transfers made *before* 30 November 1993 (called 'rolled-up indexation'). [*TCGA 1992, s 55(7)–(9); FA 1994, s 93(4)*].

(b) The principles illustrated in this example apply equally to inter-spouse transfers (except that, for inter-spouse transfers, indexation allowance cannot be computed beyond April 1998 — see note (d) to (A) above).

# Indexation 210.2

**(D) Intra-group transfers — asset acquired by group after 31 March 1982 — loss on ultimate disposal** [*TCGA 1992, ss 56(2)–(4), 171; FA 1994, s 93(5)*]

L Ltd, M Ltd and N Ltd are members of a 75% group of companies. L Ltd acquired a property in June 1990 for £50,000 and transferred it to M Ltd in June 1993. M Ltd transferred the property to N Ltd in June 1996, and N Ltd sold it outside the group in June 1999 for £55,000. The relevant indexation factors are as follows:

| | |
|---|---|
| June 1990 to June 1993 | 0.113 |
| June 1993 to June 1996 | 0.085 |

### (i) Disposal in June 1993
Consideration deemed to be such that neither gain nor loss arises.

| | £ |
|---|---|
| Cost of asset to L Ltd | 50,000 |
| Indexation allowance £50,000 × 0.113 | 5,650 |
| Cost of asset to M Ltd | £55,650 |

### (ii) Disposal in June 1996

| | |
|---|---|
| Cost of asset to M Ltd | 55,650 |
| Indexation allowance £55,650 × 0.085 | 4,730 |
| Cost of asset to N Ltd | £60,380 |

### (iii) Disposal in June 1999

| | |
|---|---|
| Proceeds | 55,000 |
| Cost (as above) | 60,380 |
| Loss before adjustment under *Sec 56(3)* | 5,380 |
| *Deduct* Indexation on June 1996 disposal | 4,730 |
| Allowable loss | £650 |

### Notes

(*a*) Where a loss accrues on the ultimate disposal, it is reduced by any indexation allowance included in the cost of the asset by virtue of a no gain/no loss disposal made *after* 29 November 1993. If this adjustment would otherwise convert a loss into a gain, the disposal is treated as giving rise to neither a gain nor a loss. [*TCGA 1992, s 56(3); FA 1994, s 93(5)*].

(*b*) The principles illustrated in this example apply equally to inter-spouse transfers (except that, for inter-spouse transfers, indexation allowance cannot be computed beyond April 1998 — see note (*d*) to (A) above).

## 211.1 Interest on Overpaid Tax

## 211 Interest on Overpaid Tax

[*TCGA 1992, s 283; FA 1994, 19 Sch 46, 26 Sch Pt V(23); FA 1997, s 92(5)(6)*]

### 211.1 PRE-SELF-ASSESSMENT

L realised net chargeable gains (after the annual exemption) of £20,000 in 1995/96. An assessment was raised on 15 January 1997, charging tax of £8,000. L paid the tax on 30 January 1997. In December 1998, L made a claim under *TCGA 1992, s 152* (rollover relief) and the 1995/96 assessment was reduced to £8,000, with tax payable of £3,200. A repayment of £4,800 was made by payable order issued on 15 April 1999.

**Repayment supplement is as follows**                £

| | | |
|---|---|---:|
| 6.4.97 – 5.8.97 | £4,800 × 4% × $\frac{4}{12}$ | 64.00 |
| 6.8.97 – 5.1.99 | £4,800 × 4.75% × $\frac{17}{12}$ | 323.00 |
| 6.1.99 – 5.3.99 | £4,800 × 4% × $\frac{2}{12}$ | 32.00 |
| 6.3.99 – 5.5.99 | £4,800 × 3% × $\frac{2}{12}$ | 24.00 |
| | | £443.00 |

### 211.2 SELF-ASSESSMENT

M's tax return for 1997/98 included a chargeable gain of £52,500 on the sale of some unquoted shares. His self-assessment showed capital gains tax payable of £18,400, i.e. £52,500 – £6,500 (annual exemption) = £46,000 @ 40% (M's marginal rate of income tax). M paid the tax on 27 January 1999. However, the computation included an estimated valuation of the shares as at 31 March 1982 and, following negotiations, the value was finally agreed at a figure in excess of M's estimate, resulting in a reduction of £8,000 in the chargeable gain. Thus, tax of £3,200 (£8,000 @ 40%) became repayable to M, and repayment was duly made on 9 August 1999.

**Repayment supplement is as follows**

| | | |
|---|---|---:|
| 27.1.99 – 5.3.99 | £3,200 × 4% × $\frac{38}{365}$ | 13.33 |
| 6.3.99 – 9.8.99 | £3,200 × 3% × $\frac{156}{365}$ | 41.03 |
| | | £54.36 |

**Note**

(*a*) Supplement runs from the date the tax was paid (even if before the due date — 31 January 1999 in this case) to the date the repayment order is issued. [*TCGA 1992, s 283(1)(2); FA 1994, 19 Sch 46; FA 1997, s 92(5)(6)*].

## 212 Interest and Surcharges on Unpaid Tax

212.1 **SELF-ASSESSMENT** [*TMA 1970, ss 59C, 69, 86; FA 1994, ss 194, 196, 199, 19 Sch 20; FA 1995, ss 109, 110*]

Mr Watson's 1997/98 capital gains tax liability as shown in his self-assessment amounts to £5,000. On 1 May 1999 Mr Watson pays £2,000 and on 3 August 1999 he pays the £3,000 balance.

Mr Watson will be charged as follows.

*Interest and Surcharge due*

|  | £ | £ |
|---|---|---|
| *Interest* | | |
| £2,000 × 8.5% × $\frac{34}{365}$ (31.1.99 – 5.3.99) | 15.84 | |
| £2,000 × 7.5% × $\frac{56}{365}$ (6.3.99 – 1.5.99) | 23.01 | 38.85 |
| £3,000 × 8.5% × $\frac{34}{365}$ (31.1.99 – 5.3.99) | 23.75 | |
| £3,000 × 7.5% × $\frac{150}{365}$ (6.3.99 – 3.8.99) | 92.47 | 116.22 |
| | | £155.07 |
| *Surcharge* | | |
| £5,000 × 5% | | 250.00 |
| £3,000 × 5% | | 150.00 |
| | | £400.00 |

**Notes**

(*a*) Under self-assessment, capital gains tax is due on 31 January following the year of assessment.

(*b*) If any tax is paid more than 28 days late, a 5% surcharge is levied in addition to interest. An additional surcharge is also levied if the tax is outstanding for more than 6 months. On appeal, surcharges may be set aside if the Commissioners accept that the taxpayer had a 'reasonable excuse' for late payment. Interest is chargeable on a surcharge and accrues from a date which is 30 days after the surcharge is imposed. [*TMA 1970, s 59C; FA 1994, s 194; FA 1995, s 109*].

## 213.1 Land

## 213 Land

213.1 **SMALL PART DISPOSALS** [*TCGA 1992, s 242; FA 1996, 21 Sch 37*]

C owns farmland which cost £134,000 in May 1986. In February 1994, a small plot of land is exchanged with an adjoining landowner for another piece of land. The value placed on the transaction is £18,000. The value of the remaining estate excluding the new piece of land is estimated at £250,000. In March 2000, C sells the whole estate for £300,000.

| Indexation factors | | |
|---|---|---|
| May 1986 to February 1994 | | 0.452 |
| February 1994 to April 1998 (note (*d*)) | | 0.144 |
| May 1986 to April 1998 (note (*d*)) | | 0.662 |

**(i) No claim made under *TCGA 1992, s 242(2)***

|  |  | £ | £ |
|---|---|---:|---:|
| (*a*) | *Disposal in February 1994* | | |
| | Disposal proceeds | | 18,000 |
| | Allowable cost $\dfrac{18,000}{18,000 + 250,000} \times £134,000$ | | 9,000 |
| | Unindexed gain | | 9,000 |
| | Indexation allowance £9,000 × 0.452 | | 4,068 |
| | Chargeable gain 1993/94 | | £4,932 |
| (*b*) | *Disposal in March 2000* | | |
| | Disposal proceeds | | 300,000 |
| | Allowable cost | | |
| | Original land £(134,000 − 9,000) | 125,000 | |
| | Exchanged land | 18,000 | 143,000 |
| | Unindexed gain | | 157,000 |
| | Indexation allowance | | |
| | Original land £125,000 × 0.662 | 82,750 | |
| | Exchanged land £18,000 × 0.144 | 2,592 | 85,342 |
| | Chargeable gain 1999/2000 (subject to any available TAPER RELIEF (226)) | | £71,658 |

**(ii) Claim made under *TCGA 1992, s 242(2)***

|  |  | |
|---|---|---:|
| (*a*) | *No disposal in February 1994* | |
| | Allowable cost of original land | 134,000 |
| | *Deduct* disposal proceeds | 18,000 |
| | Adjusted allowable cost | £116,000 |
| | Allowable cost of additional land | £18,000 |

# Land 213.1

|  |  | £ | £ |
|---|---|---:|---:|
| (b) | *Disposal in March 2000* |  |  |
|  | Disposal proceeds |  | 300,000 |
|  | Allowable cost |  |  |
|  | Original land | 116,000 |  |
|  | Additional land | 18,000 | 134,000 |
|  | Unindexed gain |  | 166,000 |
|  | Indexation allowance |  |  |
|  | Original land £134,000 × 0.662 | 88,708 |  |
|  | Additional land £18,000 × 0.144 | 2,592 |  |
|  |  | 91,300 |  |
|  | Receipt set-off £18,000 × 0.144 | 2,592 | 88,708 |
|  | Chargeable gain 1999/2000 (subject to any available TAPER RELIEF (226)) |  | £77,292 |

**Notes**

(a) A claim under *TCGA 1992, s 242* may be made where the consideration for the part disposal does not exceed one-fifth of the value of the whole, up to a maximum of £20,000.

(b) If the second disposal had also been made in 1993/94 no claim under *Sec 242(2)* could have been made on the part disposal as proceeds of all disposals of land in the year would have exceeded £20,000.

(c) If the original land had been held at 31 March 1982 and the part disposal took place after that date, the disposal proceeds, on a claim under *Sec 242(2)*, would be deducted from the 31 March 1982 value for the purpose of the re-basing provisions.

(d) Other than for the purposes of corporation tax on chargeable gains, indexation allowance is frozen at its April 1998 level. Therefore, the indexation factor for April 1998 is used in respect of disposals in a later month (and expenditure incurred in April 1998 or later does not attract indexation allowance at all). See 210 INDEXATION.

## 213.2 Land

**213.2 COMPULSORY PURCHASE** [*TCGA 1992, ss 243–248; FA 1996, s 141(4)(6), 21 Sch 38*]

### (A) Rollover where new land acquired

#### (i) Rollover not claimed

D owns freehold land purchased for £77,000 in 1978. Part of the land is made the subject of a compulsory purchase order. The compensation of £70,000 is agreed on 10 August 1999. The market value of the remaining land is £175,000. The value of the total freehold land at 31 March 1982 was £98,000. The indexation factor for the period March 1982 to April 1998 (see note (*a*)) is 1.047.

|  | £ | £ |
|---|---|---|
| Disposal consideration | 70,000 | 70,000 |
| Cost £77,000 × $\dfrac{70{,}000}{70{,}000 + 175{,}000}$ | 22,000 | |
| Market value 31.3.82 | | |
| £98,000 × $\dfrac{70{,}000}{70{,}000 + 175{,}000}$ | | 28,000 |
| Unindexed gain | 48,000 | 42,000 |
| Indexation allowance £28,000 × 1.047 | 29,316 | 29,316 |
| Gain after indexation | £18,684 | £12,684 |
| Chargeable gain (subject to any available TAPER RELIEF (226)) | | £12,684 |

#### (ii) Rollover claimed under *TCGA 1992, s 247*

If, in (i), D acquires new land costing, say, £80,000 in, say, December 1999, relief may be claimed as follows.

|  | £ |
|---|---|
| Allowable cost of land compulsorily purchased | 28,000 |
| Indexation allowance | 29,316 |
| Deemed consideration for disposal | 57,316 |
| Actual consideration | 70,000 |
| Chargeable gain rolled over | £12,684 |
| Allowable cost of new land (£80,000 − £12,684) | £67,316 |

**Note**

(*a*) Other than for the purposes of corporation tax on chargeable gains, indexation allowance is frozen at its April 1998 level. Therefore, the indexation factor for April 1998 is used in respect of disposals in a later month (and expenditure incurred in April 1998 or later does not attract indexation allowance at all). See 210 INDEXATION.

## (B) Small disposals

### (i) No rollover relief claimed

T inherited land in June 1986 at a probate value of £290,000. Under a compulsory purchase order, a part of the land is acquired for highway improvements. Compensation of £32,000 and a further £10,000 for severance, neither sum including any amount in respect of loss of profits, is agreed on 15 May 1999. The value of the remaining land is £900,000. Prior to the compulsory purchase, the value of all the land had been £950,000. The indexation factor for the period June 1986 to April 1998 (note (*c*)) is 0.663.

|  | £ |
|---|---:|
| Total consideration for disposal (£32,000 + £10,000) | 42,000 |
| *Deduct* allowable cost $\dfrac{42,000}{42,000 + 900,000} \times £290,000$ | 12,930 |
| Unindexed gain | 29,070 |
| Indexation allowance £12,930 × 0.663 | 8,573 |
| Chargeable gain (subject to any available TAPER RELIEF (226)) | £20,497 |

### (ii) Rollover relief claimed under *TCGA 1992, s 243*

Total consideration for disposal is £42,000, less than 5% of the value of the estate before the disposal (£950,000). T may therefore claim that the consideration be deducted from the allowable cost of the estate.

Revised allowable cost (£290,000 − £42,000)      £248,000

### Notes

(*a*) An indexation adjustment in respect of the amount deducted will be required on a subsequent disposal of the estate. [*TCGA 1992, ss 53(3), 57*]. For an example of the computation, see 206.4(E) DISPOSAL.

(*b*) From 24 February 1997, the Revenue additionally regard consideration of £3,000 or less as 'small', whether or not it would pass the 5% test illustrated here. (Revenue Tax Bulletin February 1997, p 397).

## 213.3 Land

### 213.3 LEASES

**(A) Short leases which are not initially wasting assets** [*TCGA 1992, 8 Sch 1*]

On 31 August 1994, N purchased the remaining term of a lease of commercial premises for £55,000. The lease was subject to a 25-year sub-lease granted on 1 July 1972 at a fixed rental of £1,000 a year. The market rental was estimated at £15,000 a year. The term of the lease held by N is 60 years from 1 April 1970. The value of the lease in 1997, when the sub-lease expired, was estimated at 31 August 1994 as being £70,000. Immediately upon expiry of the sub-lease, N has refurbishment work done at a cost of £50,000 (payable on 30 July 1997), £40,000 of which qualifies as enhancement expenditure. On 31 March 2000, N sells the lease for £130,000.

| Indexation factors | | |
|---|---|---|
| August 1994 to April 1998 (note (*b*)) | | 0.124 |
| July 1997 to April 1998 (note (*b*)) | | 0.032 |

| | | |
|---|---|---|
| Term of lease at date of expiry of sub-lease | 32 years 9 months | |
| Relevant percentage $89.354 + \frac{9}{12} \times (90.280 - 89.354)$ | 90.049% | |
| | | |
| Term of lease at date of assignment | 30 years | |
| Relevant percentage | 87.330% | |

| | £ | £ |
|---|---|---|
| Disposal consideration | | 130,000 |
| *Deduct* allowable cost | 55,000 | |
| enhancement costs | 40,000 | |
| | 95,000 | |
| *Less* Wasted | | |
| $\dfrac{90.049 - 87.330}{90.049} \times 95{,}000$ | 2,868 | |
| | | 92,132 |
| Unindexed gain | | 37,868 |
| Indexation allowance: | | |
| Cost of lease | | |
| $0.124 \times \dfrac{55{,}000}{95{,}000} \times £92{,}132$ | 6,614 | |
| Enhancement costs | | |
| $0.032 \times \dfrac{40{,}000}{95{,}000} \times £92{,}132$ | 1,241 | 7,855 |
| Chargeable gain 1999/2000 (subject to any available TAPER RELIEF (226)) | | £30,013 |

**Note**

(*a*) The head-lease becomes a wasting asset on the expiry of the sub-lease. [*TCGA 1992, 8 Sch 1(2)*].

(*b*) Other than for the purposes of corporation tax on chargeable gains, indexation allowance is frozen at its April 1998 level. Therefore, the indexation factor for April 1998 is used in respect of disposals in a later month (and expenditure incurred in April 1998 or later does not attract indexation allowance at all). See 210 INDEXATION.

## Land 213.3

**(B) Grant of long lease** [*TCGA 1992, s 42, 8 Sch 2*]
In 1980, K acquired a long lease by assignment for £24,000. At the time he acquired it, the lease had an unexpired term of 82 years. On 10 April 1999, he granted a 55-year sub-lease for a premium of £110,000 and a peppercorn rent. The value of the reversion plus the capitalised value of the rents is £10,000. The value of the lease at 31 March 1982 was estimated at £54,000. The indexation factor for the period March 1982 to April 1998 (see note (*b*) to (A) above) is 1.047.

|  | £ | £ |
|---|---:|---:|
| Disposal consideration | 110,000 | 110,000 |
| Cost £24,000 × $\dfrac{110{,}000}{110{,}000 + 10{,}000}$ | 22,000 | |
| Market value 31.3.82 | | |
| £54,000 × $\dfrac{110{,}000}{110{,}000 + 10{,}000}$ | | 49,500 |
| Unindexed gain | 88,000 | 60,500 |
| Indexation allowance £49,500 × 1.047 | 51,827 | 51,827 |
| Gain after indexation | £36,173 | £8,673 |
| Chargeable gain 1999/2000 (subject to any available TAPER RELIEF (226)) | | £8,673 |

## 213.3 Land

**(C) Grant of short lease** [*ICTA 1988, s 34; TCGA 1992, 8 Sch 2, 5; FA 1998, s 40, 5 Sch 15, 63*]

L is the owner of a freehold factory which he leases for a term of 25 years commencing in December 1999. The cost of the factory was £100,000 in April 1992. The lease is granted for a premium of £30,000 and an annual rent. The reversion to the lease plus the capitalised value of the rents amount to £120,000. The indexation factor for April 1992 to April 1998 (see note (*c*)) is 0.171.

|  | £ | £ |
|---|---|---|
| **Amount chargeable to income tax** | | |
| Amount of premium | | 30,000 |
| *Deduct* excluded $\dfrac{25-1}{50} \times £30,000$ | | 14,400 |
| Amount chargeable to income tax | | £15,600 |
| | | |
| **Chargeable gain** | | |
| Premium received | 30,000 | |
| *Deduct* charged to income tax | 15,600 | |
| | | 14,400 |
| Allowable cost $\dfrac{14,400}{30,000 + 120,000} \times £100,000$ | | 9,600 |
| | | |
| Unindexed gain | | 4,800 |
| Indexation allowance £9,600 × 0.171 | | 1,642 |
| Chargeable gain 1999/2000 (subject to any available TAPER RELIEF (226)) | | £3,158 |

**Notes**

(*a*) A short lease is one the duration of which, at the time of grant, does not exceed 50 years.

(*b*) The amount chargeable to income tax is not deducted from the amount of premium appearing in the denominator of the apportionment fraction.

(*c*) Other than for the purposes of corporation tax on chargeable gains, indexation allowance is frozen at its April 1998 level. Therefore, the indexation factor for April 1998 is used in respect of disposals in a later month (and expenditure incurred in April 1998 or later does not attract indexation allowance at all). See 210 INDEXATION.

# Land 213.3

**(D) Disposal by assignment of short lease: without enhancement expenditure** [*TCGA 1992, 8 Sch 1*]

X buys a lease for £200,000 on 1 October 1995. The lease commenced on 1 June 1986 for a term of 60 years. X assigns the lease for £300,000 at the end of March 2000. The indexation factor for October 1995 to April 1998 (note (*a*)) is 0.085.

| | | |
|---|---|---|
| Term of lease unexpired at date of acquisition | 50 years 8 months | |
| Relevant percentage | 100% | |
| | | |
| Term of lease unexpired at date of assignment | 46 years 2 months | |
| Relevant percentage $98.490 + \frac{2}{12} \times (98.902 - 98.490)$ | 98.559% | |

| | £ | £ |
|---|---|---|
| Disposal consideration | | 300,000 |
| Allowable cost | 200,000 | |
| *Deduct* Wasted $\frac{100 - 98.559}{100} \times £200,000$ | 2,882 | |
| | | 197,118 |
| Unindexed gain | | 102,882 |
| Indexation allowance £197,118 × 0.085 | | 16,755 |
| Chargeable gain 1999/2000 (subject to any available TAPER RELIEF (226)) | | £86,127 |

**Note**

(*a*)  Other than for the purposes of corporation tax on chargeable gains, indexation allowance is frozen at its April 1998 level. Therefore, the indexation factor for April 1998 is used in respect of disposals in a later month (and expenditure incurred in April 1998 or later does not attract indexation allowance at all). See 210 INDEXATION.

**(E) Disposal by assignment of short lease held at 31 March 1982** [*TCGA 1992, s 35, 8 Sch 1*]

A buys a lease for £100,000 on 1 March 1981. The lease commenced on 31 March 1971 for a term of 60 years. Its value at 31 March 1982 was estimated at £104,000. On 31 March 2000, A assigns the lease for £240,000. The indexation factor for the period March 1982 to April 1998 (note (*d*)) is 1.047.

**(i) The computation without re-basing to 1982 is as follows**

| | |
|---|---|
| Term of lease unexpired at date of acquisition (1.3.81) | 50 years 1 month |
| Relevant percentage | 100% |
| | |
| Term of lease unexpired at date of assignment | 31 years 0 months |
| Relevant percentage | 88.371% |

## 213.3 Land

|  | £ | £ |
|---|---:|---:|
| Disposal consideration |  | 240,000 |
| Cost | 100,000 |  |
| Deduct Wasted $\dfrac{100 - 88.371}{100} \times £100,000$ | 11,629 | 88,371 |
| Unindexed gain |  | 151,629 |
| Indexation allowance (see (ii) below) |  | 96,556 |
| Gain after indexation |  | £55,073 |

### (ii) The computation with re-basing to 1982 is as follows

| Term of lease unexpired at deemed date of acquisition (31.3.82) | 49 years |
|---|---|
| Relevant percentage | 99.657% |
| Term of lease unexpired at date of assignment | 31 years |
| Relevant percentage | 88.371% |

|  | £ | £ |
|---|---:|---:|
| Disposal consideration |  | 240,000 |
| Market value 31.3.82 | 104,000 |  |
| Deduct Wasted $\dfrac{99.657 - 88.371}{99.657} \times £104,000$ | 11,778 | 92,222 |
| Unindexed gain |  | 147,778 |
| Indexation allowance £92,222 × 1.047 |  | 96,556 |
| Gain after indexation |  | £51,222 |

| Chargeable gain 1999/2000 (subject to any available TAPER RELIEF (226)) | £51,222 |
|---|---:|

### Notes

(a) A is deemed, under *TCGA 1992, s 35*, to have disposed of and immediately re-acquired the lease on 31 March 1982 at its market value at that date.

(b) Both calculations produce a gain with the re-basing calculation producing the smaller gain. Therefore, re-basing applies. [*Sec 35(2)(3)(a)*].

(c) Indexation is based, in both calculations, on the assumption that the asset was sold and re-acquired at market value on 31 March 1982 since this gives a greater allowance than if based on original cost as reduced by the wasting asset provisions. [*TCGA 1992, s 55(1)(2)*].

(d) Other than for the purposes of corporation tax on chargeable gains, indexation allowance is frozen at its April 1998 level. Therefore, the indexation factor for April 1998 is used in respect of disposals in a later month (and expenditure incurred in April 1998 or later does not attract indexation allowance at all). See 210 INDEXATION.

**(F) Disposal by assignment of short lease: with enhancement expenditure** [*TCGA 1992, 8 Sch 1*]

D Ltd acquires the lease of office premises for £100,000 on 1 July 1991. On 1 January 1993, the company contracts for complete refurbishment of the premises at a total cost of £180,000, of which £120,000 can be regarded as capital enhancement expenditure. The work is done at the beginning of January 1993, and the money is payable in equal tranches in March 1993 and May 1993. The lease is for a term of 50 years commencing 1 April 1984. On 1 January 2000, the lease is assigned to a new lessee for £450,000.

| Indexation factors (assumed) | | |
|---|---|---|
| July 1991 to January 2000 | | 0.250 |
| March 1993 to January 2000 | | 0.180 |
| May 1993 to January 2000 | | 0.170 |

Term of lease unexpired at date of acquisition — 42 years 9 months
Relevant percentage $96.593 + \frac{9}{12} \times (97.107 - 96.593)$ — 96.978%

Term of lease unexpired at date of expenditure
incurred (January 1993 — see note (*a*)) — 41 years 3 months
Relevant percentage $96.041 + \frac{3}{12} \times (96.593 - 96.041)$ — 96.179%

Term of lease unexpired at date of assignment — 34 years 3 months
Relevant percentage $91.156 + \frac{3}{12} \times (91.981 - 91.156)$ — 91.362%

| | £ | £ | £ |
|---|---:|---:|---:|
| Disposal consideration | | | 450,000 |
| Cost of acquisition | 100,000 | | |
| *Deduct* Wasted | | | |
| $\dfrac{96.978 - 91.362}{96.978} \times 100,000$ | 5,791 | 94,209 | |
| Enhancement expenditure | 120,000 | | |
| *Deduct* Wasted | | | |
| $\dfrac{96.179 - 91.362}{96.179} \times 120,000$ | 6,010 | 113,990 | 208,199 |
| Unindexed gain | | | 241,801 |
| Indexation allowance | | | |
| Cost of lease £94,209 × 0.250 | | 23,552 | |
| Enhancement costs | | | |
| March 1993 £56,995 × 0.180 | | 10,259 | |
| May 1993 £56,995 × 0.170 | | 9,689 | |
| | | | 43,500 |
| Chargeable gain | | | £198,301 |

**Note**
(*a*)  The wasting provisions apply to enhancement expenditure by reference to the time when it is first reflected in the nature of the lease. The indexation provisions apply by reference to the date the expenditure became due and payable. [*TCGA 1992, s 54(4)(b), 8 Sch 1(4)(b)*].

## 213.3 Land

**(G) Sub-lease granted out of short lease: premium not less than potential premium**
[TCGA 1992, 8 Sch 4, 5; FA 1998, 5 Sch 63]
On 1 November 1997, S purchased a lease of shop premises then having 50 years to run for a premium of £100,000 and an annual rental of £40,000. After occupying the premises for the purposes of his own business, S granted a sub-lease to N Ltd. The sub-lease was for a term of 21 years commencing on 1 August 1999, for a premium of £50,000 and an annual rental of £30,000. It is agreed that, had the rent under the sub-lease been £40,000, the premium obtainable would have been £20,000. The indexation factor for November 1997 to April 1998 (note (*b*)) is 0.019.

| | |
|---|---:|
| Term of lease at date granted | 50 years |
| Relevant percentage | 100% |
| | |
| Term of lease at date sub-lease granted | 48 years 3 months |
| Relevant percentage $99.289 + \frac{3}{12} \times (99.657 - 99.289)$ | 99.381% |
| | |
| Term of lease at date sub-lease expires | 27 years 3 months |
| Relevant percentage $83.816 + \frac{3}{12} \times (85.053 - 83.816)$ | 84.125% |

**Premium chargeable on S under Schedule A**    £
Amount of premium                               50,000

$Deduct \dfrac{21 - 1}{50} \times £50,000$      20,000

Amount chargeable under Schedule A              £30,000

**Chargeable gain**
Disposal consideration                          50,000
Allowable expenditure

$£100,000 \times \dfrac{99.381 - 84.125}{100}$  15,256

Unindexed gain                                  34,744
Indexation allowance £15,256 × 0.019            290

Chargeable gain                                 34,454
*Deduct* Amount chargeable under Schedule A     30,000

Net chargeable gain (subject to any available
   TAPER RELIEF (226))                          £4,454

**Notes**
(*a*) If the amount chargeable under Schedule A exceeded the chargeable gain, the net gain would be nil. The deduction cannot create or increase a loss. [TCGA 1992, 8 Sch 5(2)].

(*b*) Other than for the purposes of corporation tax on chargeable gains, indexation allowance is frozen at its April 1998 level. Therefore, the indexation factor for April 1998 is used in respect of disposals in a later month (and expenditure incurred in April 1998 or later does not attract indexation allowance at all). See 210 INDEXATION.

**(H) Sub-lease granted out of short lease: premium less than potential premium**
[*TCGA 1992, 8 Sch 4, 5; FA 1998, 5 Sch 63*]
C bought a lease of a house on 1 May 1995, when the unexpired term was 49 years. The cost of the lease was £20,000, and the ground rent payable is £500 p.a. C then let the house on a monthly tenancy until 30 November 1999 when he granted a 10-year lease for a premium of £5,000 and an annual rent of £8,000. Had the rent under the sub-lease been £500 a year, the premium obtainable would have been £40,000. C does not at any time occupy the house as a private residence. The indexation factor for May 1995 to April 1998 (note (*b*)) is 0.087.

| | |
|---|---:|
| Term of lease at date of acquisition | 49 years |
| Relevant percentage | 99.657% |
| | |
| Term of lease when sub-lease granted | 44 years 5 months |
| Relevant percentage $97.595 + \frac{5}{12} \times (98.059 - 97.595)$ | 97.788% |
| | |
| Term of lease when sub-lease expires | 34 years 5 months |
| Relevant percentage $91.156 + \frac{5}{12} \times (91.981 - 91.156)$ | 91.500% |

| | £ |
|---|---:|
| **Amount chargeable under Schedule A** | |
| Amount of premium | 5,000 |
| *Deduct* exclusion $\dfrac{10-1}{50} \times 5{,}000$ | 900 |
| Chargeable under Schedule A | £4,100 |
| | |
| Disposal consideration | 5,000 |
| *Deduct* allowable expenditure | |
| $£20{,}000 \times \dfrac{97.788 - 91.500}{99.657} \times \dfrac{5{,}000}{40{,}000}$ | 158 |
| | |
| Unindexed gain | 4,842 |
| Indexation allowance £158 × 0.087 | 14 |
| Chargeable gain | 4,828 |
| *Deduct* Amount chargeable under Schedule A | 4,100 |
| Net chargeable gain | £728 |

**Notes**
(*a*) If the amount chargeable under Schedule A exceeded the chargeable gain, the net gain would be nil. The deduction cannot create or increase a loss. [*TCGA 1992, 8 Sch 5(2)*].

(*b*) Other than for the purposes of corporation tax on chargeable gains, indexation allowance is frozen at its April 1998 level. Therefore, the indexation factor for April 1998 is used in respect of disposals in a later month (and expenditure incurred in April 1998 or later does not attract indexation allowance at all). See 210 INDEXATION.

## 214.1 Losses

## 214 Losses

**Cross-references.** See IT 10.2 LOSSES for the set-off of trading losses against chargeable gains made by individuals. See 201.2 ANNUAL RATES AND EXEMPTIONS for the interaction between losses and the annual exemption. See also 226.1(B) TAPER RELIEF.

### 214.1 GENERAL

On 30 April 1999 Q sells for £40,000 a part of the land which he owns. The market value of the remaining estate is £160,000. Q bought the land for £250,000 in March 1990.

|  | £ |
|---|---|
| Disposal consideration | 40,000 |
| Allowable cost $\dfrac{40,000}{40,000 + 160,000} \times £250,000$ | 50,000 |
| Allowable loss | £10,000 |

**Note**

(a) Indexation allowance cannot increase or create a loss for CGT purposes. [*TCGA 1992, s 53; FA 1994, s 93(1)–(3)*].

### 214.2 LOSSES ON SHARES IN UNLISTED TRADING COMPANIES [*ICTA 1988, ss 574–576; FA 1994, s 210, 20 Sch 8; FA 1996, 38 Sch 6(1)(2)(9); FA 1998, s 80*]

P subscribed for 3,000 £1 ordinary shares at par in W Ltd, a qualifying trading company, in June 1988. In September 1995, P acquired a further 2,200 shares at £3 per share from another shareholder. In December 1999, P sold 3,900 shares at 40p per share.

| Indexation factors | June 1988 to September 1995 | 0.413 |
|---|---|---|
|  | September 1995 to April 1998 (note (*c*)) | 0.080 |

**Procedure**

Firstly, establish the '*section 104* holding' pool.

|  | Shares | Qualifying expenditure £ | Indexed pool £ |
|---|---|---|---|
| June 1988 subscription | 3,000 | 3,000 | 3,000 |
| Indexation to September 1995 |  |  |  |
| £3,000 × 0.413 |  |  | 1,239 |
| September 1995 acquisition | 2,200 | 6,600 | 6,600 |
|  | 5,200 | 9,600 | 10,839 |
| Indexed rise: September 1995 to April 1998 |  |  |  |
| £10,839 × 0.080 |  |  | 867 |
|  | 5,200 | 9,600 | 11,706 |
| December 1999 disposal | (3,900) | (7,200) | (8,780) |
| Pool carried forward | 1,300 | £2,400 | £2,926 |

# Losses 214.2

*Step 1.* Calculate the CGT loss in the normal way, as follows

|  | £ |
|---|---|
| Disposal consideration 3,900 × £0.40 | 1,560 |
| Allowable cost $\dfrac{3,900}{5,200} \times £9,600$ | 7,200 |
| Allowable loss | £5,640 |

*Step 2.* Applying a LIFO basis, identify the qualifying shares (1,700) and the non-qualifying shares (2,200) comprised in the disposal.

*Step 3.* Calculate the proportion of the loss attributable to the qualifying shares.

Loss referable to 1,700 qualifying shares $\dfrac{1,700}{3,900} \times £5,640$     £2,458

*Step 4.* Compare the loss in Step 3 with the actual cost of the qualifying shares, *viz.*

Cost of 1,700 qualifying shares $\dfrac{1,700}{3,000} \times £3,000$     £1,700

The loss available against income is restricted to £1,700 (being lower than £2,458).

The loss not relieved against income remains an allowable loss for CGT purposes.

£5,640 − £1,700 =     £3,940

### Notes

(a) Steps 1 to 4 illustrated in this example are those identified by the Revenue Capital Gains Manual at CG 58377.

(b) For shares issued after 5 April 1998 (not illustrated above), a company is a qualifying trading company for the purposes of this relief only if it would be a qualifying company for the purposes of the Enterprise Investment Scheme (EIS), although it is not a condition that the company issued the shares under the EIS or that any EIS income tax relief has been, or could have been, claimed in respect of them. [*ICTA 1988, s 576(4)–(4B); FA 1998, s 80(3)(5)*].

(c) Other than for the purposes of corporation tax on chargeable gains, indexation allowance is frozen at its April 1998 level. Therefore, the indexation factor for April 1998 is used in respect of disposals in a later month (and expenditure incurred in April 1998 or later does not attract indexation allowance at all). See 210 INDEXATION.

(d) For further examples on this topic, see IT 10.5 LOSSES and CT 118.4 LOSSES.

## 215.1 Married Persons

## 215 Married Persons

**Cross-reference.** See 226.3 TAPER RELIEF.

215.1 **INTER-SPOUSE TRANSFERS AND RATES OF TAX** [*TCGA 1992, ss 4, 58*]

### (A) No inter-spouse transfer
Paul and Heidi are a married couple with total income of £30,000 and £35,000 respectively for 1999/2000. On 4 April 2000, Heidi sells a painting which she had acquired in June 1994 at a cost of £5,000. Net sale proceeds amount to £17,900 and the indexation factor for the period June 1994 to April 1998 (note (*a*)) is 0.124. Neither spouse disposed of any other chargeable assets during 1999/2000.

**Chargeable gain — Heidi**

|  | £ |
|---|---:|
| Net proceeds | 17,900 |
| Cost | 5,000 |
| Unindexed gain | 12,900 |
| Indexation allowance £5,000 × 0.124 | 620 |
| Chargeable gain | 12,280 |
| Annual exemption | 7,100 |
| Taxable gain | £5,180 |
| | |
| Total income | 35,000 |
| Personal allowance | 4,335 |
| Taxable income | £30,665 |

Basic rate limit = £28,000, so gain of £5,180 is all taxed at 40%.

Tax payable £5,180 × 40%      £2,072.00

**Note**

(*a*) Other than for the purposes of corporation tax on chargeable gains, indexation allowance is frozen at its April 1998 level. Therefore, the indexation factor for April 1998 is used in respect of disposals in a later month (and expenditure incurred in April 1998 or later does not attract indexation allowance at all). See 210 INDEXATION.

## (B) Inter-spouse transfer

The facts are as in (A) above except that in January 2000, Heidi gives the painting to Paul who then makes the sale on 4 April 2000.

### Chargeable gain — Heidi

|  | £ |
|---|---:|
| Deemed consideration (January 2000) | 5,620 |
| Cost | 5,000 |
| Unindexed gain | 620 |
| Indexation allowance (to April 1998) £5,000 × 0.124 | 620 |
| Chargeable gain | Nil |

### Chargeable gain — Paul

|  | £ |
|---|---:|
| Net proceeds (4.4.2000) | 17,900 |
| Cost (January 2000) | 5,620 |
| Chargeable gain | 12,280 |
| Annual exemption | 7,100 |
| Taxable gain | £5,180 |
| | |
| Total income | 30,000 |
| Personal allowance | (4,335) |
| Taxable income | £25,665 |

Taxable income falls short of the basic rate limit (£28,000) by £2,335, so gain of £5,180 is taxed as follows.

|  |  |
|---|---:|
| £2,335 at 20% | 467.00 |
| 2,845 at 40% | 1,138.00 |
| Tax payable | £1,605.00 |
| | |
| Tax saving compared with (A) above | £467.00 |

### Notes

(a) The inter-spouse transfer is deemed to be for such consideration as to ensure that no gain or loss accrues. [*TCGA 1992, s 58*]. Effectively, the consideration is equal to cost plus indexation (to April 1998 see 210.1 INDEXATION). See 210.2(A)(B) INDEXATION for further examples. The principles in 210.2(C)(D) INDEXATION also apply.

(b) The fact that transfers of assets between husband and wife are no gain/no loss transfers enables savings to be made by ensuring that disposals are made by a spouse with an unused annual exemption and/or lower tax rates.

(c) An inter-spouse transfer followed by a sale could be attacked by the Revenue as an anti-avoidance device. To minimise the risk, there should be a clear time interval between the two transactions and no arrangements made to effect the ultimate sale until after the transfer. The gift should be outright with no strings attached and with no 'arrangement' for eventual proceeds to be passed to the transferor.

## 215.2 Married Persons

### 215.2 JOINTLY OWNED ASSETS

Derek and Raquel are a married couple. Derek had for many years owned an investment property which he purchased for £70,000 in May 1987. On 5 January 1995, he transferred to Raquel a 10% share in the property which was thereafter held in their joint names under a joint tenancy. No declaration is made for income tax purposes under *ICTA 1988, s 282B*, with the result that the rental income from the property is treated, by virtue of *ICTA 1988, s 282A* as arising in equal shares. On 29 June 1999, the property is sold for £140,000.

| | |
|---|---:|
| Indexation factors May 1987 to January 1995 | 0.433 |
| May 1987 to April 1998 (note (*d*)) | 0.596 |
| January 1995 to April 1998 (note (*d*)) | 0.114 |

**(i) Inter-spouse transfer**

| | £ |
|---|---:|
| Deemed consideration (January 1995) | 10,031 |
| Cost £70,000 × 10% (see note (*c*)) | 7,000 |
| Unindexed gain | 3,031 |
| Indexation allowance £7,000 × 0.433 | 3,031 |
| Chargeable gain | Nil |

**(ii) 1999/2000 disposal**

| | Derek £ | Raquel £ |
|---|---:|---:|
| Disposal proceeds | 126,000 | 14,000 |
| Cost: Derek (£70,000 − £7,000) | 63,000 | |
| Raquel (see (i) above) | | 10,031 |
| Unindexed gain | 63,000 | 3,969 |
| Indexation allowance: £63,000 × 0.596 | 37,548 | |
| £10,031 × 0.114 | | 1,144 |
| Chargeable gains | £25,452 | £2,825 |

**Notes**

(*a*) Where a joint declaration of unequal beneficial interests is made under *Sec 282B*, it is presumed that the same split applies for capital gains tax purposes. In the absence of a declaration, and regardless of the income tax treatment of income derived from the asset, a gain on an asset held in the joint names of husband and wife is apportioned in accordance with their respective beneficial interests at the time of disposal. (Revenue Press Release 21 November 1990).

(*b*) See 215.1 above as to how the consideration for the inter-spouse transfer is arrived at.

(*c*) The allowable expenditure on the inter-spouse transfer should be apportioned in accordance with the part disposal rules in *TCGA 1992, s 42* (see *Sec 42(5)* and 206.2 DISPOSAL). In this case, as the property is to be held on a joint tenancy with neither spouse being free to dispose separately of his or her share, it is assumed that the value of a 10% share and a 90% share is, respectively, 10% and 90% of the value of the property as a whole.

(*d*) Other than for the purposes of corporation tax on chargeable gains, indexation allowance is frozen at its April 1998 level. Therefore, the indexation factor for April 1998 is used in respect of disposals in a later month (and expenditure incurred in April 1998 or later does not attract indexation allowance at all). See 210 INDEXATION.

# 216 Mineral Royalties

**Cross-reference.** See also IT 12.1 MINERAL ROYALTIES.

**216.1 GENERAL** [*ICTA 1988, s 122; TCGA 1992, ss 201–203*]

L Ltd, an investment company preparing accounts to 31 December, is the holder of a lease of land acquired in 1986 for £66,000, when the lease had an unexpired term of 65 years. In January 1994, L Ltd grants a 10-year licence to a mining company to search for and exploit minerals beneath the land. The licence is granted for £60,000 plus a mineral royalty calculated on the basis of the value of any minerals won by the licensee. The market value of the retained land (exclusive of the mineral rights) is then £10,000. L Ltd receives mineral royalties as follows

|  |  | £ |
|---|---|---|
| Year ended | 31 December 1994 | 12,000 |
|  | 31 December 1995 | 19,000 |
|  | 31 December 1996 | 29,000 |
|  | 31 December 1997 | 38,000 |
|  | 31 December 1998 | 17,000 |
|  | 31 December 1999 | 10,000 |

On 2 January 2000, L Ltd relinquishes its rights under the lease and receives no consideration from the lessor.

### (i) Chargeable gains 1994

| | | £ |
|---|---|---|
| (a) Disposal proceeds | | 60,000 |
| Allowable cost $\dfrac{60,000}{60,000 + 10,000} \times £66,000$ | | 56,571 |
| Chargeable gain before indexation | | £3,429 |
| (b) $\frac{1}{2} \times £12,000$ | | £6,000 |

### (ii) Chargeable gains 1995 to 1999

| | | £ |
|---|---|---|
| 1995 | $\frac{1}{2} \times £19,000$ | 9,500 |
| 1996 | $\frac{1}{2} \times £29,000$ | 14,500 |
| 1997 | $\frac{1}{2} \times £38,000$ | 19,000 |
| 1998 | $\frac{1}{2} \times £17,000$ | 8,500 |
| 1999 | $\frac{1}{2} \times £10,000$ | 5,000 |

### (iii) Loss 2000

| | | |
|---|---|---|
| Proceeds of disposal of lease | | Nil |
| Allowable cost £66,000 − £56,571 | note (*a*) | 9,429 |
| Allowable loss | | £9,429 |

## 216.1 Mineral Royalties

(iv) **The loss may be set off against the chargeable gains arising on the mineral royalties as follows**

|  | £ |
|---|---|
| 1999 (whole) | 5,000 |
| 1998 (part) | 4,429 |
|  | £9,429 |

**Note**
(a) Under *ICTA 1988, s 122* and *TCGA 1992, s 201*, one half of mineral royalties is taxed as income and one half as a chargeable gain. The gain is deemed to accrue in the year of assessment or company accounting period for which the royalties are receivable and is not capable of being reduced by any expenditure or by indexation allowance.

# 217 Overseas Matters

## 217.1 OVERSEAS RESIDENT SETTLEMENTS

### (A) Charge under *TCGA 1992*, s 87

M, resident and domiciled in the UK, is the sole beneficiary of a discretionary settlement administered in the Cayman Islands. The trustees are all individuals resident in the Cayman Islands. The settlement was created in 1987 by M's father, who is resident and domiciled in the UK throughout. For 1987/88 to 1998/99 the trustees have chargeable gains and allowable losses, and make capital payments to M, as follows

|  | Chargeable gains £ | Allowable losses £ | Capital payments £ |
|---|---|---|---|
| 1987/88 | 50,000 | 60,000 | 20,000 |
| 1988/89 | 80,000 | 30,000 | 50,000 |
| 1989/90 | 95,000 | — | — |
| 1990/91 | — | — | 35,000 |
| 1991/92 | 32,000 | 7,000 | 20,000 |
| 1992/93 | — | — | 27,000 |
| 1993/94–1998/99 | 101,000 | — | — |

See also (B) below.

**1987/88**

| | £ | £ |
|---|---|---|
| Trust gains (£50,000 – £60,000) | | — |
| Capital payment | | 20,000 |
| Balance of capital payment carried forward | | £20,000 |
| Trust losses carried forward | | £10,000 |

**1988/89**

| | £ | £ |
|---|---|---|
| Trust gains (£80,000 – £30,000 – £10,000) | | £40,000 |
| Capital payment | 50,000 | |
| Brought forward | 20,000 | £70,000 |
| Chargeable gains assessable on M | | £40,000 |
| Capital payment carried forward (£70,000 – £40,000) | | £30,000 |

**1989/90**

| | £ |
|---|---|
| Trust gains | £95,000 |
| Capital payment brought forward | £30,000 |
| Chargeable gains assessable on M | £30,000 |
| Trust gains carried forward (£95,000 – £30,000) | £65,000 |

## 217.1 Overseas Matters

**1990/91**

| | £ |
|---|---:|
| Trust gains | — |
| Trust gains brought forward | 65,000 |
| | £65,000 |
| Capital payment | £35,000 |
| Chargeable gains assessable on M | £35,000 |
| Trust gains carried forward (£65,000 − £35,000) | £30,000 |

**1991/92**

| | £ |
|---|---:|
| Trust gains (£32,000 − £7,000) | 25,000 |
| Trust gains brought forward | 30,000 |
| | £55,000 |
| Capital payment | £20,000 |
| Chargeable gains assessable on M | £20,000 |
| Trust gains carried forward (£55,000 − £20,000) | £35,000 |

**1992/93**

| | £ |
|---|---:|
| Trust gains | — |
| Trust gains brought forward | 35,000 |
| | £35,000 |
| Capital payment | £27,000 |
| Chargeable gains assessable on M | £27,000 |
| Trust gains carried forward | £8,000 |

**1993/94–1998/99**

| | £ |
|---|---:|
| Cumulative trust gains | 101,000 |
| Trust gains brought forward | 8,000 |
| Trust gains carried forward | £109,000 |

**Note**

(*a*) As regards gains and losses accruing to the trustees after 16 March 1998 and capital payments received by beneficiaries after that date, these provisions apply regardless of the domicile and residence status of the settlor when the settlement was made or during the tax year in question. [*TCGA 1992, s 87; FA 1998, s 130*].

# Overseas Matters 217.1

**(B) Surcharge on CGT under TCGA 1992, s 87** [*TCGA 1992, ss 91–93, 97*]

The facts are as in (A) above. In 1999/2000, the trustees make a capital payment of £100,000. For both 1992/93 and 1999/2000, M is liable to CGT at the rate of 40% on chargeable gains attributed to him under *TCGA 1992, s 87,* and he has utilised his annual exemptions against personal gains.

**(i) Determination of qualifying amounts** [*Sec 92(1)(2)*]

| | |
|---|---:|
| Qualifying amount for 1990/91 (equivalent to trust gains carried forward at 5.4.91) | £30,000 |
| Qualifying amount for 1991/92 (i.e. trust gains for that year only) | £25,000 |

**(ii) Matching capital payments made after 5.4.91** [*Sec 92(3)–(6)*]

£20,000 paid in 1991/92 is matched (on first in, first out basis) with qualifying amount for 1990/91, leaving an unmatched qualifying amount of £10,000 for 1990/91.

£27,000 paid in 1992/93. £10,000 is matched with balance of qualifying amount for 1990/91 and £17,000 is matched with qualifying amount for 1991/92, leaving an unmatched qualifying amount of £8,000 for 1991/92.

£100,000 paid in 1999/2000. £8,000 is matched with balance of qualifying amount for 1991/92 (leaving £92,000 to be matched with post-1991/92 qualifying amounts and £9,000 unmatched).

**(iii) Surcharge payable by M** [*Secs 91–93*]

**1991/92**

No surcharge is payable in respect of capital payments made before 6.4.92.

**1992/93**

As only part of the capital payment is matched with a qualifying amount for a year of assessment falling before that immediately preceding the year in which the payment is made, only that part (i.e. £10,000 — see (ii) above) is liable to surcharge, and the balance is ignored. [*Sec 93(3)*].

| | £ |
|---|---:|
| CGT payable by M (subject to surcharge): | |
| £27,000 × 40% | 10,800 |
| Surcharge £10,000 × 40% = £4,000 × 10% × 2 years | |
| (1.12.91–30.11.93) [*Sec 91(3)(4)(5)(a)*] | 800 |
| Total tax payable | £11,600 |

| **1999/2000** | £ |
|---|---:|
| CGT payable by M (subject to surcharge): | |
| £100,000 × 40% | 40,000 |
| Surcharge on part of payment matched with 1991/92 qualifying amount: | |
| £8,000 × 40% = £3,200 × 10% × 6 years (1.12.94–30.11.2000) [*Sec 91(3)(4)(5)(b)*] | 1,920 |
| Surcharge on balance of payment (not illustrated) | X |
| Total tax payable | X |

## 217.1 Overseas Matters

**Note**
(a) The surcharge is 10% per annum for a maximum of 6 years. [*TCGA 1992, s 91(3)–(5)*].

**(C) Charge under *TCGA 1992, s 87* — further example**

T and M are the only beneficiaries under a Jersey settlement set up by their grandfather. None of the trustees is resident in the UK.

T is resident in the UK but M is neither resident nor ordinarily resident in the UK. Both beneficiaries have a UK domicile. In 1998/99, the trustees sell shares realising a chargeable gain of £102,000. No disposals are made in 1999/2000.

The trustees make capital payments of £60,000 to M in 1998/99. In 1999/2000 they make capital payments of £60,000 to T and £10,000 to M.

| 1998/99 | £ |
|---|---|
| Trust gains | 102,000 |
| Capital payment | 60,000 |
| Trust gains carried forward | £42,000 |

M has chargeable gains of £60,000 but is not subject to CGT.

| 1999/2000 | £ |
|---|---|
| Trust gains (brought forward) | 42,000 |
| Capital payments (£60,000 + £10,000) | 70,000 |
| Balance of capital payments carried forward | £28,000 |

The chargeable gains are apportioned as follows

| | | £ |
|---|---|---|
| T | $\dfrac{60,000}{70,000} \times £42,000$ | 36,000 |
| M | $\dfrac{10,000}{70,000} \times £42,000$ (not assessable) | 6,000 |
| | | £42,000 |

The capital payments carried forward are apportioned as follows

| | £ |
|---|---|
| T £60,000 − £36,000 | 24,000 |
| M £10,000 − £6,000 | 4,000 |
| | £28,000 |

## Overseas Matters 217.1

**(D) Distributions of income and gains** [*ICTA 1988, s 740(6); TCGA 1992, ss 87, 97*]

A Liechtenstein foundation was created in 1965 by a UK resident domiciled in Scotland. None of the trustees is resident in the UK and the trust administration is carried on in Switzerland. The foundation has the following income and chargeable gains for 1997/98 to 1999/2000.

|  | Income £ | Chargeable gains £ |
|---|---|---|
| 1997/98 | 15,000 | 5,000 |
| 1998/99 | 24,000 | 12,000 |
| 1999/2000 | 30,000 | 3,000 |

L, who is resident and domiciled in the UK and is the only current beneficiary, receives payments of £28,000 in 1997/98 and £50,000 in 1999/2000.

|  | Total £ | Income £ | Chargeable gains £ |
|---|---|---|---|
| **1997/98** | | | |
| Total income/gains | 20,000 | 15,000 | 5,000 |
| Payment | 28,000 | 15,000 | 5,000 |
| Balance | Nil | Nil | Nil |
| Balance of payment c/f | £8,000 | | |
| **1998/99** | | | |
| Total income/gains | 36,000 | 24,000 | 12,000 |
| Payment (balance b/f) | 8,000 | 8,000 | — |
| Balance c/f | £28,000 | £16,000 | £12,000 |
| **1999/2000** | | | |
| Total income/gains | 33,000 | 30,000 | 3,000 |
| Brought forward | 28,000 | 16,000 | 12,000 |
|  | 61,000 | 46,000 | 15,000 |
| Payment | 50,000 | 46,000 | 4,000 |
| Balance c/f against future payments | £11,000 | — | £11,000 |

**Summary of taxable amounts**

|  | Schedule D, Case VI £ | Capital gains tax £ |
|---|---|---|
| 1997/98 | 15,000 | 5,000 |
| 1998/99 | 8,000 | — |
| 1999/2000 | 46,000 | 4,000 |

## 217.2 Overseas Matters

217.2 **COMPANY MIGRATION** [*TCGA 1992, ss 185, 187*]
Z Ltd is a company incorporated in Ruritania, but regarded as resident in the UK by virtue of its being managed and controlled in the UK. It is the 75% subsidiary of Y plc, a UK resident company. On 1 October 1999, the management and control of Z Ltd is transferred to Ruritania and it thus ceases to be UK resident, although it continues to trade in the UK, on a much reduced basis, via a UK branch.

Details of the company's chargeable assets immediately before 1 October 1999 were as follows.

|  | Market value | Capital gain after indexation (where applicable) if all assets sold |
|---|---|---|
|  | £ | £ |
| Factory in UK | 480,000 | 230,000 |
| Warehouse in UK | 300,000 | 180,000 |
| Factory in Ruritania | 350,000 | 200,000 |
| Warehouse in Ruritania | 190,000 | 100,000 |
| UK quoted investments | 110,000 | 80,000 |
| Foreign trade investments | 100,000 | Loss (60,000) |

The UK warehouse continues to be used in the UK trade. The UK factory does not, and is later sold. On 1 June 2000, the Ruritanian warehouse is sold for the equivalent of £210,000. On 1 October 2001, Y plc sells its shareholding in Z Ltd.

Prior to becoming non-UK resident, Z Ltd had unrelieved capital losses brought forward of £40,000.

**The corporation tax consequences assuming no election under *TCGA 1992, s 187* are as follows**

Chargeable gain accruing to Z Ltd on 1.10.99

|  | £ |
|---|---|
| Factory (UK) | 230,000 |
| Factory (Ruritania) | 200,000 |
| Warehouse (Ruritania) | 100,000 |
| UK quoted investments | 80,000 |
| Foreign trade investments | (60,000) |
|  | 550,000 |
| Losses brought forward | 40,000 |
| Net gain chargeable to corporation tax | £510,000 |

The later sale of the UK factory does not attract corporation tax as the company is non-resident and the factory has not, since the deemed reacquisition immediately before 1 October 1999, been used in a trade carried on in the UK through a branch or agency. Similarly, the sale of the overseas warehouse, and of any other overseas assets, is outside the scope of corporation tax on chargeable gains. Any subsequent disposal of the UK warehouse *will* be within the charge to corporation tax, having been omitted from the deemed disposal on 1 October 1999, due to its being used in a trade carried on in the UK through a branch. On disposal, the gain will be computed by reference to original cost, or 31.3.82 value if appropriate, rather than to market value immediately before 1 October 1999 — see also note (*d*).

Y plc will realise a capital gain (or loss) on the sale of its shareholding in Z Ltd on 1 October 2001.

## Overseas Matters 217.2

**The corporation tax consequences if an election is made under *TCGA 1992, s 187* are as follows**

Chargeable gain accruing to Z Ltd on 1.10.99

|  | £ |
|---|---:|
| Factory (UK) | 230,000 |
| UK quoted investments | 80,000 |
|  | 310,000 |
| Losses brought forward | 40,000 |
| Net gain liable to corporation tax | £270,000 |

Postponed gain on foreign assets

|  | £ |
|---|---:|
| Factory (Ruritania) | 200,000 |
| Warehouse (Ruritania) | 100,000 |
|  | 300,000 |
| Foreign trade investments | (60,000) |
|  | £240,000 |

On 1 June 2000, a proportion of the postponed gain becomes chargeable as a result of the sale, within six years of Z Ltd's becoming non-resident, of one of the assets in respect of which the postponed gain accrued. The gain chargeable to corporation tax as at 1 June 2000 on Y plc is

$$\frac{100{,}000 \text{ (postponed gain on warehouse)}}{300{,}000 \text{ (aggregate of postponed gains)}} \times £240{,}000 = £80{,}000$$

On 1 October 2001, in addition to any gain or loss arising on the sale of the shares, Y plc will be chargeable to corporation tax on the remainder of the postponed gain, i.e. on £160,000 (£240,000 – £80,000), by virtue of Z Ltd having ceased to be its 75% subsidiary as a result of the sale of shares.

The position as regards the UK warehouse is the same as if no election had been made.

**Notes**

(a) The provisions of *TCGA 1992, s 185* apply where a company ceases to be resident in the UK. All companies incorporated in the UK are regarded as UK resident. As such a company cannot therefore cease to be resident, *Sec 185* can apply only to companies incorporated abroad which are UK resident. See also Revenue Statement of Practice SP 1/90 as regards company residence generally.

(b) If, with an election, Z Ltd's unrelieved capital losses had exceeded its chargeable gains arising on 1 October 1999, the excess could have been allowed against postponed gains at the time when they become chargeable on Y plc, subject to the two companies making a joint election to that effect under *TCGA 1992, s 187(5)*.

(c) *FA 1988, ss 130–132* contain management provisions designed to secure payment of all outstanding tax liabilities on a company becoming non-UK resident. See also Revenue Statement of Practice SP 2/90.

## 217.3 Overseas Matters

(d) If the UK warehouse ceases to be a chargeable asset by virtue of Z Ltd's ceasing to carry on a trade in the UK through a branch or agency, there will be a deemed disposal at market value at that time, under *TCGA 1992, s 25*. See 217.3 below.

217.3 **NON-RESIDENTS CARRYING ON TRADE, ETC. THROUGH UK BRANCH OR AGENCY** [*TCGA 1992, ss 10, 25*]

X, who is not resident and not ordinarily resident in the UK, practises abroad as a tax consultant and also practises in the UK through a London branch, preparing accounts to 5 April. The assets of the UK branch include premises bought in 1988 for £60,000 and a computer acquired in 1997 for £20,000. On 31 January 2000, the computer ceases to be used in the UK branch and is immediately shipped abroad, and on 28 February 2000, X closes down the UK branch. He sells the premises in June 2000 for £118,000. Capital allowances claimed on the computer up to and including 1998/99 were £8,750 and short-life asset treatment had been claimed.

Relevant market values of the assets are as follows

| | £ |
|---|---|
| Computer, at 31 January 2000 | 11,000 |
| Premises, at 14 March 1989 | 65,000 |
| at 28 February 2000 | 110,000 |
| Indexation factor March 1989 to April 1998 (note (*h*)) | 0.448 |

**The UK capital gains tax consequences are as follows**

| | £ | £ |
|---|---|---|
| *Computer* | | |
| Market value 31.1.2000 | | 11,000 |
| *Deduct* cost | 20,000 | |
| *Less* capital allowances claimed    note (*f*) | 9,000 | 11,000 |
| Chargeable gain | | Nil |

| | £ |
|---|---|
| *Premises* | |
| Market value 28.2.2000 | 110,000 |
| *Deduct* market value 14.3.89 | 65,000 |
| Unindexed gain | 45,000 |
| Indexation allowance £65,000 × 0.448 | 29,120 |
| Chargeable gain | £15,880 |
| | |
| Net chargeable gains 1999/2000 (subject to TAPER RELIEF (226)) | £15,880 |

# Overseas Matters 217.4

**Notes**

(a) X is within the charge to UK capital gains tax for disposals after 13 March 1989 by virtue of his carrying on a profession in the UK through a branch or agency. Previously, the charge applied only to non-residents carrying on a *trade* in this manner. X is deemed to have disposed of (with no capital gains tax consequences) and reacquired immediately before 14 March 1989 all chargeable assets used in the UK branch at market value, so that any subsequent CGT charge will be by reference only to post-13 March 1989 gains. [*FA 1989, s 126(3)–(5); TCGA 1992, s 10(5)*].

(b) There is a deemed disposal, at market value, of the computer on 31 January 2000 as a result of its ceasing to be a chargeable asset by virtue of its becoming situated outside the UK. [*TCGA 1992, s 25(1)*].

(c) There is a deemed disposal, at market value, of the premises on 28 February 2000 as a result of the asset ceasing to be a chargeable asset by virtue of X's ceasing to carry on a trade, profession or vocation in the UK through a branch or agency. [*TCGA 1992, s 25(3)(8)*]. See also note (g) below.

(d) There are no UK CGT consequences on the actual disposal of the premises in June 2000.

(e) X is entitled to the £7,100 annual exemption against UK gains, regardless of his residence status.

(f) Where a chargeable asset has qualified for capital allowances and a loss accrues on its disposal, the allowable expenditure is restricted, under *TCGA 1992, s 41*, by the net allowances given, which in this example amount to £9,000 (writing-down allowances £8,750 plus balancing allowance £250 arising on the asset's ceasing to be used in the trade).

(g) *TCGA 1992, s 25(3)* (see note (c) above) does not apply, on a claim under *TCGA 1992, s 172*, in relation to an asset where a non-UK resident company transfers its trade (carried on through a UK branch or agency) to a UK resident group company. The asset is deemed to be transferred at no gain/no loss.

(h) Other than for the purposes of corporation tax on chargeable gains, indexation allowance is frozen at its April 1998 level. Therefore, the indexation factor for April 1998 is used in respect of disposals in a later month (and expenditure incurred in April 1998 or later does not attract indexation allowance at all). See 210 INDEXATION.

## 217.4 TRANSFER OF ASSETS TO NON-RESIDENT COMPANY [*TCGA 1992, s 140*]

Q Ltd, a UK resident company, carries on business in a foreign country through a branch there. In September 1993, it is decreed that all enterprises in that country be carried on by locally resident companies. Q Ltd forms a wholly-owned non-UK resident subsidiary R and transfers all the assets of the branch to R wholly in consideration for the issue of shares. The assets transferred include the following

## 217.4 Overseas Matters

|  | Value £ | Chargeable gains £ |
|---|---:|---:|
| Goodwill | 100,000 | 95,000 |
| Freehold land | 200,000 | 120,000 |
| Plant (items worth more than £6,000) | 50,000 | 20,000 |
| Other assets | 150,000 | — |
|  | £500,000 | £235,000 |

In March 1995, there is a compulsory acquisition of 50% of the share capital of R for £300,000 (market value). The value of the whole shareholding immediately before disposal is £750,000. The value of Q Ltd's remaining 50% holding is £300,000.

In June 1999, R is forced to sell its freehold land to the government.

**Q Ltd's capital gains position is as follows**

### 1993
The gain of £235,000 is deferred. The allowable cost of the shares in R is £500,000.

### 1995

|  | £ |
|---|---:|
| Consideration on disposal | 300,000 |
| *Add* Proportion of deferred gain £235,000 × $\frac{300,000}{750,000}$ | 94,000 |
|  | 394,000 |
| *Deduct* Cost of shares sold £500,000 × $\frac{300,000}{300,000 + 300,000}$ | 250,000 |
| Gain subject to indexation | £144,000 |

### 1999
Proportion of deferred gain chargeable

Gain arising $\frac{120,000}{235,000}$ × £235,000 £120,000

Balance of gain still held over
(£235,000 − £94,000 − £120,000)  £21,000

### Notes
(a) The 1999 gain arises under *Sec 140(5)*. If the sale of freehold land had taken place more than six years after the original transfer of assets, no part of the deferred gain would have become chargeable as a result.

(b) The 1995 gain arises under *Sec 140(4)*. In this case, there is no time limit as in (a) above.

(c) The 1995 gain is subject to indexation allowance on £250,000 from September 1993 to March 1995.

# 218 Partnerships

## 218.1 ASSETS [*TCGA 1992, s 59*]

G, H and I trade in partnership. They share capital in the ratio 5:4:3. Land occupied by the firm is sold on 15 April 1999 for £90,000, having been acquired for £30,000 in 1981. The agreed market value of the land at 31 March 1982 is £27,000. G has elected under *TCGA 1992, s 35(5)* for his personal assets held on 31 March 1982 to be treated as disposed of and re-acquired at their market value on that date. G has personal gains in 1999/2000 of £2,500, H has losses of £1,000 and I made no disposals of personal assets. None of the partners has any capital losses brought forward from earlier years. The partnership land was a business asset for taper relief purposes but the personal assets sold by G and H were non-business assets. The indexation factor for the period March 1982 to April 1998 (note (*c*)) is 1.047.

**The gains of G, H and I, without re-basing to 1982, are as follows**

|  | G ($\frac{5}{12}$) £ | H ($\frac{4}{12}$) £ | I ($\frac{3}{12}$) £ |
|---|---|---|---|
| Disposal consideration | 37,500 | 30,000 | 22,500 |
| Cost | 12,500 | 10,000 | 7,500 |
| Unindexed gain | 25,000 | 20,000 | 15,000 |
| Indexation allowance Cost × 1.047 | 13,088 | 10,470 | 7,853 |
| Gain after indexation | £11,912 | £9,530 | £7,147 |

**The gains of G, H and I, with re-basing to 1982, are as follows**

|  | G ($\frac{5}{12}$) £ | H ($\frac{4}{12}$) £ | I ($\frac{3}{12}$) £ |
|---|---|---|---|
| Disposal consideration | 37,500 | 30,000 | 22,500 |
| Market value 31.3.82 | 11,250 | 9,000 | 6,750 |
| Unindexed gain | 26,250 | 21,000 | 15,750 |
| Indexation allowance (as above) | 13,088 | 10,470 | 7,853 |
| Gain after indexation | £13,162 | £10,530 | £7,897 |

**Summary**

|  | G £ | H £ | I £ |
|---|---|---|---|
| Share of partnership gain | 11,912 | 9,530 | 7,147 |
| Personal gains/(losses) | 2,500 | (1,000) | — |
| Chargeable gain | 14,412 | 8,530 | 7,147 |
| Taper relief @ 15% on £11,912/£8,530/£7,147 | 1,787 | 1,280 | 1,072 |
|  | 12,625 | 7,250 | 6,075 |
| Annual exemption | 7,100 | 7,100 | 7,100 |
| Taxable gain | £5,525 | 150 | Nil |

**Notes**

(*a*) An individual partner's election under *Sec 35(5)* in respect of his personal assets does not extend to his share of partnership assets and *vice versa*, this being by virtue of *Sec 35(7)*. (See Revenue Statement of Practice SP 4/92, para 10(i)).

## 218.2 Partnerships

(b) For taper relief purposes, the partnership land is deemed to have been held for one extra year after 5 April 1998 by virtue of its having been acquired before 17 March 1998 by the persons making the disposal. [*TCGA 1992, s 2A(8)(9); FA 1998, s 121(1)(4)*]. For the interaction between tapered gains and untapered losses, see 226.1(B) TAPER RELIEF.

(c) Other than for the purposes of corporation tax on chargeable gains, indexation allowance is frozen at its April 1998 level. See 210 INDEXATION.

### 218.2 CHANGES IN SHARING RATIOS

J and K have traded in partnership for several years, sharing capital and income equally. The acquisition costs and 31 March 1982 values of the chargeable assets of the firm are as follows

|  | Cost £ | 31.3.82 value £ |
|---|---|---|
| Premises | 60,000 | 150,000 |
| Goodwill | 10,000 | 50,000 |

The assets have not been revalued in the firm's balance sheet. On 1 June 1999, J and K admit L to the partnership, and the sharing ratio is J 35%, K 45% and L 20%. The indexation factor for March 1982 to April 1998 (note (d)) is 1.047.

**J and K are regarded as disposing of part of their interest in the firm's assets to L as follows**

|  | £ | £ |
|---|---|---|
| **J** | | |
| *Premises* | | |
| Deemed consideration | | |
| £60,000 × (50% − 35%) | 9,000 | |
| *Add* indexation allowance (see below) | 23,558 | |
| Total deemed consideration | 32,558 | |
| Allowable cost | 9,000 | |
| Unindexed gain | 23,558 | |
| Indexation allowance (50% − 35%) × £150,000 × 1.047 | 23,558 | — |
| *Goodwill* | | |
| Deemed consideration | | |
| £10,000 × (50% − 35%) | 1,500 | |
| *Add* indexation allowance (see below) | 7,853 | |
| Total deemed consideration | 9,353 | |
| Allowable cost | 1,500 | |
| Unindexed gain | 7,853 | |
| Indexation allowance (50% − 35%) × £50,000 × 1.047 | 7,853 | — |
| Chargeable gain/allowable loss | | Nil |

**K**
*Premises*

| | | |
|---|---:|---:|
| Deemed consideration | | |
| £60,000 × (50% − 45%) | | 3,000 |
| Add indexation allowance (see below) | | 7,853 |
| Total deemed consideration | | 10,853 |
| Allowable cost | | 3,000 |
| Unindexed gain | | 7,853 |
| Indexation allowance (50% − 45%) × £150,000 × 1.047 | 7,853 | — |

*Goodwill*

| | | |
|---|---:|---:|
| Deemed consideration | | |
| £10,000 × (50% − 45%) | | 500 |
| Add indexation allowance (see below) | | 2,618 |
| Total deemed consideration | | 3,118 |
| Allowable cost | | 500 |
| Unindexed gain | | 2,618 |
| Indexation allowance (50% − 45%) × £50,000 × 1.047 | 2,618 | — |
| Chargeable gain/allowable loss | | Nil |

The allowable costs (inclusive, in L's case, of indexation allowance to April 1998) of the three partners are now

| | | Freehold land £ | Goodwill £ |
|---|---|---:|---:|
| J | | 21,000 | 3,500 |
| K | | 27,000 | 4,500 |
| L | note (c) | 43,411 | 12,471 |

**Notes**

(a) The treatment illustrated above is taken from Revenue Statement of Practice SP D12 (17.1.75), para 4 as extended by SP 1/89. Each partner's disposal consideration is equal to his share of current balance sheet value of the asset concerned plus, for disposals after 5 April 1988, indexation allowance, and each disposal treated as producing no gain and no loss.

(b) As the deemed disposals are no gain/no loss disposals, re-basing to 1982 does not apply. The incoming partner, having acquired his share in the assets by means of a no gain/no loss disposal after 31 March 1982 is regarded as having held the asset at that date for the purposes of re-basing on a subsequent disposal. (Revenue Statement of Practice SP 1/89).

(c) L's allowable costs comprise 20% of original cost, plus indexation allowance to April 1998 based on 20% of 31 March 1982 value.

(d) Other than for the purposes of corporation tax on chargeable gains, indexation allowance is frozen at its April 1998 level. Therefore, the indexation factor for April 1998 is used in respect of disposals in a later month (and expenditure incurred in April 1998 or later does not attract indexation allowance at all). See 210 INDEXATION.

(e) See 210.2(A)(C) INDEXATION for an example of the indexation adjustments required on a subsequent disposal other than a no gain/no loss disposal.

# 218.3 Partnerships

## 218.3 ACCOUNTING ADJUSTMENTS

A, B and C trade in partnership. They share income and capital profits equally. The firm's only chargeable asset is its premises which cost £51,000 in 1987. C, who is 49, decides to retire. The remaining partners agree to share profits equally. Before C retires (in May 1999), the premises are written up to market value in the accounts, estimated at £81,000. C does not receive any payment directly from the other partners on his retirement.

**The capital gains tax consequences are**
On retiring, C is regarded as having disposed of his interest in the firm's premises for a consideration equal to his share of the then book value.

|  |  | £ |
|---|---|---|
| Disposal consideration | $\frac{1}{3} \times £81,000$ | 27,000 |
| Acquisition cost | $\frac{1}{3} \times £51,000$ | 17,000 |
| Gain subject to indexation to April 1998 and taper relief |  | £10,000 |

A and B will each be treated as acquiring a $\frac{1}{6}$ ($\frac{1}{2} \times \frac{1}{3}$) share in the premises, at a cost equal to one half of C's disposal consideration. Their acquisition costs are then

|  |  | A | B |
|---|---|---|---|
|  |  | £ | £ |
| Cost of original share | $\frac{1}{3} \times £51,000$ | 17,000 | 17,000 |
| Cost of new share | $\frac{1}{2} \times £27,000$ | 13,500 | 13,500 |
| Total |  | £30,500 | £30,500 |

**Note**
(a) If C retires for reasons of ill-health, he may be entitled to RETIREMENT RELIEF (221).

## 218.4 CONSIDERATION OUTSIDE ACCOUNTS

D, E and F are partners in a firm of accountants who share all profits in the ratio 7:7:6. G is admitted as a partner in May 1999 and pays the other partners £10,000 for goodwill. The new partnership shares are D $\frac{3}{10}$, E $\frac{3}{10}$, F $\frac{1}{4}$ and G $\frac{3}{20}$. The book value of goodwill is £18,000, its cost on acquisition of the practice from the predecessor in 1987.

**The partners are treated as having disposed of shares in goodwill as follows**

**D**

$\frac{7}{20} - \frac{3}{10} = \frac{1}{20}$

| | £ | £ |
|---|---|---|
| Disposal consideration | | |
| Notional $\frac{1}{20} \times £18,000$ | 900 | |
| Actual $\frac{7}{20} \times £10,000$ | 3,500 | |
| | | 4,400 |
| Allowable cost $\frac{1}{20} \times £18,000$ | | 900 |
| Unindexed gain | | £3,500 |

**E**

$\frac{7}{20} - \frac{3}{10} = \frac{1}{20}$

| | £ |
|---|---|
| Disposal consideration (as for D) | 4,400 |
| Allowable cost (as for D) | 900 |
| Unindexed gain | £3,500 |

**F**

$\frac{6}{20} - \frac{1}{4} = \frac{1}{20}$

| | £ | £ |
|---|---|---|
| Disposal consideration | | |
| Notional $\frac{1}{20} \times £18,000$ | 900 | |
| Actual $\frac{6}{20} \times £10,000$ | 3,000 | |
| | | 3,900 |
| Allowable cost | | 900 |
| Unindexed gain | | £3,000 |

G's allowable cost of his share of goodwill is therefore

| | £ |
|---|---|
| Actual consideration paid | 10,000 |
| Notional consideration paid $\frac{3}{20} \times £18,000$ | 2,700 |
| | £12,700 |

**Note**

(a) In practice, the above calculations must be adjusted for indexation allowance to April 1998 which is added to the notional consideration and deducted from the unindexed gain — see 218.2 above and Revenue Statement of Practice SP 1/89. Any chargeable gains remaining after indexation are reduced by TAPER RELIEF (226).

## 218.5 Partnerships

### 218.5 SHARES ACQUIRED IN STAGES

Q is a partner in a medical practice. The partnership's only chargeable asset is a freehold house used as a surgery. The cost of the house to the partnership was £3,600 in 1962 and it was revalued in the partnership accounts to £50,000 in 1988. Q was admitted to the partnership in June 1964 with a share of $\frac{1}{6}$ of all profits. As a result of partnership changes, Q's profit share altered as follows

1970   $\frac{1}{5}$
1981   $\frac{1}{4}$
1999   $\frac{3}{10}$

**For capital gains tax, Q's allowable cost of his share of the freehold house is calculated as follows**

|  |  | £ |  |
|---|---|---:|---:|
| 1964 | $\frac{1}{6} \times £3,600$ |  | £600 |
| 1970 | $(\frac{1}{5} - \frac{1}{6}) \times £3,600$ | 120 |  |
| 1981 | $(\frac{1}{4} - \frac{1}{5}) \times £3,600$ | 180 |  |
| 1999 | $(\frac{3}{10} - \frac{1}{4}) \times £50,000$ | 2,500 | £2,800 |

**Notes**

(a) The pre- and post-6.4.65 costs are not pooled.

(b) On Q's acquisition of an increased share of the property in 1999 (following the revaluation in 1988), any partner with a reduced share will be treated as having made a disposal and thus a chargeable gain. The re-basing rules of *TCGA 1992, s 35* will apply to the disposal (subject to the usual comparison with the gain or loss without re-basing).

## 218.6 PARTNERSHIP ASSETS DISTRIBUTED IN KIND

R, S and T are partners sharing all profits in the ratio 4:3:3. Farmland owned by the firm is transferred in November 1999 to T for future use by him as a market gardening enterprise separate from the partnership business. No payment is made by T to the other partners but a reduction is made in T's future share of income profits. The book value of the farmland is £5,000, its cost in 1987, but the present market value is £15,000.

|  |  | £ |
|---|---|---:|
| **R** | | |
| Deemed disposal consideration | $\frac{4}{10} \times £15,000$ | 6,000 |
| Allowable cost | $\frac{4}{10} \times £5,000$ | 2,000 |
| Gain (subject to indexation allowance to April 1998 and TAPER RELIEF (226)) | | £4,000 |
| | | |
| **S** | | |
| Deemed disposal consideration | $\frac{3}{10} \times £15,000$ | 4,500 |
| Allowable cost | $\frac{3}{10} \times £5,000$ | 1,500 |
| Gain (subject to indexation allowance to April 1998 and TAPER RELIEF (226)) | | £3,000 |
| | | |
| **T** | | |
| Partnership share | $\frac{3}{10} \times £5,000$ | 1,500 |
| Market value of R's share | | 6,000 |
| Market value of S's share | | 4,500 |
| Allowable cost of land for future disposal | | £12,000 |

# 219 Private Residences

## 219.1 PERIODS OF OWNERSHIP QUALIFYING FOR EXEMPTION AND LET PROPERTY EXEMPTION [*TCGA 1992, ss 222, 223*]

**(A)**
P sold a house on 1 July 1999 realising an otherwise chargeable gain of £46,000. The house was purchased on 1 February 1980 and was occupied as a residence until 30 June 1987 when P moved to another residence, letting the house as residential accommodation. He did not re-occupy the house prior to its sale.

|  | £ |
|---|---:|
| Gain on sale | 46,000 |
| *Deduct* Exempt amount under main residence rules | |
| $\dfrac{5y\ 3m + 3y}{17y\ 3m} \times £46{,}000$ | 22,000 |
| | 24,000 |
| *Deduct* Let property exemption | 22,000 |
| Net chargeable gain | £2,000 |

**Notes**

(*a*) The final three years of ownership are always included in the exempt period of ownership. [*Sec 223(1)*].

(*b*) The period of ownership for the exemption calculation does not include any period before 31 March 1982. This applies regardless of whether the gain has been calculated by reference to cost or to 31 March 1982 value under the re-basing rules. [*Sec 223(7)*].

(*c*) The gain attributable to the letting (£24,000) is exempt to the extent that it does not exceed the lesser of £40,000 and the gain otherwise exempt (£22,000 in this example). [*Sec 223(4)*].

(*d*) No TAPER RELIEF (226) is available in this example as the property is clearly not a business asset for the purposes of that relief and has been owned for too short a period after 5 April 1998 for non-business asset taper relief to apply. If relief had been available, the gain to be tapered is the gain *after* applying all available exemptions (other than the annual exemption), i.e. £2,000.

**(B)**
Q bought a house on 1 August 1981 for £40,000 and used it as his main residence. On 10 February 1982, he was sent by his employer to manage the Melbourne branch of the firm and continued to work in Australia until 4 August 1986, the whole of his duties being performed outside the UK. The house was let as residential accommodation during that period. Q took up residence in the house once again following his return to the UK, but on 30 September 1993 moved to Switzerland for health reasons. On this occasion, the property was not let. He returned to the UK in August 1996, but did not reside in the house at any time prior to its being sold on 31 December 1999 for £212,350. The house had a market value of £50,000 at 31 March 1982 and the indexation factor for the period March 1982 to April 1998 (note (*f*)) is 1.047.

## Private Residences 219.1

**Computation of gain before applying exemptions**

|  | £ | £ |
|---|---:|---:|
| Disposal consideration | 212,350 | 212,350 |
| Cost | 40,000 |  |
| Market value 31.3.82 |  | 50,000 |
| Unindexed gain | 172,350 | 162,350 |
| Indexation allowance £50,000 × 1.047 | 52,350 | 52,350 |
| Gain after indexation | £120,000 | £110,000 |

| Gain before applying exemptions | £110,000 |
|---|---:|

**The gain is reduced by the main residence exemptions as follows**

| Period of ownership (excluding period before 31.3.82) |  | 17y 9m |
|---|---|---|
| Exempt periods since 31.3.82: |  |  |
| 31.3.82 – 30.9.93 | 11y 6m |  |
| 1.1.97 – 31.12.99 (last three years) | 3y 0m | 14y 6m |

|  | £ |
|---|---:|
| Gain as above | 110,000 |
| *Deduct* Exempt amount under main residence rules |  |
| $\dfrac{14\text{y 6m}}{17\text{y 9m}} \times £110{,}000$ | 89,859 |
|  | 20,141 |
| *Deduct* Let property exemption: |  |
| Period of letting 31.3.82 – 4.8.86     4y 4m |  |
| Gain attributable to letting $\dfrac{4\text{y 4m}}{17\text{y 9m}} \times £110{,}000 =$     £26,852 |  |
| Exemption     note (*e*) | 20,141 |
| Net chargeable gain | Nil |

### Notes

(*a*) Periods of ownership before 31 March 1982 are excluded in applying the main residence exemptions. This is the case even if re-basing to 1982 does not apply. [*Sec 223(7)*].

(*b*) The period spent in Australia (regardless of its length but excluding that part of it before 31 March 1982) counts as a period of residence, as Q worked in an employment all the duties of which were performed outside the UK and used the house as his main residence at some time before and after this period of absence. [*Sec 223(3)(b)*].

(*c*) The period spent in Switzerland would have been exempt, having not exceeded three years, but the exemption is lost as Q did not occupy the property as a main residence at any time after this period. [*Sec 223(3)(a)*].

(*d*) The last three years of ownership are always exempt providing the property has been used as the owner's only or main residence at some time during the period of

## 219.2 Private Residences

ownership, and for this purpose, 'period of ownership' is not restricted to the period after 30 March 1982. [*Secs 222, 223(1)*].

(*e*) The let property exemption is the lesser of the gain attributable to the period of letting (£26,852), the gain otherwise exempt (£89,859 in this example) and £40,000. It is further restricted in this example to the amount of the gain otherwise unrelieved, as it cannot create a loss. It is available only if the property is let as residential accommodation. [*Sec 223(4)*].

(*f*) Other than for the purposes of corporation tax on chargeable gains, indexation allowance is frozen at its April 1998 level. Therefore, the indexation factor for April 1998 is used in respect of disposals in a later month (and expenditure incurred in April 1998 or later does not attract indexation allowance at all). See 210 INDEXATION.

### 219.2 ELECTION FOR MAIN RESIDENCE [*TCGA 1992, s 222(5); FA 1996, 20 Sch 59, 41 Sch Pt V(10)*]

S purchased the long lease of a London flat on 1 June 1991. He occupied the flat as his sole residence until 31 July 1993 when he acquired a property in Shropshire. Both properties were thereafter occupied as residences by S until the lease of the London flat was sold on 28 February 2000, realising an otherwise chargeable gain of £75,000.

The possibilities open to S are

**(i) Election for London flat to be treated as main residence throughout**

Exempt gain £75,000

**(ii) Election for Shropshire property to be treated as main residence from 31.7.93 onwards**

Exempt gain $£75,000 \times \dfrac{2y\ 2m + 3y}{8y\ 9m}$      £44,286

**(iii) Election for London flat to be treated as main residence up to 28 February 1997, with election for the Shropshire property to be so treated thereafter**

Exempt gain $£75,000 \times \dfrac{5y\ 9m + 3y}{8y\ 9m}$      £75,000

**Note**

(*a*) The elections in (iii) are the most favourable, provided they could have been made by 31 July 1995 in respect of the London flat, and by 28 February 1999 in respect of the Shropshire property. Note that the last three years' ownership of the London flat is an exempt period in any case. The advantage of (iii) over (i) is that the period of ownership 1 March 1997 to 28 February 2000 of the Shropshire property will be treated as a period of residence as regards any future disposal of that property. Revenue practice is that the *initial* election (which can be varied) must be made within two years of acquisition of the second property, and this was upheld in *Griffin v Craig-Harvey Ch D 1993, 66 TC 396, [1994] STC 54.*

# 220 Qualifying Corporate Bonds

[*TCGA 1992, ss 115–117*]

**220.1 DEFINITION** [*TCGA 1992, s 117; FA 1993, s 84(1)(3); FA 1995, s 50*]
B has the following transactions in 5% unsecured loan stock issued in 1983 by F Ltd.

|  |  | £ |
|---|---|---:|
| 11.11.83 | Purchase £2,000 | 1,800 |
| 10.7.89 | Gift from wife £1,000 (original cost £800) | — |
| 30.9.94 | Purchase £2,000 | 2,100 |
| 5.6.99 | Sale £4,000 | (3,300) |

Apart from the gift on 10.7.89, all acquisitions were arm's length purchases. B's wife acquired her £1,000 holding on 11.11.83. Indexation allowance of £266 arose on the transfer from wife to husband.

For the purposes of the accrued income scheme, the sale is without accrued interest and the rebate amount is £20. The stock is a corporate bond as defined by *TCGA 1992, s 117(1)* and a 'relevant security' as defined by *TCGA 1992, s 108(1)*.

Under the rules for matching relevant securities in *TCGA 1992, s 106A*, the stock disposed of is identified with acquisitions as follows.

(i) Identify £2,000 with purchase on 30.9.94 (LIFO)

|  | £ |
|---|---:|
| Disposal consideration £3,300 × $\frac{2,000}{4,000}$ | 1,650 |
| *Add* rebate amount £20 × $\frac{2,000}{4,000}$ | 10 |
|  | 1,660 |
| Allowable cost | 2,100 |
| Loss | £440 |

The loss is *not* allowable as the £2,000 stock purchased on 30.9.94 is a qualifying corporate bond (note (*a*)). [*TCGA 1992, s 115*].

(ii) Identify £1,000 with acquisition on 10.7.89

|  | £ |
|---|---:|
| Disposal consideration £3,300 × $\frac{1,000}{4,000}$ | 825 |
| *Add* rebate amount £20 × $\frac{1,000}{4,000}$ | 5 |
|  | 830 |
| Allowable cost (including indexation to 10.7.89) | 1,066 |
| Allowable loss | £236 |

The loss is allowable as the stock acquired on 10.7.89 is not a qualifying corporate bond (note (*b*)).

(iii) Identify £1,000 with purchase on 11.11.83

|  | £ |
|---|---:|
| Disposal consideration £3,300 × $\frac{1,000}{4,000}$ | 825 |
| *Add* rebate amount £20 × $\frac{1,000}{4,000}$ | 5 |
|  | 830 |
| Allowable cost £1,800 × $\frac{1,000}{2,000}$ | 900 |
| Allowable loss | £70 |

## 220.2 Qualifying Corporate Bonds

The loss is allowable as the stock acquired on 11.11.83 is not a qualifying corporate bond (note (*c*)).

**Notes**
(*a*) The acquisition on 30.9.94 is a qualifying corporate bond as it was acquired after 13 March 1984 otherwise than as a result of an excluded disposal. [*TCGA 1992, s 117(7)(b)*].

(*b*) The acquisition on 10.7.89 was the result of an excluded disposal, being a no gain/no loss transfer between spouses where the first spouse had acquired the stock before 14 March 1984. It is therefore not a qualifying corporate bond. [*TCGA 1992, s 117(7)(b)(8)*].

(*c*) Securities acquired before 14 March 1984 cannot be qualifying corporate bonds in the hands of the person who so acquired them.

(*d*) See IT 22.1 SCHEDULE D, CASE VI for the income tax effects of the accrued income scheme.

## 220.2 REORGANISATION OF SHARE CAPITAL [*TCGA 1992, s 116*]

D holds 5,000 £1 ordinary shares in H Ltd. He acquired the shares in April 1990 by subscription at par. On 1 August 1993, he accepted an offer for the shares from J plc. The terms of the offer were one 25p ordinary share of J plc and £10 J plc 10% unsecured loan stock (a qualifying corporate bond) for each H Ltd ordinary share. Both the shares and the loan stock are listed on the Stock Exchange. In December 1999, D sells £20,000 loan stock at its quoted price of £105 per cent.

The value of J plc ordinary shares at 1 August 1993 was £3.52 per share and the loan stock was £99.20 per cent. The indexation factor for April 1990 to August 1993 is 0.129.

The cost of the H Ltd shares must be apportioned between the J plc ordinary shares and loan stock.

|  | £ |
|---|---|
| Value of J plc shares | |
| 5,000 × £3.52 | 17,600 |
| Value of J plc loan stock | |
| £50,000 × 99.2% | 49,600 |
| | £67,200 |

**Allowable cost of J plc shares**

$$\frac{17,600}{67,200} \times £5,000 \qquad £1,310$$

**Allowable cost of J plc loan stock**

$$\frac{49,600}{67,200} \times £5,000 \qquad £3,690$$

## Qualifying Corporate Bonds 220.2

**Chargeable gain on H Ltd shares attributable to J plc loan stock to date of exchange**

|  | £ |
|---|---|
| Deemed disposal consideration | 49,600 |
| Allowable cost | 3,690 |
| Unindexed gain | 45,910 |
| Indexation allowance £3,690 × 0.129 | 476 |
| Deferred chargeable gain | £45,434 |

**Deferred chargeable gain accruing on disposal of loan stock in December 1999**

| Loan stock sold (nominal) | £20,000 |
|---|---|
| Total holding of loan stock before disposal (nominal) | £50,000 |

Deferred chargeable gain accruing in 1999/2000

$$\frac{20,000}{50,000} \times £45,434 \qquad £18,174$$

**Notes**

(a) The gain on the sale of J plc loan stock is exempt (as the stock is a qualifying corporate bond) except for that part which relates to the gain on the previous holding of H Ltd shares. [*TCGA 1992, ss 115, 116(10)*]. There will also be income tax consequences under the accrued income scheme (see IT 22.1 SCHEDULE D, CASE VI).

(b) For taper relief purposes, the deferred gain is deemed to arise in August 1993 (and not in December 1999). [*TCGA 1992, A1 Sch 16; FA 1998, s 121(2)(4), 20 Sch*]. Thus, there can be no taper relief due in this example.

(c) The qualifying corporate bond is treated as acquired at the date of the reorganisation, so even if the original shares had been held at 31 March 1982, re-basing could *not* apply on the subsequent disposal of the loan stock. However, where the original shares were acquired before 31 March 1982, the reorganisation took place before 6 April 1988, and the qualifying corporate bonds are disposed of after 5 April 1988, the deferred chargeable gain is halved. [*TCGA 1992, 4 Sch 4*].

(d) The exchange of J plc ordinary shares for H Ltd shares is dealt with under *TCGA 1992, ss 127–130*, and no gain or loss will arise until the J plc shares are disposed of. See 224.4 SHARES AND SECURITIES.

## 221.1 Retirement Relief

## 221 Retirement Relief

[*TCGA 1992, ss 163, 164, 6 Sch; FA 1993, s 87, 7 Sch Pt I, 23 Sch Pt III(7); FA 1994, s 92; FA 1996, s 176; FA 1998, s 140, 27 Sch Pt III(31)*]

### 221.1 EXTENT OF RELIEF

#### (A) General provisions

N had been the proprietor of a retail business for more than ten years. In December 1999, when N was 51, he sold the whole of the business to a national group for £380,000. The consideration under the agreement is apportioned as follows

|  | £ |
|---|---:|
| Freehold shop | 220,000 |
| Flat over shop (occupied throughout by N as main residence) | 60,000 |
| Goodwill | 80,000 |
| Trading stock | 12,000 |
| Fixtures and fittings (one item over £6,000) | 8,000 |
|  | £380,000 |

Chargeable gains after indexation to April 1998 are

|  | £ |
|---|---:|
| Freehold shop | 177,500 |
| Goodwill | 52,000 |
| Fixture | 500 |
| Aggregate | £230,000 |

**Retirement relief is calculated as follows**

| | £ |
|---|---:|
| Gain subject to relief | 230,000 |
| Maximum available for 100% relief | |
| Qualifying period — 10 years | |
| $\dfrac{10}{10} \times £200,000$ | (200,000) |
| Maximum available for 50% relief (statutory maximum £600,000) | |
| £230,000 − £200,000 = £30,000 | |
| £30,000 × $\frac{1}{2}$ | (15,000) |
| Chargeable gain subject to TAPER RELIEF (226) | £15,000 |

**Notes**

(*a*) For disposals after 5 April 1999 and before 6 April 2000, the exemption is extended to one half of gains between £200,000 and £800,000, these limits being reduced by reference to qualifying periods of less than ten years. These figures are gradually reduced between 6 April 2000 and 5 April 2003, culminating in the abolition of retirement relief for disposals after 5 April 2003.

(*b*) The age from which a person may qualify for retirement relief, other than on ill-health grounds, is 50.

# Retirement Relief 221.1

(c) The flat over the shop is exempt from capital gains tax as it has been N's main residence throughout the period of ownership.

**(B) Retirement from business on ill-health grounds and relief restricted by reference to qualifying period** [TCGA 1992, s 163(1)–(3), 6 Sch 3, 13; FA 1994, s 92; FA 1996, 20 Sch 66]

After giving up salaried employment in June 1993 at the age of 41, R purchased a small philately business. In June 1999, R finds he is unable to continue running the business because of ill-health and sells for the following amounts.

|  | Proceeds | Chargeable gain (after indexation to April 1998) |
|---|---|---|
|  | £ | £ |
| Premises | 230,000 | 186,000 |
| Goodwill | 30,000 | 22,800 |
| Fixtures and fittings (none over £6,000) | 8,000 | — |
| Stock | 25,000 | — |
|  |  | £208,800 |

**Retirement relief is given as follows**

|  | £ |
|---|---|
| Gains eligible for relief | 208,800 |

Maximum available for 100% relief
Qualifying period — 6 years

$$\frac{6}{10} \times £200,000 \qquad (120,000)$$

Ceiling for 50% relief

$$\frac{6}{10} \times £800,000 = £480,000$$

£208,800 (being less than £480,000) – £120,000 = £88,800
£88,800 × ½     (44,400)

Chargeable gain subject to TAPER RELIEF (226)     £44,400

**Note**

(a) Relief is given where an individual has retired below the age of 50 on ill-health grounds provided he has ceased work and is likely to remain permanently incapable of that kind of work. Claims for relief on the grounds of ill-health must be made to the Board by the first anniversary of 31 January following the tax year in which the disposal occurred. [TCGA 1992, 6 Sch 3, 5(2)(4); FA 1996, 20 Sch 66, 21 Sch 44(3)].

## 221.1 Retirement Relief

**(C) Operative date — ceasing to be a full-time working officer or employee** [*TCGA 1992, s 163(5)(7), 6 Sch 1; FA 1993, s 87, 7 Sch Pt I*]

Q gave up full-time work at the age of 51 in June 1999 when she had been a director of Q Ltd, her personal company, for five years. She continued as a director, working three four-hour mornings per week until January 2000 when she sold her 40% shareholding in Q Ltd realising a chargeable gain of £490,000.

**Retirement relief is given as follows**

|  | £ |
|---|---:|
| Gain eligible for relief | 490,000 |

Maximum available for 100% relief
Qualifying period — 5 years

$\frac{5}{10} \times £200,000$ (100,000)

Ceiling for 50% relief

$\frac{5}{10} \times £800,000 = £400,000$

£400,000 − £100,000 = £300,000
£300,000 × $\frac{1}{2}$ (150,000)

Chargeable gain 1999/2000 (subject to TAPER RELIEF (226)) £240,000

**Note**

(*a*) If an individual ceases to be a full-time working officer or employee of a company but remains an officer or employee and works an average of ten hours per week in a technical or managerial capacity until the date of disposal, the operative date is deemed to be the date of ceasing to be a full-time working officer or employee. This enables retirement relief to be given, but by reference to the qualifying period ended on that earlier date rather than on the date of disposal.

# Retirement Relief 221.1

**(D) Share for share exchange — relief available** [*TCGA 1992, 6 Sch 2; FA 1996, 21 Sch 44(1)(2)*]

In November 1999, D, aged 67, accepts an offer to exchange his 60% holding of 1,200 shares in C Ltd for shares in M plc on the basis of 10 for 1. He has been a full-time working officer of C Ltd for 15 years. He receives 12,000 shares in M plc valued at £180,000. The holding in C Ltd cost £50,000 in August 1984. D elects *not* to treat the new shares and the holding disposed of as the same asset under *TCGA 1992, s 127*.

The indexation factor from August 1984 to April 1998 (note (*b*)) is 0.808.

C Ltd had no non-business assets.

**The chargeable gain is calculated as follows**

|  | £ |
|---|---:|
| Disposal consideration | 180,000 |
| Cost | 50,000 |
| Unindexed gain | 130,000 |
| Indexation allowance £50,000 × 0.808 | 40,400 |
| Gain after indexation | £89,600 |
| | |
| Gain subject to retirement relief | 89,600 |
| Retirement relief available (maximum £200,000 at 100% and £600,000 at 50%) | 89,600 |
| Chargeable gain | Nil |

**Notes**

(*a*) The base cost for D's holding of M plc shares is £180,000.

(*b*) Other than for the purposes of corporation tax on chargeable gains, indexation allowance is frozen at its April 1998 level. Therefore, the indexation factor for April 1998 is used in respect of disposals in a later month (and expenditure incurred in April 1998 or later does not attract indexation allowance at all). See 210 INDEXATION.

## 221.2 Retirement Relief

### 221.2 GAINS QUALIFYING FOR RELIEF

**(A) Non-business chargeable assets** [*TCGA 1992, 6 Sch 6, 7, 12; FA 1993, s 87, 7 Sch Pt I*]

P Ltd carries on a trade of printing and bookbinding. Its full-time working directors include C who owns 10% of the issued share capital and of the voting rights. In December 1999, on reaching the age of 63, C gives his shares to his sister. At the date of transfer, the company's assets are valued as follows

|  | £ | £ | Market value £ | Cost £ |
|---|---|---|---|---|
| Leasehold printing works |  |  | 190,000 | 50,000 |
| Goodwill |  |  | 60,000 | — |
| Stocks of materials |  |  | 80,000 | 75,000 |
| Plant |  |  |  |  |
| Printing presses No 1 | 8,000 |  |  | 3,000 |
| No 2 | 8,500 |  |  | 3,500 |
| No 3 | 6,500 | 23,000 |  | 2,000 |
| Typesetter |  | 10,500 |  | 15,000 |
| Binding machine |  | 16,500 |  | 12,000 |
| Small tools, type etc. |  | 7,000 |  | 10,000 |
| Motor cars |  | 20,000 |  | 30,000 |
| Office fixtures and fittings (items under £6,000) |  | 9,000 | 86,000 | 15,000 |
| Shares in associated publishing company |  |  | 60,000 | 40,000 |
| Cash at bank and in hand |  |  | 7,500 | — |
| Debtors |  |  | 11,500 | — |

The chargeable gain (after indexation to April 1998) arising on the shares given to C's sister is £75,000.

**The value of the company's chargeable assets is as follows**

|  | Business £ | Non-business £ |
|---|---|---|
| Leasehold | 190,000 | — |
| Goodwill | 60,000 | — |
| Plant (£23,000 + £10,500 + £16,500) | 50,000 | — |
| Shares | — | 60,000 |
|  | £300,000 | £60,000 |

Gain eligible for retirement relief is therefore

$£75,000 \times \dfrac{300,000}{300,000 + 60,000}$ £62,500

**Notes**

(a) Chargeable assets are all assets other than those on which any gain accruing on a disposal immediately before the end of the qualifying period would not be a chargeable gain.

(b) The balance of the gain after retirement relief will qualify for TAPER RELIEF (226).

## Retirement Relief 221.2

**(B) Shares in holding company — group holding non-business assets.** [*TCGA 1992, 6 Sch 6, 8, 12; FA 1993, s 87, 7 Sch Pt I*]

D, a full-time working director aged 60, gives 20% of his shares in his personal company, N Ltd, to his son. The business of manufacturing and distributing double glazing units is carried on through two subsidiaries, X Ltd and Y Ltd. At the date of disposal in November 1999, the market value of the assets of the group are as follows.

|  | Assets | Chargeable assets Business | Chargeable assets Non-business |
|---|---|---|---|
|  | £ | £ | £ |
| **N Ltd** |  |  |  |
| Leasehold of factory | 150,000 | 150,000 |  |
| Investment in subsidiaries |  |  |  |
| X (100%) | 60,000 |  |  |
| Y (60%) | 40,000 |  |  |
| Quoted shares | 10,000 |  | 10,000 |
| **X Ltd (100% owned)** |  |  |  |
| Plant | 32,000 | 32,000 |  |
| Stock, debtors and cash | 18,000 |  |  |
|  |  | £182,000 | £10,000 |
| **Y Ltd (60% owned)** |  |  |  |
| Freehold shop (half let) | 50,000 | 25,000 | 25,000 |
| Plant and machinery | 15,000 | 15,000 |  |
| Stock, debtors and cash | 9,000 |  |  |
|  |  | £40,000 | £25,000 |
| 60% thereof |  | £24,000 | £15,000 |
| Total |  | £206,000 | £25,000 |

The chargeable gain (after indexation to April 1998) on the gift of shares is £57,750.

**The gain eligible for retirement relief is therefore**

$$£57,750 \times \frac{206,000}{206,000 + 25,000} = £51,500$$

### Notes
(a) A shareholding in another member of the trading group is not counted as a chargeable asset.

(b) Chargeable business and non-business assets of a part-owned subsidiary are reduced in proportion to the share capital owned.

(c) It is assumed that none of the items of plant and machinery are covered by the £6,000 chattel exemption.

(d) The balance of the gain after retirement relief will qualify for TAPER RELIEF (226).

## 221.2 Retirement Relief

**(C) Associated disposal by trustees** [*TCGA 1992, s 164(3)–(5), 6 Sch 13; FA 1993, s 87, 7 Sch Pt I*]

B has carried on a business for more than ten years in premises held by a family trust in which he has a life interest of 40%.

In May 1998 B, who is then 54, sells the business, realising a chargeable gain of £173,000. The trustees sell the property on 30 April 1999, at a chargeable gain of £89,000.

**Disposal by B**

|  | £ |
|---|---:|
| Chargeable gain | 173,000 |
| Retirement relief (100%) | (173,000) |
| Chargeable gain | Nil |

**Disposal by trustees**

|  | £ |
|---|---:|
| Chargeable gain | 89,000 |

Gain subject to retirement relief: 40% × £89,000 = £35,600

| | |
|---|---:|
| Relief available at 100% £(200,000 – 173,000) | (27,000) |
| Relief available at 50% £(35,600 – 27,000) | (4,300) |
| Chargeable gain | £57,700 |

**Notes**

(*a*) For the purposes of calculating the maximum available retirement relief, a trustees' disposal is regarded as a qualifying disposal by the beneficiary. If disposals by trustees and a beneficiary are made on the same day, relief is given first to the gain by the beneficiary.

(*b*) The qualifying period of full-time working must end not more than one year before the trustees' disposal. If the trustees' sale were deferred to, say, June 1999, no relief would be available except at the Board's discretion.

**(D) Associated disposal — restriction for non-business use, qualifying period and rent** [*TCGA 1992, 6 Sch 10; FA 1996, 20 Sch 66(4)*]

In May 1999, X, who had been a full-time working officer for 10 years and was aged 53, sold his qualifying holding of shares in W Ltd realising a chargeable gain of £90,000. The company had, since 1989, used a warehouse acquired by X personally in 1984. It was agreed that whilst the company would continue to carry on the trade, it would vacate the warehouse (for which it paid a rent of 75% market rate) after six months. X then sold the warehouse in December 1999 realising a chargeable gain of £47,250.

Disposal of shares

| | £ |
|---|---|
| Chargeable gain | 90,000 |
| Retirement relief (100%) | (90,000) |
| | Nil |

Disposal of warehouse

| | £ |
|---|---|
| Chargeable gain | 47,250 |

Gain subject to retirement relief
  (i) Proportion of business use

$$\frac{10 \text{ years}}{15 \text{ years}} \times £47{,}250 = £31{,}500$$

  (ii) Qualifying period of ownership

$$\frac{10}{10\frac{1}{2}} \times £31{,}500 = £30{,}000 \quad \text{note } (b)$$

  (iii) Proportion rent-free
  25% × £30,000 = £7,500

Balance of relief available (at 100%) £(200,000 − 90,000) = £110,000

| | |
|---|---|
| Retirement relief (restricted to £7,500 × 100%) | 7,500 |
| Chargeable gain subject to TAPER RELIEF (226) | £39,750 |

**Notes**

(a) Restricted retirement relief is available where the asset has not been used for business purposes throughout the period of ownership or where the individual was not concerned in carrying on the trade during part of the period of use in the business or where rent has been paid for the use of the asset. The part qualifying for relief is that which is 'just and reasonable'.

(b) For the final six months of use of the warehouse in the business, W Ltd was not X's personal company. (Note that for taper relief purposes, this will also restrict the period for which the warehouse is a business asset by reference to X's disposal — see 226.2 TAPER RELIEF.)

## 221.2 Retirement Relief

**(E) Partnerships** [*TCGA 1992, s 163(8), 6 Sch 10; FA 1996, 20 Sch 66(4)*]

U, V and W trade in partnership. They have shared income and capital in the ratio 5:3:2 since 1976. On 30 April 1999, V retires aged 63 after 30 years as a partner and receives a lump sum of £50,000 from the other partners. Of the £50,000, £35,000 is expressed to relate to V's interest in the freehold depot, £10,000 to goodwill and £5,000 to non-chargeable assets. V also transfers to the firm, for £120,000, office premises which the firm has occupied for business purposes, paying an annual rent to V of £3,000. The open market rent for the property is £5,000 per annum. V's chargeable gain on the property is £82,000. The book values of the firm's chargeable assets are as follows.

| | |
|---|---|
| Freehold depot | £40,000 (cost on 1.5.87) |
| Goodwill | £10,000 (valuation on 31.3.82) |

| | | |
|---|---|---|
| Indexation factors | May 1987 to April 1998 | 0.596 |
| | March 1982 to April 1998 | 1.047 |

**Chargeable gains eligible for retirement relief are**

| | £ | £ | £ |
|---|---:|---:|---:|
| Freehold depot: Consideration | 35,000 | | |
| Allowable cost $\frac{3}{10}$ × £40,000 | 12,000 | | |
| Unindexed gain | | 23,000 | |
| Indexation allowance £12,000 × 0.596 | | 7,152 | |
| | | | 15,848 |
| Goodwill: Consideration | 10,000 | | |
| Allowable cost $\frac{3}{10}$ × £10,000 | 3,000 | | |
| Unindexed gain | | 7,000 | |
| Indexation allowance £3,000 × 1.047 | | 3,141 | |
| | | | 3,859 |
| Office premises Chargeable gain | £82,000 | | |
| Fraction eligible | | | |
| $\frac{3}{10} + \left(\frac{7}{10} \times \frac{5,000 - 3,000}{5,000}\right) = \frac{29}{50} \times £82,000$ | | | 47,560 |
| | | | £67,267 |

**Notes**

(a) The whole of the £67,267 attracts 100% retirement relief. V is therefore chargeable only on the non-eligible part of the gain on the office premises of £34,440 (£82,000 − £47,560), and this is subject to TAPER RELIEF (226).

(b) Where rent, but at less than market rent, is paid by the partnership, *TCGA 1992, 6 Sch 10* gives relief for a 'just and reasonable' amount of the gain. The formula shown above is used by the Revenue (Revenue Capital Gains Manual, CG 63836, CG 63838).

(c) See (D) above for restriction of relief where an asset has not been used for business purposes throughout the period of ownership.

## Retirement Relief 221.2

**(F) Capital distribution** [*TCGA 1992, s 163(1)(2)(4), 6 Sch 11, 12(5)(6); FA 1993, s 87, 7 Sch Pt I; FA 1996, 21 Sch 44(4)*].

At 60, M decides to put his personal trading company into voluntary liquidation. He holds all the share capital and has been a full-time working officer for 20 years. In November 1998, the company sold off machinery for £7,000. The company ceases to trade in February 1999, and in November 1999 the liquidator pays M a cash distribution of £12,000 and transfers to him the lease of its premises, then worth £24,000.

M's chargeable gain for 1999/2000 (after indexation to April 1998) on disposal of his shares is £27,000.

At cessation, the company's assets (at market value) were

|  | Assets | Chargeable Business | Chargeable Non-business |
|---|---|---|---|
|  | £ | £ | £ |
| Lease of premises | 25,000 | 25,000 |  |
| Flat over premises (let) | 5,000 |  | 5,000 |
| Plant, fixtures | 13,000 | 13,000 |  |
| Motor cars | 8,000 |  |  |
| Stock, debtors, cash | 19,000 |  |  |

M elects under *TCGA 1992, 6 Sch 12(5)* to substitute the machinery sold in November 1998 for the proceeds of its sale held at cessation in order to increase the proportion of chargeable business assets.

**The chargeable gain is calculated as follows**

|  | £ |
|---|---|
| Gain on disposal | 27,000 |

Restricted to cash portion of distribution   note *(b)*

$$\frac{12{,}000}{12{,}000 + 24{,}000} \times £27{,}000 = £9{,}000$$

Allowable for retirement relief (at 100%)

$$\frac{25{,}000 + 13{,}000 + 7{,}000}{25{,}000 + 13{,}000 + 7{,}000 + 5{,}000} \times £9{,}000 \qquad 8{,}100$$

Chargeable gain subject to TAPER RELIEF (226)   £18,900

### Notes

(*a*) The liquidator's distribution must be within one year of the date of cessation of business or such longer period as the Board allows. (See definition of 'permitted period' in *TCGA 1992, 6 Sch 1(2)*.)

(*b*) No retirement relief is available on that part of the gain attributable to the proportion of the capital distribution consisting of chargeable business assets. [*TCGA 1992, 6 Sch 11*].

(*c*) It is assumed that no item of the plant and fixtures is covered by the £6,000 chattel exemption.

## 221.3 Retirement Relief

### 221.3 AMOUNT OF RELIEF

**(A) Aggregation of earlier business periods** [*TCGA 1992, 6 Sch 14; FA 1996, 39 Sch 7*]

A sold the hotel he had owned and run for ten years in July 1991. In January 1992 he reinvested £65,000 in a similar business, rolling over the earlier chargeable gain of £50,000. When he was 51, in January 2000, the hotel was severely damaged by fire and A decided to retire. He received £200,000 from the insurance company and £45,000 for the sale of the land. The indexation factor for the period January 1992 to April 1998 (note (*b*)) is 0.199.

|  | £ | £ |
|---|---:|---:|
| Disposal proceeds — sale of land | 45,000 | |
| — insurance monies | 200,000 | |
|  |  | 245,000 |
| Cost | 65,000 | |
| *Less* rolled over gain | 50,000 | |
|  |  | 15,000 |
|  |  | 230,000 |
| Indexation allowance £15,000 × 0.199 |  | 2,985 |
|  |  | 227,015 |
| Maximum retirement relief available at 100% £200,000 |  |  |
| Restricted by qualifying period |  |  |
| $\dfrac{8 + 1\frac{1}{2}}{10} \times £200,000 \times 100\%$    note (*a*) |  | 190,000 |
|  |  | 37,015 |

Maximum retirement relief available at 50%:

$£800,000 \times \dfrac{9\frac{1}{2}}{10} = £760,000 - £190,000 = £570,000$

| £227,015 − £190,000 = £37,015 × 50% | 18,508 |
|---|---:|
| Chargeable gain subject to TAPER RELIEF (226) | **£18,507** |

**Notes**

(*a*) The two business periods falling within the ten-year qualifying period are aggregated but the qualifying period is restricted by the gap between the ownership of the two businesses.

(*b*) Other than for the purposes of corporation tax on chargeable gains, indexation allowance is frozen at its April 1998 level. Therefore, the indexation factor for April 1998 is used in respect of disposals in a later month (and expenditure incurred in April 1998 or later does not attract indexation allowance at all). See 210 INDEXATION.

# Retirement Relief 221.3

**(B) Relief given on earlier disposal** [*TCGA 1992, 6 Sch 15*]
P, who was born in 1937, carried on the following businesses, and made gains qualifying for retirement relief on disposals of them at cessation, as follows.

| Business A | 1.4.81 – 30.6.93 | £500,000 |
|---|---|---|
| Business B | 1.4.95 – 30.6.99 | £176,000 |

## His entitlement to retirement relief is calculated as follows

*Business A*

| | | |
|---|---|---|
| Gains qualifying for relief | | £500,000 |
| Qualifying period | | 10 years |

Maximum available for 100% relief:

| | | £ |
|---|---|---|
| 10/10 × £150,000 × 100% | | 150,000 |

| | | |
|---|---|---|
| Maximum available for 50% relief: | | |
| 10/10 × £450,000 | £450,000 | |
| Excess of gains £500,000 – £150,000 | £350,000 | |
| £350,000 × 50% | | 175,000 |
| Relief given 1993/94 | | £325,000 |
| | | |
| Chargeable gain 1993/94 | | £175,000 |
| | | |
| Underlying gains | | |
| (£150,000 + (2 × £175,000)) | | £500,000 |

*Business B*

(1) Before restriction applied:

| | | |
|---|---|---|
| Gains qualifying for relief | | £176,000 |

Qualifying period (extended under *TCGA 1992, 6 Sch 14* as gap between businesses less than 2 years — 10 years (maximum) less 1.75 years from 1.7.93 to 31.3.95)     8.25 years

Maximum available for 100% relief:

| | | £ |
|---|---|---|
| 8.25/10 × 200,000 × 100% | | 165,000 |

| | | |
|---|---|---|
| Maximum available for 50% relief: | | |
| 8.25/10 × £600,000 | £495,000 | |
| Excess of gains £176,000 – 165,000 | £11,000 | |
| £11,000 × 50% | | 5,500 |
| Relief due subject to (2) below | | £170,500 |

## 221.3 Retirement Relief

(2) Applying *TCGA 1992, 6 Sch 15* restriction:

|  |  | £ |
|---|---|---|
| Gains qualifying for relief |  | 176,000 |
| *Add:* Underlying gains on earlier disposal |  | 500,000 |
|  |  | £676,000 |

| | | |
|---|---|---|
| Qualifying period for later disposal (as above) | 8.25 years | |
| Extended by qualifying period for earlier disposal but up to a maximum of 10 years | 1.75 years | 10 years |

Maximum available for 100% relief:

|  |  | £ |
|---|---|---|
| 10/10 × £200,000 × 100% |  | 200,000 |

| | | |
|---|---|---|
| Maximum available for 50% relief: | | |
| 10/10 × £600,000 | £600,000 | |
| Excess of gains £676,000 − 200,000 | £476,000 | |
| £476,000 × 50% | | 238,000 |
| | | 438,000 |
| *Less:* Relief given on disposal of Business A | | 325,000 |
| Relief due (as less than £170,500 in (1) above) | | £113,000 |
| | | |
| Chargeable gain 1999/2000 (£176,000 − £113,000) | | £63,000 |

**Note**
(*a*) The 1999/2000 chargeable gain of £63,000 is subject to TAPER RELIEF (226).

**(C) Married persons — aggregation of spouses' qualifying periods — transfer on death** [*TCGA 1992, 6 Sch 16; FA 1996, 21 Sch 44(5)*]
R acquired her late husband's 30% shareholding in X Ltd on his death in June 1995. She took over the office he had held for 15 years as a full-time working officer until, at the age of 63, she sold her shares in June 1999 incurring an otherwise chargeable gain of £264,000 (after indexation and before taper relief).

**The chargeable gain is calculated as follows**

|  | £ |
|---|---|
| Gain eligible for relief | 264,000 |
| Maximum available for 100% relief | |
| $\dfrac{4+6}{10} \times £200{,}000 \times 100\%$ | (200,000) |
| Maximum available for 50% relief | |
| $\dfrac{4+6}{10} \times £800{,}000 = £800{,}000 - £200{,}000 = £600{,}000$ | |
| £264,000 − £200,000 = £64,000 × 50% | (32,000) |
| Chargeable gain 1999/2000 subject to TAPER RELIEF (226) | £32,000 |

**Note**

(*a*) Written election must be made, by the first anniversary of 31 January following the tax year in which the disposal occurs, for the qualifying period to be extended by the spouse's qualifying period.

**(D) Married persons — aggregation of spouses' qualifying periods — lifetime transfer** [*TCGA 1992, 6 Sch 16; FA 1996, 21 Sch 44(5)*]

In May 1992, J, who was 65 that month, gave 40% of the shares in Y Ltd, a trading company, to his son realising an otherwise chargeable gain of £40,000. He had been a full-time working director for 12 years. His wife G, aged 54, already held 20% of the share capital and both she and the son became full-time directors. Later that year, J's health failed and he transferred his remaining 40% holding to G who continued as a full-time working director until November 1999 when she gave her shares to her son realising an otherwise chargeable gain of £240,000 (after indexation and before taper relief). All the company's chargeable assets are chargeable business assets.

| Gift by J to son | £ |
|---|---|
| Gain eligible for relief | 40,000 |
| Retirement relief available (£40,000 × 100%) | 40,000 |
| Chargeable gain | Nil |

## 221.3 Retirement Relief

**Disposal by G**

*No election to aggregate qualifying periods*
Gain eligible for relief                                                          240,000
Maximum available for 100% relief

$$\frac{7\frac{1}{2}}{10} \times £200{,}000 \qquad\qquad (150{,}000)$$

Ceiling for 50% relief

$$\frac{7\frac{1}{2}}{10} \times £800{,}000 = £600{,}000 - £150{,}000 = £450{,}000$$

£240,000 − £150,000 = £90,000 × 50%                                (45,000)

Chargeable gain 1999/2000 (subject to TAPER
  RELIEF (226))                                                                         £45,000

*Election made to aggregate qualifying periods*                              £
Gain eligible for relief                                                          240,000
Maximum available for 100% relief

$$\frac{10}{10} \times £200{,}000 = \qquad\qquad 200{,}000$$

*Deduct* Relief at 100% previously given          40,000      (160,000)

Ceiling for 50% relief

$$\frac{10}{10} \times £800{,}000 = £800{,}000 - £200{,}000 = £600{,}000$$

£240,000 − £160,000 = £80,000 × 50%                                (40,000)

Chargeable gain 1999/2000 (subject to TAPER
  RELIEF (226))                                                                         £40,000

**The election is beneficial.**

**Notes**
(a) Where, following a lifetime gift, the election is made for aggregation, retirement relief on the later disposal is restricted to that available if that disposal had been made by the transferor spouse. [*TCGA 1992, 6 Sch 16(3)(4)*]. Thus, in this example, the relief must take into account retirement relief already given to the transferor spouse on an earlier disposal (see (B) above). [*TCGA 1992, 6 Sch 15*].

(b) G and her son could make a joint claim for the gain on her gift to be held-over under *TCGA 1992, s 165*, but retirement relief takes priority. See 209.2 HOLD-OVER RELIEFS for examples including the interaction between the two.

# 222 Rollover Relief — Replacement of Business Assets

**Cross-reference.** See also 204.2 ASSETS HELD ON 31 MARCH 1982 for relief under *TCGA 1992, s 36, 4 Sch* for certain gains accruing before 31 March 1982.

[*TCGA 1992, ss 152–158*]

## 222.1 NATURE OF RELIEF [*TCGA 1992, s 152*]

**(A)**

N Ltd carries on a manufacturing business. It makes the following disposals and acquisitions of assets during the company's accounting periods ended 31 December 1997, 31 December 1998 and 31 December 1999.

|  | Asset | Bought/(sold) £ | Chargeable gains £ |
|---|---|---|---|
| 1.10.97 | Freehold depot | 18,000 | — |
| 12.12.97 | Leasehold warehouse | (50,000) | 28,000 |
| 19.6.98 | Business formerly carried on by another company: | | |
|  | Goodwill | 20,000 | — |
|  | Freehold factory unit | 90,000 | — |
| 1.2.99 | Land adjacent to main factory, now surplus to requirements | (40,000) | 19,000 |
| 8.9.99 | Industrial mincer (fixed plant) | (30,000) | 5,000 |
| 1.11.99 | Extension to new factory | 35,000 | — |

**(i) The gain on the leasehold warehouse may be rolled over against the following**

| | Cost £ | | Gain £ |
|---|---|---|---|
| Freehold depot | 18,000 | $\dfrac{18,000}{50,000} \times £28,000$ | 10,080 |
| Goodwill | 20,000 | $\dfrac{20,000}{50,000} \times £28,000$ | 11,200 |
| Freehold factory (part) | 12,000 | $\dfrac{12,000}{50,000} \times £28,000$ | 6,720 |
| | £50,000 | | £28,000 |

See note (*b*)

**(ii) The gain on the surplus land may then be rolled over as follows**

| | | | |
|---|---|---|---|
| Freehold factory (part) | £40,000 | Gain rolled over | £19,000 |

**(iii) The gain on the industrial mincer may be rolled over as follows**

| | | | |
|---|---|---|---|
| Extension to new factory (part) | £30,000 | Gain rolled over | £5,000 |

## 222.1 Rollover Relief — Replacement of Business Assets

**The position at 31 December 1999 is then as follows**

|  | £ |
|---|---:|
| Freehold depot | |
| Cost | 18,000 |
| *Deduct* gains rolled over | 10,080 |
| Allowable cost | £7,920 |
| Goodwill | |
| Cost | 20,000 |
| *Deduct* gains rolled over | 11,200 |
| Allowable cost | £8,800 |
| | |
| Freehold factory | |
| Cost | 90,000 |
| *Deduct* gains rolled over (£6,720 + £19,000) | 25,720 |
| Allowable cost | £64,280 |
| | |
| Extension to new factory | |
| Cost | 35,000 |
| *Deduct* gains rolled over | 5,000 |
| Allowable cost | £30,000 |

**Notes**

(*a*) The expenditure still available to match against disposal proceeds is

Extension to factory (£35,000 − £30,000)     £5,000

The expenditure is available only against disposals up to 31 October 2000.

(*b*) There is no statutory rule prescribing the way in which the gain on an asset must be rolled over against a number of different assets. The taxpayer's allocation of the rolled over gain against the cost of the new assets should be accepted by the Revenue, providing specified amounts of consideration are positively earmarked and set against the cost of specified new assets (Revenue Capital Gains Manual, CG 60775). In (i) the chargeable gain has been rolled over rateably to the costs of the items, but bringing in only part (i.e. the balance of proceeds) of the cost of the freehold factory.

# Rollover Relief — Replacement of Business Assets

**(B)**
L Ltd carries on a vehicle repair business. In December 1997 it sells a workshop for £90,000 net of costs. The workshop had cost £45,000 inclusive in April 1990. A new workshop is purchased for £144,000 (including incidental costs of acquisition) on 11 January 1998 and sold for £168,000 on 14 January 2000.

| Indexation factors | April 1990 to December 1997 | 0.279 |
|---|---|---|
| | January 1998 to January 2000 (estimated) | 0.060 |

L Ltd claims rollover of the chargeable gain.

|  | £ |
|---|---:|
| Allowable cost of original workshop | 45,000 |
| Indexation allowance £45,000 × 0.279 | 12,555 |
|  | 57,555 |
| Actual disposal consideration | 90,000 |
| Chargeable gain rolled over | £32,445 |
|  |  |
| Cost of new workshop | 144,000 |
| *Deduct* amount rolled over | 32,445 |
| Deemed allowable cost | £111,555 |
|  |  |
| Disposal consideration, replacement workshop | 168,000 |
| Allowable cost | 111,555 |
| Unindexed gain | 56,445 |
| Indexation allowance £111,555 × 0.060 | 6,693 |
| Chargeable gain | £49,752 |

**(C)**
The facts are as in (B) above except that the business is carried on by M, an individual. M makes no disposals in 1999/2000 other than that of the replacement workshop. The indexation factor for the period January 1998 to April 1998 is 0.019.

The rolled over gain and the allowable cost of the replacement asset are as in (B) above.

**The computation on the disposal of the replacement workshop is as follows**

|  | £ |
|---|---:|
| Disposal consideration, replacement workshop | 168,000 |
| Allowable cost | 111,555 |
| Unindexed gain | 56,445 |
| Indexation allowance £111,555 × 0.019 | 2,119 |
| Gain subject to taper relief | £54,326 |
| Business asset taper relief: £54,326 @ 15% (note (*a*)) | 8,149 |
| Chargeable gain 1999/2000 | £46,177 |

**Notes**
(*a*)  The qualifying holding period for taper relief purposes runs from 6 April 1998 to 14 January 2000, comprising one complete year, plus the bonus year for assets acquired before 17 March 1998. [*TCGA 1992, s 2A; FA 1998, s 121(1)*]. The period

## 222.2 Rollover Relief — Replacement of Business Assets

of ownership of the original workshop cannot be taken into account (and this would be the case even if all or part of that period was a period after 5 April 1998).

(b) Other than for the purposes of corporation tax on chargeable gains, indexation allowance is frozen at its April 1998 level. See 210 INDEXATION.

### 222.2 PARTIAL RELIEF

**(A) Assets only partly replaced** [*TCGA 1992, s 153*]

G carries on an accountancy practice. In March 1999, he agrees to acquire the practice of another sole practitioner, who is about to retire. As part of the acquisition, G pays £20,000 for goodwill. In January 2000, G moves to new premises, acquiring the remaining 70 years of a 99-year lease for £50,000. The sale of his former office on 25 February 2000 realises £80,000, and a chargeable gain (after indexation to April 1998) of £59,000 arises. (The former office had been owned since 1989.)

|  | £ | £ |
|---|---:|---:|
| Amount of proceeds of disposal of old office |  | 80,000 |
| Costs against which gains can be rolled over |  |  |
| Goodwill | 20,000 |  |
| Lease | 50,000 |  |
|  | 70,000 |  |
| Chargeable gain not rolled over |  | 10,000 |
| Business asset taper relief @ 15% |  | 1,500 |
| Chargeable gain |  | £8,500 |
| Chargeable gain rolled over (£59,000 − £10,000) |  | £49,000 |
| Allowable cost of assets (see note (a)): |  |  |
| Goodwill | 20,000 |  |
| Gain rolled over $\frac{20,000}{70,000} \times £49,000$ | 14,000 |  |
|  |  | £6,000 |
| Lease | 50,000 |  |
| Gain rolled over $\frac{50,000}{70,000} \times £49,000$ | 35,000 |  |
|  |  | £15,000 |

**Notes**

(a) There is no statutory rule prescribing the way in which a gain is to be rolled over against more than one acquisition. See note (b) to 222.1(A).

(b) It would not have been possible to roll over the gain only against the acquisition of the goodwill. The consideration not reinvested (£60,000) would be more than the gain (£59,000).

(c) The qualifying holding period for taper relief purposes runs from 6 April 1998 to 25 February 2000, comprising one complete year, plus the bonus year for assets acquired before 17 March 1998. [*TCGA 1992, s 2A; FA 1998, s 121(1)*].

(d) A gain does not qualify for taper relief to the extent that it is rolled over.

## Rollover Relief — Replacement of Business Assets 222.3

**(B) Partial business use** [*TCGA 1992, s 152(7)*]
N carries on a consultancy business from commercial premises formerly used as a shop. N has owned the property since 1 July 1979, but it was let until 1 March 1991 when N moved in, following the expiry of the lease held by the former tenant. The property cost £8,000. On 1 February 2000, N sells the property for £100,000, moving to a new office with a long lease which he acquires for £60,000 and which is wholly used for his business. The value at 31 March 1982 of the property sold was £40,000 and N has made the global re-basing election under *TCGA 1992, s 35(5)*. The indexation factor for March 1982 to April 1998 (note (*d*)) is 1.047.

**For rollover relief purposes**, N is treated as having disposed of two separate assets, one representing his occupation and professional use of the property, the other his ownership of it as an investment. In practice, the proceeds and chargeable gain may be allocated by a simple time apportionment.

*Proceeds attributable to business use*

Proceeds £100,000 × $\frac{8y\ 11m}{17y\ 10m}$   note (*c*)                                             £50,000

*Chargeable gain attributable to business use*

[£100,000 − £40,000 − (£40,000 × 1.047)] = £18,120 × $\frac{8y\ 11m}{17y\ 10m}$            £9,060

**Notes**
(*a*)   The proceeds attributable to business use are less than the cost of the new office, so that the whole of the chargeable gain attributable to business use can be rolled over. The allowable cost of the new office is then £50,940 (£60,000 − £9,060).

(*b*)   The balance of the chargeable gain, £9,060 (£18,120 − £9,060) is not eligible for rollover. It *is* eligible for business asset taper relief by reference solely to the use of the property after 5 April 1998 (see 226.2 TAPER RELIEF).

(*c*)   The time apportionment takes into account only the period of ownership after 30 March 1982. [*TCGA 1992, s 152(9)*].

(*d*)   Other than for the purposes of corporation tax on chargeable gains, indexation allowance is frozen at its April 1998 level. Therefore, the indexation factor for April 1998 is used in respect of disposals in a later month (and expenditure incurred in April 1998 or later does not attract indexation allowance at all). See 210 INDEXATION.

## 222.3 WASTING ASSETS [*TCGA 1992, s 154*]

**(A) Crystallisation of held-over gain**
In March 1995, a father and son partnership carrying on a car dealing trade sold a freehold showroom for £400,000 realising a chargeable gain (after indexation) of £190,000. On 30 June 1995, the firm purchased for £450,000 the remaining term of a lease due to expire on 30 June 2025 and used the premises as a new showroom. The whole of the gain on the old asset was held over under *TCGA 1992, s 154* on the acquisition of the new asset. In consequence of the father's decision to retire from the business and the resulting need to downsize the operation, the firm assigns the lease for £490,000 on 1 July 1999. The indexation factor for the period June 1995 to April 1998 (note (*c*)) is 0.085.

## 222.3 Rollover Relief — Replacement of Business Assets

**The chargeable gains to be apportioned between the two partners for 1999/2000 are as follows**

|  | £ | £ |
|---|---:|---:|
| Proceeds of assignment |  | 490,000 |
| Cost (see note (*a*)) | 450,000 |  |
| *Deduct* Wasted $\dfrac{87.330 - 82.496}{87.330} \times £450{,}000$ | 24,909 | 425,091 |
| Unindexed gain |  | 64,909 |
| Indexation allowance £425,091 × 0.085 |  | 36,133 |
| Chargeable gain 1999/2000 (see also note (*b*)) |  | £28,776 |
| Held-over gain becoming chargeable under *TCGA 1992, s 154(2)(a)* |  | £190,000 |

**Notes**

(*a*) The gain of £190,000 is deferred as opposed to being rolled over and does not reduce the cost of the new asset.

(*b*) Each of the partners will be entitled to taper relief on their share of the gain of £28,776 to the extent that it is not reduced by the offset of capital losses (and the father's share may in any case be covered by retirement relief). Taper relief on the deferred gain of £190,000 operates by reference to the date of disposal and period of ownership of the old asset, and none is due in this case as the disposal was before 6 April 1998. See 226.4 TAPER RELIEF. The deferred gain cannot be covered by retirement relief as the disposal giving rise to it did not take place on retirement.

(*c*) Other than for the purposes of corporation tax on chargeable gains, indexation allowance is frozen at its April 1998 level. Therefore, the indexation factor for April 1998 is used in respect of disposals in a later month (and expenditure incurred in April 1998 or later does not attract indexation allowance at all). See 210 INDEXATION.

(*d*) See also 213.3(D)–(F) LAND for further examples on the assignment of short leases.

## Rollover Relief — Replacement of Business Assets 222.3

**(B) Rollover of held-over gain**

C Ltd, a manufacturing company, sells an item of fixed plant for £30,000 in February 1995. A chargeable gain of £7,200 arises. In 1997, the company buys storage facilities on a 20-year lease for £40,000. In 1999, an extension to the company's freehold factory is completed at a cost of £25,000.

**The position is as follows**

(i) The company may claim holdover of the £7,200 chargeable gain in 1995, against the cost of the lease.

(ii) In 1999, part of the chargeable gain can be rolled over against the cost of the factory extension, as follows

|  | £ |
|---|---|
| Expenditure available for rollover | 25,000 |
| Maximum capable of rollover | |
| £7,200 – (£30,000 – £25,000) | 2,200 |
| Adjusted base cost of extension | £22,800 |

**Notes**

(*a*) The balance of the chargeable gain, £5,000 (£7,200 – £2,200) may continue to be held over against the cost of the lease, either until it crystallises or until further rollover is possible.

(*b*) Had the company not claimed holdover against the cost of the lease, a claim against the cost of the extension in 1999 would not have been possible, as the expenditure was incurred outside the normal time limit.

## 223.1 Settlements

## 223 Settlements

**Cross-reference.** See 217.1 OVERSEAS MATTERS as regards capital gains of non-resident settlements.

223.1 **ANNUAL EXEMPTIONS AND RATES OF TAX** [*TCGA 1992, ss 3, 4(1AA), 1 Sch 2; FA 1998, s 120; FA 1999, s 26(3)*]

The trustees of the E settlement, created in 1973, realise net chargeable gains and allowable losses, adjusted for taper relief where appropriate, as follows

|  | Chargeable gain/ (allowable loss) £ |
|---|---|
| 1995/96 | (2,250) |
| 1996/97 | 1,100 |
| 1997/98 | 4,400 |
| 1998/99 | 3,100 |
| 1999/2000 | 10,150 |

The settlor does not have an interest in the settlement (see note (*b*)).

**The trustees' capital gains tax liability is computed as follows**

|  | £ |
|---|---|
| **1995/96** | |
| Taxable amount | Nil |
| Losses carried forward | £2,250 |
| **1996/97** | |
| Net chargeable gains | 1,100 |
| Losses brought forward | — |
| Taxable amount (covered by annual exemption of £3,150) | £1,100 |
| CGT | Nil |
| Losses carried forward | £2,250 |
| **1997/98** | |
| Net chargeable gains | 4,400 |
| Losses brought forward | 1,150 |
| Taxable amount (covered by annual exemption) | £3,250 |
| CGT | Nil |
| Losses carried forward (£2,250 − £1,150) | £1,100 |
|  | £ |
| **1998/99** | |
| Net chargeable gains | 3,100 |
| Losses brought forward | — |
| Taxable amount (covered by annual exemption of £3,400) | £3,100 |
| CGT | Nil |
| Losses carried forward | £1,100 |

# Settlements 223.1

**1999/2000**

| | |
|---|---:|
| Net chargeable gains | 10,150 |
| Losses brought forward | 1,100 |
| Taxable amount | £9,050 |
| CGT at 34% on £5,500 (9,050 − 3,550) | £1,870.00 |
| Losses carried forward | Nil |

**Notes**

(a) For 1998/99 onwards, the rate of capital gains tax on gains accruing to the trustees of any settlement, whether it be an interest in possession trust or an accumulation and maintenance trust is equivalent to the 'rate applicable to trusts' under *ICTA 1988, s 686*. The rate is 34% for 1999/2000. [*TCGA 1992, s 4(1AA); ICTA 1988, s 686(1A); FA 1993, 6 Sch 8; FA 1998, s 120; FA 1999, s 26(3)*].

(b) If the settlor had an interest in the settlement (as defined by *TCGA 1992, s 77(2)–(5)*) at any time during 1999/2000, the gain of £9,050 (after deducting losses but before deducting the annual exemption) would be chargeable on the settlor and not on the trustees. His own annual exemption of £7,100 may be set against the gain (see also 201.2(B) ANNUAL RATES AND EXEMPTIONS). Any tax payable could be recovered from the trustees. See also 223.2 below. [*TCGA 1992, ss 77–79; FA 1995, s 74, 17 Sch 27–29*].

(c) See *TCGA 1992, 1 Sch 2(4)–(6)* for the annual exemption available to two or more settlements made by the same settlor after 6 June 1978.

## 223.2 Settlements

### 223.2 SETTLEMENT IN WHICH SETTLOR HAS AN INTEREST [*TCGA 1992, ss 77–79; FA 1995, s 74, 17 Sch 27–29*]

In May 1998 Henry, a UK resident, settled £25,000 on trust to his wife for her life with the remainder to his adult daughter absolutely. The trustees are resident in the UK. For 1998/99, the trustees make disposals on which they incur losses of £300. For 1999/2000, they realise gains of £3,500 and losses of £700 (these figures being net of any available taper relief). Henry has personal gains of £5,300 for 1999/2000 (again after any available taper relief) with no losses brought forward. Henry's taxable income for 1999/2000 is £50,000 and he is thus liable to tax at 40% on capital gains.

**Henry's capital gains tax liability for 1999/2000 is calculated as follows**

|  |  | £ | £ |
|---|---|---:|---:|
| Personal gains |  |  | 5,300 |
| Settlement gains |  | 3,500 |  |
| *Deduct* Losses |  | 700 |  |
|  |  | 2,800 |  |
| *Deduct* Losses b/f |  | 300 | 2,500 |
|  |  |  | 7,800 |
| *Deduct* Annual exemption |  |  | 7,100 |
| Gain liable to CGT |  |  | £700 |
| CGT payable at 40% |  |  | £280.00 |
| CGT recoverable from trustees | note (*a*) |  | £280.00 |

**Notes**

(*a*) The settlement gains are regarded as forming the highest part of the total amount on which Henry is liable to CGT. His personal gains are therefore fully covered by his annual exemption and the whole of the liability relates to the settlement gains; it is thus fully recoverable from the trustees. [*TCGA 1992, s 78*].

(*b*) Note that for 1999/2000 onwards gains attributed to the settlor in this way cannot be covered by any personal capital losses of his. This is illustrated at 201.2(B) ANNUAL RATES AND EXEMPTIONS.

(*c*) If either Henry or his wife died during 1999/2000, or if they ceased to be married during that year, *Secs 77–79* would not apply and the settlement gain of £2,800 (before deducting losses brought forward) would be covered by the trustees' annual exemption of £3,550, with losses of £300 carried forward to 2000/01. [*TCGA 1992, s 77(6); FA 1995, 17 Sch 27*].

## 223.3 CREATION OF A SETTLEMENT [*TCGA 1992, s 70*]

**(A)**

In December 1999, C transfers to trustees of a settlement for the benefit of his children 10,000 shares in W plc, a quoted company. The value of the gift is £85,000. C bought the shares in 1981 for £20,000 and their value at 31 March 1982 was £35,000. The indexation factor for March 1982 to April 1998 (note (*b*)) is 1.047.

|  | £ | £ |
|---|---:|---:|
| Deemed disposal consideration | 85,000 | 85,000 |
| Cost | 20,000 | |
| Market value 31.3.82 | | 35,000 |
| Unindexed gain | 65,000 | 50,000 |
| Indexation allowance £35,000 × 1.047 | 36,645 | 36,645 |
| Gain after indexation | £28,355 | £13,355 |
| Chargeable gain | | £13,355 |
| Trustees' allowable cost | | £85,000 |

**Notes**

(*a*) If the transfer had been a chargeable lifetime transfer for inheritance tax purposes, or would be one but for the annual inheritance tax exemption, C could have elected under *TCGA 1992, s 260* to roll the gain over against the trustees' base cost of the shares. The trustees do not join in any such election. This would normally cover only a transfer to a discretionary settlement. Where taper relief is otherwise available, it is the untapered gain that is held over.

(*b*) Other than for the purposes of corporation tax on chargeable gains, indexation allowance is frozen at its April 1998 level. See 210 INDEXATION.

## 223.4 Settlements

**(B)**

In late April 1999 H settles farmland on trust for himself for life, with interests in reversion to his children. The land cost £20,000 in 1972 and its agreed values are £60,000 at 31 March 1982 and £125,000 at the date of settlement. H's interest in possession in the settled property is valued at £90,000. The indexation factor from March 1982 to April 1998 (note (*c*)) is 1.047.

**The chargeable gain is computed as follows**

|  | £ | £ |
|---|---:|---:|
| Deemed disposal proceeds | 125,000 | 125,000 |
| Cost | 20,000 | |
| Market value 31.3.82 | | 60,000 |
| Unindexed gain | 105,000 | 65,000 |
| Indexation allowance £60,000 × 1.047 | 62,820 | 62,820 |
| Gain after indexation | £42,180 | £2,180 |
| | | |
| Chargeable gain | | £2,180 |

**Notes**

(*a*) The value of H's interest in the settled property is ignored and the transfer is not treated as a part disposal.

(*b*) For as long as H has an interest in the settlement the provisions of *TCGA 1992*, ss 77–79 will apply to any settlement gains, with the effect that they will be chargeable on the settlor and not on the trustees. See 223.2 above.

(*c*) Other than for the purposes of corporation tax on chargeable gains, indexation allowance is frozen at its April 1998 level. See 210 INDEXATION.

## 223.4 PERSON BECOMING ABSOLUTELY ENTITLED TO SETTLED PROPERTY
[*TCGA 1992, s 71*]

**(A)**

M is a beneficiary entitled to an interest in possession in settled property, under a settlement made by her mother. The trustees exercise a power of appointment to advance capital to M, and, in September 1999, transfer to her a house valued at £80,000. The house was acquired by the trustees by gift from the settlor in 1995, when its value was £45,000.

**The trustees realise an unindexed gain** of £35,000 (£80,000 – £45,000) on the advancement of capital to M.

**Notes**

(*a*) An indexation allowance (computed to April 1998 — see 210.1(B) INDEXATION) is available to the trustees and will be based on their deemed acquisition cost of £45,000.

(*b*) If, while it was settled property, the house had been occupied by M as her private residence with the permission of the trustees, then all or part of the gain would be exempt under *TCGA 1992, s 225*.

# Settlements 223.4

**(B) Transfer of settlement losses** [*TCGA 1992, s 71(2)–(2D); FA 1999, s 75*]

F is the sole remaining beneficiary of an accumulation and maintenance settlement established under his late uncle's will and in which he became entitled to an interest in possession upon reaching the age of 18 in 1992. On 18 September 1999, his 25th birthday, he becomes absolutely entitled as against the trustees to the capital of the trust. At that date, the trust capital consists of the following:

- cash of £12,000,
- 10,000 shares in ABC Ltd (purchased for £6,000 in May 1998 and currently valued at £11,000), and
- 15,000 shares in DEF Ltd (transferred into the trust at a CGT value of £27,000 but now valued at only £13,000).

On 30 June 1999, the trustees had sold shares in GHK Ltd at a gain of £3,000 (after deducting indexation allowance to April 1998). On 7 July 1999, they sold shares in LMN Ltd at a loss of £500. None of the above-mentioned trust investments were business assets for taper relief purposes. At 6 April 1999, the trustees had allowable capital losses of £1,000 brought forward from earlier years.

In December 1999, F sells the ABC Ltd shares for £11,600. He also disposes of other assets in 1999/2000 realising chargeable gains of £9,000 (with no taper relief due). In 2000/01, he sells the DEF Ltd shares for £15,500 and also disposes of other assets realising chargeable gains of £8,500 (all attracting 5% taper relief) and allowable losses of £1,500. For the purposes of this example, the annual exemption for 2000/01 is assumed to be £7,300.

### F takes over entitlement to trust losses as follows

|  | £ | £ |
|---|---:|---:|
| Loss on DEF Ltd shares transferred to F £(27,000–13,000) |  | 14,000 |
| *Deduct* trustees' 'pre-entitlement gains' (*Sec 71(2A)*): |  |  |
|     (i) gain on ABC Ltd shares transferred to F | 5,000 |  |
|     (ii) other gains in period 6.4.99–18.9.99 | 3,000 | 8,000 |
| Loss treated as accruing to F (note (*a*)) |  | £6,000 |

### F's CGT position for 1999/2000 and 2000/01 is as follows

*1999/2000*

|  | £ |
|---|---:|
| Gain on sale of ABC Ltd shares £(11,600 – 11,000) | 600 |
| Other gains | 9,000 |
|  | 9,600 |
| *Deduct* annual exemption | 7,100 |
| Gains chargeable to tax | £2,500 |
| Ex-trust losses carried forward | £6,000 |

## 223.4 Settlements

*2000/01*

|  | £ | £ |
|---|---:|---:|
| Gain on sale of DEF Ltd shares £(15,500–13,000) | 2,500 | |
| *Deduct* ex-trust losses brought forward and treated as a loss for the year | 2,500 | — |
| Other gains | 8,500 | |
| *Deduct* losses for the year | 1,500 | |
| | 7,000 | |
| *Deduct* taper relief @ 5% | 350 | 6,750 |
| | | 6,750 |
| *Deduct* annual exemption | | 7,300 |
| Gains chargeable to tax | | Nil |

|  | £ |
|---|---:|
| Ex-trust losses brought forward | 6,000 |
| Utilised in 2000/01 | 2,500 |
| Unused balance (note (*b*)) | £4,000 |

**Notes**

(*a*) Trust losses of £1,000 brought forward and £500 accruing in 1999/2000 cannot be transferred to F and in this case are wasted. The 'pre-entitlement gains' cannot be reduced by those losses before being set against the loss on DEF Ltd shares. If F had become absolutely entitled before 16 June 1999, those losses would have been transferable in addition to the £6,000 transferred in this example.

(*b*) In F's hands, the loss can only be set against a gain on the DEF Ltd shares on which it arose. As all those shares are sold in 2000/01, the loss cannot be carried forward any further and the unused balance of £4,000 has to be written off. If F had become absolutely entitled before 16 June 1999, losses transferred to him from the trust could have been used against his chargeable gains without restriction.

## 223.5 TERMINATION OF INTEREST IN POSSESSION ON DEATH [*TCGA 1992, s 72; FA 1996, 39 Sch 5*]

**(A)**

K is entitled to an interest in possession under a settlement. The settled property consists of shares and cash. On K's death, L is entitled to a life interest in succession to K. K dies on 1 December 1999, when the shares are valued at £200,000. The trustees' allowable cost in respect of the shares is £40,000.

**On K's death**, the trustees are deemed to have disposed of and immediately reacquired the shares for £200,000, thus uplifting the CGT base cost, but no chargeable gain then arises.

**(B)**

In 1974, E created a settlement for the benefit of his children M and N and his grandchildren, transferring an investment property valued at £10,000 to the trustees. The terms of the settlement were that M and N each have a life interest in half of the trust income, with the remainder passing to E's grandchildren. In 1988, N assigned his interest to P, an unrelated party, for £35,000, its then market value. In 1999, N dies. The value of a half share of the trust property is then £65,000.

**On N's death**, his life interest terminates. There is no effect on the trustees as N was no longer the person entitled to the life interest within the meaning of *TCGA 1992, s 72*.

**Notes**

(*a*) No chargeable gain arises on the disposal by N of his interest. [*TCGA 1992, s 76*].

(*b*) P may claim an allowable loss on extinction of the interest. For an example of the computation if the interest is a wasting asset, see 227.3 WASTING ASSETS.

## 224.1 Shares and Securities

## 224 Shares and Securities

**Cross-references.** See also 203 ASSETS HELD ON 6 APRIL 1965, 204 ASSETS HELD ON 31 MARCH 1982, 210 INDEXATION, 220 QUALIFYING CORPORATE BONDS and 225 SHARES AND SECURITIES — IDENTIFICATION RULES.

### 224.1 REORGANISATION OF SHARE CAPITAL — VALUATION OF DIFFERENT CLASSES OF SHARE ON SUBSEQUENT DISPOSAL [*TCGA 1992, ss 126–131*]

**(A) Unquoted shares**

V acquired 10,000 ordinary shares in X Ltd, an unquoted trading company, in April 1996 at a cost of £15,000. In April 1999, as part of a reorganisation of share capital, V was additionally allotted 3,000 new 9% preference shares in X Ltd for which he paid £3,900. In June 1999, V sold his ordinary shareholding, in an arm's length transaction, for £20,000, but retained his preference shares, then valued at £4,000. The indexation factor for the period April 1996 to April 1998 (see note (*b*)) is 0.066.

**The chargeable gain on the disposal of the ordinary shares is calculated as follows**

| | £ |
|---|---:|
| Disposal consideration | 20,000 |
| Cost (£15,000 + £3,900) × $\dfrac{20,000}{20,000 + 4,000}$ | 15,750 |
| Unindexed gain | 4,250 |
| Indexation allowance $\dfrac{15,000}{18,900}$ × £15,750 × 0.066 | 825 |
| Chargeable gain (subject to any available TAPER RELIEF (226)) | £3,425 |
| Allowable cost of 3,000 preference shares (£15,000 + £3,900 − £15,750) | 3,150 |
| Indexation allowance to April 1998 $\dfrac{15,000}{18,900}$ × £3,150 × 0.066 | 165 |
| Indexed cost | £3,315 |

**Notes**

(*a*) The ordinary shares and preference shares held after the reorganisation (the 'new holding') constitute a single asset. [*TCGA 1992, s 127*]. A disposal of part of the new holding is thus a part disposal. If neither class of shares comprising the new holding is quoted on a recognised stock exchange at any time not later than three months after the reorganisation, acquisition cost on a part disposal is apportioned by reference to market values at the date of disposal. [*TCGA 1992, s 129*].

(*b*) Other than for the purposes of corporation tax on chargeable gains, indexation allowance is frozen at its April 1998 level. Therefore, the indexation factor for April 1998 is used in respect of disposals in a later month (and expenditure incurred in April 1998 or later does not attract indexation allowance at all). See 210 INDEXATION.

## (B) Quoted shares

Assume the facts to be as in (A) above except that both the ordinary and preference shares are quoted on a recognised stock exchange. On the first day of dealing after the reorganisation took effect, the ordinary shares were quoted at £1.85 and the preference shares at £1.35. V's holdings were therefore valued at £18,500 and £4,050 respectively.

**The chargeable gain on the disposal of the ordinary shares is calculated as follows**

|  | £ |
|---|---|
| Disposal consideration | 20,000 |
| Cost (£15,000 + £3,900) × $\dfrac{18,500}{18,500 + 4,050}$ | 15,506 |
| Unindexed gain | 4,494 |
| Indexation allowance $\dfrac{15,000}{18,900}$ × £15,506 × 0.066 | 812 |
| Chargeable gain | £3,682 |
| Allowable cost of 3,000 preference shares (£15,000 + £3,900 − £15,506) | 3,394 |
| Indexation allowance to April 1998 $\dfrac{15,000}{18,900}$ × £3,394 × 0.066 | 178 |
| Indexed cost | £3,572 |

### Note

(a) Where one or more of the classes of shares or debentures comprising the new holding is quoted on a recognised stock exchange at any time not later than three months after the reorganisation, acquisition cost on a part disposal is apportioned by reference to market values on the first day of dealing on which the prices quoted reflect the reorganisation. [*TCGA 1992, s 130*].

## (C) Quoted shares — reorganisation after 31 March 1982, original holding acquired on or before that date

In 1980, W subscribed for 5,000 £1 ordinary shares at par in L plc, a quoted company. The value of his holding at 31 March 1982 was £8,000. In November 1990, L plc offered ordinary shareholders two 7% preference shares at £1 per share in respect of each five ordinary shares held. W took up his entitlement of 2,000 preference shares. On the first day of dealing after the reorganisation, the ordinary shares were quoted at £3.00 (making W's holding worth £15,000) and the preference shares at £1.02 (valuing W's holding at £2,040). In June 1999, W sells his preference shares on the market at £1.40 (total proceeds £2,800). (For simplicity, costs of acquisition and disposal are ignored in this example.) The indexation factor from March 1982 to April 1998 (see note (*b*)) is 1.047 and from November 1990 to April 1998 it is 0.251.

## 224.1 Shares and Securities

**The gain on the disposal of the preference shares is computed as follows**

**The calculation, without re-basing to 1982, is**

| | £ |
|---|---|
| Disposal consideration | 2,800 |
| Cost (£5,000 + £2,000) × $\dfrac{2,040}{2,040 + 15,000}$ | 838 |
| Unindexed gain | 1,962 |
| Indexation allowance (see below) | 1,063 |
| Gain after indexation | £899 |

**The calculation, with re-basing to 1982, is**

| | £ |
|---|---|
| Disposal consideration | 2,800 |
| (31.3.82 value £8,000 + cost £2,000) × $\dfrac{2,040}{2,040 + 15,000}$ | 1,197 |
| Unindexed gain | 1,603 |

Indexation allowance $\dfrac{8,000}{10,000} \times £1,197 \times 1.047 = £1,003$

$\dfrac{2,000}{10,000} \times £1,197 \times 0.251 = \underline{\phantom{00}60}$

| | |
|---|---|
| | 1,063 |
| Gain after indexation | £540 |
| Chargeable gain | £540 |

**Notes**

(a) On a subsequent disposal of the ordinary shares, their cost would be £6,162 (£5,000 + £2,000 − £838) or, if re-basing applied, £8,803 (£8,000 + £2,000 − £1,197). In either case, indexation would be based on £8,803.

(b) Other than for the purposes of corporation tax on chargeable gains, indexation allowance is frozen at its April 1998 level. Therefore, the indexation factor for April 1998 is used in respect of disposals in a later month (and expenditure incurred in April 1998 or later does not attract indexation allowance at all). See 210 INDEXATION.

# Shares and Securities 224.2

## 224.2 BONUS ISSUES [*TCGA 1992, ss 126–128, 130*]

### (A) Bonus of same class

In October 1990, Y plc made a scrip issue of one ordinary share for every 10 held. L held 5,000 ordinary shares, which he acquired in May 1985 for £5,500, and therefore received 500 shares in the bonus issue. In October 1999, L sells 3,000 of his shares for £7,000. The indexation factor for the period May 1985 to April 1998 (see note (*a*)) is 0.708.

| Section 104 holding | Shares | Qualifying expenditure £ | Indexed pool £ |
|---|---|---|---|
| May 1985 acquisition | 5,000 | 5,500 | 5,500 |
| October 1990 bonus issue | 500 | | |
| Indexed rise: May 1985 – April 1998 £6,500 × 0.708 | | | 3,894 |
| | 5,500 | 5,500 | 9,394 |
| October 1999 disposal | (3,000) | (3,000) | (5,124) |
| Pool carried forward | 2,500 | £2,500 | £4,270 |

**Calculation of chargeable gain**                                    £

Disposal consideration                                                7,000

Allowable cost $\dfrac{3,000}{5,500} \times £5,500$                   3,000

Unindexed gain                                                        4,000

Indexation allowance

$\dfrac{3,000}{5,500} \times £9,394 = £5,124$

£5,124 − £3,000                                                       2,124

Chargeable gain                                                       £1,876

### Note

(*a*) Other than for the purposes of corporation tax on chargeable gains, indexation allowance is frozen at its April 1998 level. Therefore, the indexation factor for April 1998 is used in respect of disposals in a later month (and expenditure incurred in April 1998 or later does not attract indexation allowance at all). See 210 INDEXATION.

The indexed pool is upgraded as if the entire holding had been disposed of at the end of 5 April 1998 but is not adjusted for any subsequent indexed rise in expenditure. [*TCGA 1992, s 110A; FA 1998, s 125(2)(4)(5)*].

## 224.2 Shares and Securities

### (B) Bonus of different class
At various dates after 5 April 1982 and before 6 April 1985, R bought a total of 2,000 'A' shares in T plc for £3,800. The value of the indexed pool immediately before 6 April 1985 was £4,460. In June 1989, R bought a further 500 'A' shares for £800. In October 1993 T plc made a bonus issue of 2 'B' shares for each 5 'A' shares held, and R received 1,000 'B' shares, valued at £1.20 each (total value £1,200) on the first dealing day after the issue. On the same day, the 'A' shares were quoted at £2 each (total value £5,000). In December 1999 R sells his 1,000 'B' shares for £2,000.

| Indexation factors | | |
|---|---|---|
| April 1985 to June 1989 | | 0.218 |
| June 1989 to October 1993 | | 0.229 |
| October 1993 to April 1998 (note (c)) | | 0.147 |

| *Section 104* holding – 'A' shares | Shares | Qualifying expenditure £ | Indexed pool £ |
|---|---|---|---|
| Pool at 6.4.85 | 2,000 | 3,800 | 4,460 |
| Indexed rise: April 1985 to June 1989 £4,460 × 0.218 | | | 972 |
| June 1989 acquisition | 500 | 800 | 800 |
| | 2,500 | 4,600 | 6,232 |
| Indexed rise: June 1989 to October 1993 £6,232 × 0.229 | | | 1,427 |
| | 2,500 | 4,600 | 7,659 |
| October 1993 bonus issue of 'B' shares: transfer proportion of expenditure and indexed pool to 'B' shares (see note (a)) | | (890) | (1,482) |
| | 2,500 | 3,710 | 6,177 |
| Indexed rise: October 1993 to April 1998 £6,177 × 0.147 | | | 908 |
| Pool of 'A' shares carried forward | 2,500 | £3,710 | £7,085 |

| *Section 104* holding — 'B' shares | | | |
|---|---|---|---|
| October 1993 bonus issue: proportion of pools transferred from 'A' shares holding | 1,000 | 890 | 1,482 |
| Indexed rise: October 1993 to April 1998 £1,482 × 0.147 | | | 218 |
| | 1,000 | 890 | 1,700 |
| December 1999 disposal | 1,000 | 890 | 1,700 |
| | — | — | — |

| Calculation of chargeable gain on disposal of 'B' shares | £ |
|---|---|
| Disposal consideration | 2,000 |
| Allowable cost (as allocated) | 890 |
| Unindexed gain | 1,110 |
| Indexation allowance £1,700 − £890 | 810 |
| Chargeable gain | £300 |

# Shares and Securities 224.2

**Notes**

(a) The cost of the 'A' shares is apportioned between 'A' and 'B' shares by reference to market values on the first day of dealing after the reorganisation. The indexed pool is apportioned in the same way.

Proportion of qualifying expenditure £4,600 × $\dfrac{1{,}200}{1{,}200 + 5{,}000}$ £890

Proportion of indexed pool £7,659 × $\dfrac{1{,}200}{1{,}200 + 5{,}000}$ £1,482

(Revenue Capital Gains Manual CG 51965 et seq.).

(b) A different basis of apportionment applies to unquoted shares (see Revenue Capital Gains Manual CG 51919 et seq.).

(c) Other than for the purposes of corporation tax on chargeable gains, indexation allowance is frozen at its April 1998 level. Therefore, the indexation factor for April 1998 is used in respect of disposals in a later month (and expenditure incurred in April 1998 or later does not attract indexation allowance at all). See 210 INDEXATION.

The indexed pool is upgraded as if the entire holding had been disposed of at the end of 5 April 1998 but is not adjusted for any subsequent indexed rise in expenditure. [*TCGA 1992, s 110A; FA 1998, s 125(2)(4)(5)*].

## 224.3 Shares and Securities

### 224.3 RIGHTS ISSUES [*TCGA 1992, ss 42, 123(1), 128(4)*]

**Cross-reference.** See 224.8(B) below as regards sale of rights.

**(A) Rights issue of same class**

W plc is a quoted company which in June 1991 made a rights issue of one £1 ordinary share for every eight £1 ordinary shares held, at £1.35 payable on allotment. V, who held 16,000 £1 ordinary shares purchased in May 1984 for £15,000, took up his entitlement in full, and was allotted 2,000 shares. In December 1999, he sells 6,000 of his shares for £12,000.

| Indexation factors | | |
|---|---|---|
| May 1984 to April 1985 | | 0.065 |
| April 1985 to June 1991 | | 0.415 |
| June 1991 to April 1998 (note (*a*)) | | 0.213 |

*Section 104* **holding**

| | Shares | Qualifying expenditure £ | Indexed pool £ |
|---|---|---|---|
| May 1984 acquisition | 16,000 | 15,000 | 15,000 |
| Indexed rise: May 1984 – April 1985 | | | |
| £15,000 × 0.065 | | | 975 |
| Pool at 6.4.85 | 16,000 | 15,000 | 15,975 |
| Indexed rise: April 1985 – June 1991 | | | |
| £15,975 × 0.415 | | | 6,630 |
| June 1991 rights issue | 2,000 | 2,700 | 2,700 |
| | 18,000 | 17,700 | 25,305 |
| Indexed rise: June 1991 – April 1998 | | | |
| £25,305 × 0.213 | | | 5,390 |
| | | | 30,695 |
| December 1999 disposal | (6,000) | (5,900) | (10,232) |
| Pool carried forward | 12,000 | £11,800 | £20,463 |

**Calculation of chargeable gain**

| | £ |
|---|---|
| Disposal consideration | 12,000 |
| Allowable cost $\dfrac{6,000}{18,000} \times £17,700$ | 5,900 |
| Unindexed gain | 6,100 |
| Indexation allowance | |
| $\dfrac{6,000}{18,000} \times £30,695 = £10,232$ | |
| £10,232 − £5,900 | 4,332 |
| Chargeable gain | £1,768 |

**Note**

(*a*) Other than for the purposes of corporation tax on chargeable gains, indexation allowance is frozen at its April 1998 level. Therefore, the indexation factor for April 1998 is used in respect of disposals in a later month (and expenditure incurred in April 1998 or later does not attract indexation allowance at all). See 210 INDEXATION.

## Shares and Securities 224.3

The indexed pool is upgraded as if the entire holding had been disposed of at the end of 5 April 1998 but is not adjusted for any subsequent indexed rise in expenditure. [*TCGA 1992, s 110A; FA 1998, s 125(2)(4)(5)*].

**(B) Rights issue of different class**
At 6 April 1985, A's 'section 104 holding' of 6,000 quoted £1 ordinary shares in S plc has a pool of expenditure of £7,800 and an indexed pool of £9,200. In October 1991, S plc made a rights issue of one 50p 'B' share for every five £1 ordinary shares held, at 60p payable in full on application. A took up his entitlement in full, acquiring 1,200 'B' shares. On the first dealing day after issue, the 'B' shares were quoted at 65p and the £1 ordinary shares at £1.50. A sells his 'B' shares in December 1999 for £2,000.

| | | | |
|---|---|---|---|
| Indexation factors | April 1985 to October 1991 | | 0.425 |
| | October 1991 to April 1998 (note (*c*)) | | 0.204 |

| *Section 104* holding — ordinary shares | Shares | Qualifying expenditure £ | Indexed pool £ |
|---|---|---|---|
| Pool at 6.4.85 | 6,000 | 7,800 | 9,200 |
| Indexed rise: April 1985 to October 1991 £9,200 × 0.425 | | | 3,910 |
| October 1991 rights issue of 'B' shares | — | 720 | 720 |
| | 6,000 | 8,520 | 13,830 |
| Transfer proportion of expenditure and indexed pool to 'B' shares    note (*a*) | | (680) | (1,103) |
| | 6,000 | 7,840 | 12,727 |
| Indexed rise: October 1991 to April 1998 £12,727 × 0.204 | | | 2,596 |
| Pool of ordinary shares carried forward | 6,000 | £7,840 | £15,323 |

| *Section 104* holding — 'B' shares | | | |
|---|---|---|---|
| October 1991 rights issue: proportion of pools transferred from ordinary shares holding | 1,200 | 680 | 1,103 |
| Indexed rise: October 1991 to April 1998 £1,103 × 0.204 | | | 225 |
| | 1,200 | 680 | 1,328 |
| December 1999 disposal | (1,200) | (680) | (1,328) |
| | — | — | — |

| Calculation of chargeable gain on disposal of 'B' shares | £ |
|---|---|
| Disposal consideration | 2,000 |
| Allowable cost (as allocated) | 680 |
| Unindexed gain | 1,320 |
| Indexation allowance £1,328 − £680 | 648 |
| Chargeable gain | £672 |

## 224.3 Shares and Securities

**Notes**

(a) The cost of the original shares is apportioned between the original shares and the 'B' shares by reference to market values on the first day of dealing after the reorganisation. The indexed pool is apportioned in the same way.

Proportion of qualifying expenditure

$$£8,520 \times \frac{1,200 \times 0.65}{(1,200 \times 0.65) + (6,000 \times 1.50)} \qquad \underline{£680}$$

Proportion of indexed pool

$$£13,830 \times \frac{1,200 \times 0.65}{(1,200 \times 0.65) + (6,000 \times 1.50)} \qquad \underline{£1,103}$$

(Revenue Capital Gains Manual CG 51965 et seq.).

(b) A different basis of apportionment applies to unquoted shares (see Revenue Capital Gains Manual CG 51919 et seq.).

(c) Other than for the purposes of corporation tax on chargeable gains, indexation allowance is frozen at its April 1998 level. Therefore, the indexation factor for April 1998 is used in respect of disposals in a later month (and expenditure incurred in April 1998 or later does not attract indexation allowance at all). See 210 INDEXATION.

The indexed pool is upgraded as if the entire holding had been disposed of at the end of 5 April 1998 but is not adjusted for any subsequent indexed rise in expenditure. [*TCGA 1992, s 110A; FA 1998, s 125(2)(4)(5)*].

**(C) Rights issue of same class: disposal out of *section 104* holding and 1982 holding**

G has purchased 100,000 25p ordinary shares in C plc as follows

| Date | Number of shares acquired | Cost £ |
|---|---|---|
| 22.5.80 | 20,000 | 0.78 |
| 5.11.83 | 15,000 | 1.10 |
| 14.9.84 | 40,000 | 1.00 |
| 30.4.98 | 25,000 | 2.30 |

In May 1992, C made a rights issue of one ordinary share for every five held, at £1.50 payable in full on application. G took up his rights in full (15,000 ordinary shares). He sells 105,000 shares in August 1999 for £2.50 per share. The shares were quoted at 90p on 31 March 1982. Incidental costs of acquisition and disposal are disregarded for the purposes of this example.

| Indexation factors | | |
|---|---|---|
| | March 1982 to April 1998 (note (*c*)) | 1.047 |
| | November 1983 to April 1985 | 0.094 |
| | September 1984 to April 1985 | 0.052 |
| | April 1985 to May 1992 | 0.470 |
| | May 1992 to April 1998 (note (*c*)) | 0.167 |

# Shares and Securities 224.3

### Section 104 holding

| | Shares | Qualifying expenditure £ | Indexed pool £ |
|---|---|---|---|
| 5.11.83 acquisition | 15,000 | 16,500 | 16,500 |
| Indexed rise: November 1983 to April 1985 £16,500 × 0.094 | | | 1,551 |
| 14.9.84 acquisition | 40,000 | 40,000 | 40,000 |
| Indexed rise: September 1984 to April 1985 £40,000 × 0.052 | | | 2,080 |
| Pool at 6.4.85 | 55,000 | 56,500 | 60,131 |
| Indexed rise: April 1985 to May 1992 £60,131 × 0.470 | | | 28,262 |
| May 1992 rights issue | 11,000 | 16,500 | 16,500 |
| | 66,000 | 73,000 | 104,893 |
| Indexed rise: May 1992 to April 1998 £104,893 × 0.167 | | | 17,517 |
| | 66,000 | 73,000 | 122,410 |
| August 1999 disposal | (66,000) | (73,000) | (122,410) |
| | — | — | — |

### 1982 holding

| | Shares | Cost £ | Market value 31.3.82 £ |
|---|---|---|---|
| 22.5.80 acquisition | 20,000 | 15,600 | 18,000 |
| May 1992 rights issue note (*a*) | 4,000 | 6,000 | 6,000 |
| | 24,000 | 21,600 | 24,000 |
| August 1999 disposal | (14,000) | (12,600) | (14,000) |
| Pool carried forward | 10,000 | £9,000 | £10,000 |

### Calculation of chargeable gain

(i) Identify 25,000 shares sold with shares acquired on 30 April 1998.

| | £ |
|---|---|
| Disposal consideration 25,000 × £2.50 | 62,500 |
| Allowable cost 25,000 × £2.30 | 57,500 |
| Chargeable gain | £5,000 |

(ii) Identify 66,000 shares sold with *section 104* holding

| | £ |
|---|---|
| Disposal consideration 66,000 × £2.50 | 165,000 |
| Allowable cost | 73,000 |
| Unindexed gain | 92,000 |
| Indexation allowance £122,410 − £73,000 | 49,410 |
| Chargeable gain | £42,590 |

## 224.3  Shares and Securities

(iii) Identify 14,000 shares with 1982 holding

**Without re-basing to 1982**

|  | £ |
|---|---:|
| Disposal consideration 14,000 × £2.50 | 35,000 |
| Cost $\dfrac{14,000}{24,000} \times £21,600$ | 12,600 |
| Unindexed gain | 22,400 |
| Indexation allowance (see below) | 11,579 |
| Gain after indexation | £10,821 |

**With re-basing to 1982**

|  |  | £ |
|---|---:|---:|
| Disposal consideration |  | 35,000 |
| Allowable expenditure $\dfrac{14,000}{24,000} \times £24,000$ |  | 14,000 |
| Unindexed gain |  | 21,000 |
| Indexation allowance | £ |  |
| $£14,000 \times \dfrac{18,000}{24,000} \times 1.047$ | 10,994 |  |
| $£14,000 \times \dfrac{6,000}{24,000} \times 0.167$ | 585 |  |
|  |  | 11,579 |
| Gain after indexation |  | £9,421 |
| Chargeable gain |  | £9,421 |
| Total chargeable gain £5,000 + £42,590 + £9,421 |  | £57,011 |

**Notes**

(a) The 1982 holding cannot be increased by an 'acquisition', but can be increased by a rights issue as this is not treated as involving an acquisition. [*TCGA 1992, ss 109(2), 127, 128*].

(b) Other than for the purposes of corporation tax on chargeable gains, disposals after 5 April 1998 are identified firstly with shares acquired on the same day, next with acquisitions in the following 30 days, then on a LIFO basis with post-5 April 1998 acquisitions as in (i) above, then with the '*section 104* holding' at 5 April 1998 as in (ii) above, then with the '1982 holding' as in (iii) above, and then on a LIFO basis with acquisitions on or before 6 April 1965. [*TCGA 1992, ss 105, 106A; FA 1998, s 124(1)(2)(7)*].

(c) Other than for the purposes of corporation tax on chargeable gains, indexation allowance is frozen at its April 1998 level. Therefore, the indexation factor for April 1998 is used in respect of disposals in a later month (and expenditure incurred in April 1998 or later does not attract indexation allowance at all). See 210 INDEXATION.

# Shares and Securities 224.4

The indexed pool is upgraded as if the entire holding had been disposed of at the end of 5 April 1998 but is not adjusted for any subsequent indexed rise in expenditure. [*TCGA 1992, s 110A; FA 1998, s 125(2)(4)(5)*].

## 224.4 COMPANY AMALGAMATIONS [*TCGA 1992, ss 135, 137, 138*]

### (A) Takeover by quoted company

S was a shareholder in N Ltd, an unquoted company. He subscribed for his 20,000 50p ordinary shares at 60p per share in 1977 and the shares were valued at £3 each at 31 March 1982. In July 1987, the shareholders accepted an offer by a public company, M plc, for their shares. Each ordinary shareholder received one £1 ordinary M plc share plus 45p cash for every two N Ltd shares held. S acquired 10,000 M plc shares and received cash of £4,500. The M plc shares were valued at £7.50 each at the time of the acquisition. In April 1999, S sells 4,000 of the M shares for £54,000.

| Indexation factors | March 1982 to July 1987 | 0.281 |
|---|---|---|
| | March 1982 to April 1998 | 1.047 |

### (i) On the merger in 1987/88, S makes a disposal only to the extent that he receives cash

| | £ |
|---|---|
| Disposal consideration | 4,500 |
| Allowable cost $\dfrac{4,500}{4,500 + (10,000 \times £7.50 = £75,000)} \times £12,000$ | 679 |
| Gross gain | 3,821 |
| Indexation allowance £679 × 0.281 | 191 |
| Chargeable gain | £3,630 |

### Note

(*a*) The fraction applied to allowable cost corresponds to 5.66%. If the percentage had not exceeded 5% the cash distribution of £4,500 would have been regarded as 'small' and could have been deducted from allowable cost (Revenue Tax Bulletin November 1992 p 46). [*TCGA 1992, s 122*]. No gain would then have arisen in 1986/87, but the allowable cost would have been reduced by £4,500. See also 224.8(B) below. (A distribution made after 23 February 1997 can additionally be regarded as 'small' if it does not exceed £3,000 — Revenue Tax Bulletin February 1997 p 397.)

### (ii) The chargeable gain on disposal in 1999/2000 is

#### Without re-basing to 1982

| | £ |
|---|---|
| Consideration for disposal of M plc shares | 54,000 |
| Allowable cost $(12,000 - 679) \times \dfrac{4,000}{10,000}$ | 4,528 |
| Unindexed gain | 49,472 |
| Indexation allowance (see below) | 23,706 |
| Gain after indexation | £25,766 |

## 224.4 Shares and Securities

**With re-basing to 1982**

| | £ |
|---|---:|
| Disposal consideration (as above) | 54,000 |
| Market value 31.3.82 | |
| £(20,000 × £3) × $\dfrac{75,000}{75,000 + 4,500}$ × $\dfrac{4,000}{10,000}$  note (*b*) | 22,642 |
| Unindexed gain | 31,358 |
| Indexation allowance £22,642 × 1.047 | 23,706 |
| Gain after indexation | £7,652 |
| Chargeable gain | £7,652 |

**Notes**

(*a*) The M plc shares are regarded as the same asset as the original N Ltd shares. [*TCGA 1992, ss 127, 135*]. Re-basing to 31 March 1982 can thus apply, as the original shares were held on that date.

(*b*) Where there has been a part disposal after 31 March 1982 and before 6 April 1988 of an asset held on the earlier of those dates, and this is followed by a disposal after 5 April 1988 to which re-basing applies, the re-basing rules are deemed to have applied to the part disposal. [*TCGA 1992, 3 Sch 4(1)*].


**(B) Takeover by unquoted company**

Y Ltd, a small unquoted company, is taken over in June 1995 by another unquoted company, C Ltd. The terms of the acquisition are that holders of £1 ordinary shares in Y Ltd receive two £1 ordinary shares and one £1 deferred share in C Ltd in exchange for every two ordinary shares held.

B acquired his holding of 500 Y Ltd shares on the death of his wife in May 1991, at probate value of £10,000. In May 1999, B sells his 250 C Ltd deferred shares for £4,500. The value of his 500 C Ltd ordinary shares is then £25,000. The indexation factor for May 1991 to April 1998 (note (*a*)) is 0.218.

**There is no CGT disposal in 1995/96. The chargeable gain on the 1999/2000 disposal is calculated as follows**

| | £ |
|---|---:|
| Disposal consideration | 4,500 |
| Allowable cost $\dfrac{4,500}{4,500 + 25,000}$ × £10,000 | 1,525 |
| Unindexed gain | 2,975 |
| Indexation allowance £1,525 × 0.218 | 332 |
| Chargeable gain | £2,643 |
| The allowable cost carried forward of the 500 C Ltd ordinary shares is | |
| (£10,000 − £1,525) | £8,475 |

## Shares and Securities

**Note**

(a) Other than for the purposes of corporation tax on chargeable gains, indexation allowance is frozen at its April 1998 level. Therefore, the indexation factor for April 1998 is used in respect of disposals in a later month (and expenditure incurred in April 1998 or later does not attract indexation allowance at all). See 210 INDEXATION.

### (C) Earn-outs

K owns 10,000 ordinary shares in M Ltd, which he acquired for £12,000 in December 1996. In July 1999, the whole of the issued share capital of M Ltd was acquired by P plc. Under the terms of the takeover, K receives £2 per share plus the right to further consideration up to a maximum of £1.50 per share depending on future profit performance. The initial consideration is receivable in cash, but the deferred consideration is to be satisfied by the issue of shares in P plc. In December 2000, K duly receives 2,000 ordinary shares valued at £6 per share in full settlement of his entitlement. The right to future consideration is valued at £1.40 per share in July 1999. The indexation factor for the period December 1996 to April 1998 (note (c)) is 0.053.

**Without a claim by K under *TCGA 1992, s 138A* the position would be**

**1999/2000**

| | £ | £ |
|---|---:|---:|
| Disposal proceeds 10,000 × £2 | 20,000 | |
| Value of rights   10,000 × £1.40 | 14,000 | 34,000 |
| Cost | 12,000 | |
| Indexation allowance £12,000 × 0.053 | 636 | 12,636 |
| Chargeable gain | | £21,364 |

**2000/01**

| | £ |
|---|---:|
| Disposal of rights to deferred consideration: | |
| Proceeds — 2,000 P plc shares @ £6 | 12,000 |
| Deemed cost of acquiring rights | 14,000 |
| Allowable loss | £2,000 |
| | |
| Cost for CGT purposes of 2,000 P plc shares | £12,000 |

**With an election, the position would be**

**1999/2000**

| | £ |
|---|---:|
| Proceeds (cash) (as above) | 20,000 |
| Cost £12,000 × $\dfrac{20,000}{20,000 + 14,000}$ | 7,059 |
| Unindexed gain | 12,941 |
| Indexation allowance £7,059 × 0.053 | 374 |
| Chargeable gain | £12,567 |
| | |
| Cost of earn-out right for CGT purposes (£12,000 − £7,059) | £4,941 |

## 224.4 Shares and Securities

**2000/01**

The shares in P plc stand in the place of the right to deferred consideration and will be regarded as having been acquired in December 1996 for £4,941. No further gain or loss arises until a disposal of the shares takes place.

**Notes**

(a) Under *TCGA 1992, s 138A*, on an election by the vendor, the right to deferred consideration (the 'earn-out right') is treated as a security within *TCGA 1992, s 132*. The gain on the original shares (to the extent that it does not derive from cash consideration) can then be held over against the value of the new shares. [*TCGA 1992, s 138A; FA 1997, s 89*]. Similar provisions previously operated by concession (ESC D27).

(b) Various conditions must be satisfied for an election under *section 138A* to be possible. In particular, the value or quantity of the securities to be received as deferred consideration must be 'unascertainable' (as defined). Any right to receive cash and/or an ascertainable amount of securities as part of the deferred consideration does not fall within these provisions and must be distinguished from the earn-out right, though this does not prevent these provisions from applying to the earn-out right.

(c) Other than for the purposes of corporation tax on chargeable gains, indexation allowance is frozen at its April 1998 level. Therefore, the indexation factor for April 1998 is used in respect of disposals in a later month (and expenditure incurred in April 1998 or later does not attract indexation allowance at all). See 210 INDEXATION.

(d) See 206.3(B)(C) DISPOSAL above for deferred consideration generally.

## Shares and Securities 224.6

**224.5 SCHEMES OF RECONSTRUCTION OR AMALGAMATION** [*TCGA 1992, s 136*]

N Ltd carries on a manufacturing and wholesaling business. In 1992, it was decided that the wholesaling business should be carried on by a separate company. Revenue clearance under *TCGA 1992, s 138* was obtained, and a company, R Ltd, was formed which, in consideration for the transfer to it by N Ltd of the latter's wholesaling undertaking, issued shares to the shareholders of N Ltd. Each holder of ordinary shares in N Ltd additionally received one ordinary share in R Ltd for each N Ltd share he held. W, who purchased his 2,500 N shares for £10,000 in December 1989, received 2,500 R shares. None of the shares involved is quoted. In August 1999, W sells 1,500 of his N shares for £6 each, a total of £9,000, agreed to be their market value. The value of W's remaining N shares is also £6 per share, and the value of his R shares is £4.50 per share. The indexation factor for the period December 1989 to April 1998 (note (*a*)) is 0.369.

|  | £ |
|---|---:|
| Disposal consideration | 9,000 |
| Allowable cost £10,000 × $\dfrac{9,000}{9,000 + (1,000 \times £6) + (2,500 \times £4.50)}$ | 3,429 |
| Unindexed gain | 5,571 |
| Indexation allowance £3,429 × 0.369 | 1,265 |
| Chargeable gain | £4,306 |

**Note**

(*a*) Other than for the purposes of corporation tax on chargeable gains, indexation allowance is frozen at its April 1998 level. Therefore, the indexation factor for April 1998 is used in respect of disposals in a later month (and expenditure incurred in April 1998 or later does not attract indexation allowance at all). See 210 INDEXATION.

**224.6 CONVERSION OF SECURITIES** [*TCGA 1992, s 132; FA 1997, s 88*]

N bought £10,000 8% convertible loan stock in S plc, a quoted company, in June 1989. The cost was £9,800. In August 1993, N exercised his right to convert the loan stock into 'B' ordinary shares of the company, on the basis of 50 shares for £100 loan stock, and acquired 5,000 shares. In June 1999, N sells 3,000 of the shares for £5.00 each. The indexation factor for June 1989 to April 1998 (note (*c*)) is 0.409.

|  | £ |
|---|---:|
| Disposal consideration | 15,000 |
| Cost $\dfrac{3,000}{5,000} \times £9,800$ | 5,880 |
| Unindexed gain | 9,120 |
| Indexation allowance £5,880 × 0.409 | 2,405 |
| Chargeable gain | £6,715 |

**Notes**

(*a*) The shares acquired on the conversion in 1993 stand in the shoes of the original loan stock. [*TCGA 1992, s 132*].

(*b*) The loan stock cannot be a corporate bond (and thus cannot be a qualifying corporate bond) as it is convertible into securities other than corporate bonds, i.e. into ordinary shares. [*ICTA 1988, 18 Sch 1(5); TCGA 1992, s 117(1)*].

## 224.7 Shares and Securities

(c) Other than for the purposes of corporation tax on chargeable gains, indexation allowance is frozen at its April 1998 level. Therefore, the indexation factor for April 1998 is used in respect of disposals in a later month (and expenditure incurred in April 1998 or later does not attract indexation allowance at all). See 210 INDEXATION.

**224.7 SCRIP DIVIDENDS** [*TCGA 1992, ss 141, 142; ICTA 1988, ss 249, 251(2)–(4); FA 1998, s 126*]

D holds ordinary 20p shares in PLC, a quoted company. The company operates a scrip dividend (also known as a stock dividend) policy whereby shareholders are given the option to take dividends in cash or in new fully-paid ordinary 20p shares, the option being exercisable separately in relation to each dividend. D purchased 2,000 shares for £1,500 in March 1980 and a further 3,000 shares for £8,100 in May 1992 and up until the end of 1997 he has always taken cash dividends. In January 1998, he opts for a scrip dividend and receives 25 shares instead of a cash dividend of £100. On 20 April 1998, he purchases a further 1,000 shares for £3,950. In July 1998, he opts for a scrip dividend of 44 shares instead of a cash dividend of £180. He opts for cash dividends thereafter. In December 1999, he sells 2,069 shares for £8,550 (ex div), leaving himself with a holding of 4,000.

In the case of both scrip dividends taken by D, the market value of the new shares is equivalent to the cash dividend forgone. The 'appropriate amount in cash' (see *TCGA 1992, s 142*) is thus the amount of that dividend. [*ICTA 1988, s 251(2)*]. Relevant indexation factors are as follows.

| | |
|---|---|
| May 1992 to January 1998 | 0.145 |
| January 1998 to April 1998 (note (*b*)) | 0.019 |

**The gain on the disposal in December 1999 is calculated as follows**

(i) Identify 44 shares sold with those received by way of scrip dividend in July 1998 (LIFO) (note (*a*))

| | £ |
|---|---|
| Proceeds £8,550 × 44/2069 | 182 |
| Cost (equal to 'appropriate amount in cash') | 180 |
| Chargeable gain | £2 |

(ii) Identify 1,000 shares sold with those acquired on 20 April 1998

| | £ |
|---|---|
| Proceeds £8,550 × 1,000/2,069 | 4,132 |
| Cost | 3,950 |
| Chargeable gain | £182 |

## Shares and Securities  224.7

(iii) Identify remaining 1,025 shares sold with '*section 104* holding' at 5 April 1998

***Section 104* holding**

|  | Shares | Qualifying expenditure £ | Indexed pool £ |
|---|---|---|---|
| May 1992 acquisition | 3,000 | 8,100 | 8,100 |
| Indexed rise: May 1992 to January 1998 £8,100 × 0.145 |  |  | 1,175 |
|  | 3,000 | 8,100 | 9,275 |
| January 1998 scrip dividend 25 × 3,000/5,000 (note (*a*)) | 15 | 60 | 60 |
|  | 3,015 | 8,160 | 9,335 |
| Indexed rise: January 1998 to April 1998 £9,335 × 0.019 |  |  | 177 |
| Pool at 5.4.98 | 3,015 | 8,160 | 9,512 |
| December 1999 disposal | (1,025) | (2,775) | (3,234) |
| Pool carried forward | 1,990 | £5,385 | £6,278 |

|  | £ |
|---|---|
| Proceeds £8,550 × 1,025/2,069 | 4,236 |
| Cost £8,160 × 1,025/3,015 | 2,775 |
| Unindexed gain | 1,461 |
| Indexation allowance £9,512 × 1,025/3,015 = £3,234 |  |
| £3,234 − £2,775 | 459 |
| Chargeable gain | £1,002 |
| **Total chargeable gain 1999/2000** (£2 + £182 + £1,002) | £1,186 |

The remaining holding of 4,000 shares consists of a '*section 104* holding' of 1,990 as illustrated above and a '1982 holding' of 2,010 (which was irrelevant to the December 1998 disposal) consisting of 2,000 purchased in March 1980 and 10 scrip dividend shares acquired in January 1998 and equated with the said purchase (see note (*a*)).

**Notes**

(*a*) Scrip dividends after 5 April 1998 are treated as free-standing acquisitions. Previously, a scrip dividend received by an individual was treated as a reorganisation within *TCGA 1992, s 128* so that the new shares equated with those already held. Thus, in this example, the January 1998 scrip dividend is split pro rata between the '1982 holding' and the '*section 104* holding'.

(*b*) Other than for the purposes of corporation tax on chargeable gains, indexation allowance is frozen at its April 1998 level. Therefore, the indexation factor for April 1998 is used in respect of disposals in a later month (and expenditure incurred in April 1998 or later does not attract indexation allowance at all). See 210 INDEXATION.

The indexed pool is upgraded as if the entire holding had been disposed of at the end of 5 April 1998 but is not adjusted for any subsequent indexed rise in expenditure. [*TCGA 1992, s 110A; FA 1998, s 125(2)(4)(5)*].

(*c*) See also 225.1 SHARES AND SECURITIES — IDENTIFICATION RULES.

## 224.8 Shares and Securities

### 224.8 CAPITAL DISTRIBUTIONS

**(A)** [*TCGA 1992, s 122*]
T holds 10,000 ordinary shares in a foreign company M SA. The shares were bought in April 1995 for £80,000. In February 2000, M SA has a capital reconstruction involving the cancellation of one-fifth of the existing ordinary shares in consideration of the repayment of £10 to each shareholder per share cancelled. T's holding is reduced to 8,000 shares, valued at £96,000. The indexation factor for the period April 1995 to April 1998 (note (*a*)) is 0.091.

|  | £ |
|---|---:|
| Disposal consideration (2,000 × £10) | 20,000 |
| Allowable cost $\dfrac{20,000}{20,000 + 96,000} \times £80,000$ | 13,793 |
| Unindexed gain | 6,207 |
| Indexation allowance £13,793 × 0.091 | 1,255 |
| Chargeable gain | £4,952 |
| The allowable cost of the remaining shares is £80,000 − £13,793 | £66,207 |

**Note**

(*a*) Other than for the purposes of corporation tax on chargeable gains, indexation allowance is frozen at its April 1998 level. Therefore, the indexation factor for April 1998 is used in respect of disposals in a later month (and expenditure incurred in April 1998 or later does not attract indexation allowance at all). See 210 INDEXATION.

**(B) Sale of rights** [*TCGA 1992, ss 122, 123; FA 1996, 20 Sch 52*]
X is a shareholder in K Ltd, owning 2,500 £1 ordinary shares which were purchased for £7,000 in October 1995. K Ltd makes a rights issue, but X sells his rights, without taking them up, for £700 in August 1999. The ex-rights value of X's 2,500 shares at the date of sale was £14,500. The indexation factor for the period October 1995 to April 1998 (note (*a*)) is 0.085.

| 'Section 104' holding' of K £1 ordinary shares | Shares | Qualifying expenditure £ | Indexed pool £ |
|---|---:|---:|---:|
| October 1995 acquisition | 2,500 | 7,000 | 7,000 |
| Indexed rise to April 1998 £7,000 × 0.085 |  |  | 595 |
|  | 2,500 | £7,000 | £7,595 |

The Revenue cannot require the capital distribution to be treated as a disposal, as the £700 received for the rights does not exceed 5% of (£700 + £14,500) and in any case does not exceed £3,000 (see Revenue Tax Bulletin February 1997 p 397). [*TCGA 1992, s 122(2); FA 1996, 20 Sch 52*]. If the transaction is not treated as a disposal, the £700 is deducted from both the acquisition cost of the shares and the indexed pool, leaving balances of, respectively, £6,300 and £6,895. If the transaction is treated as a disposal (possibly because X wishes to utilise part of his annual exemption), the computation is as follows.

## Shares and Securities 224.9

|  | £ |
|---|---|
| Disposal proceeds | 700 |
| Allowable cost $\dfrac{700}{700 + 14,500} \times £7,000$ | 322 |
| Unindexed gain | 378 |
| Indexation allowance: $£7,595 \times \dfrac{700}{700 + 14,500} = £350$ | |
| £350 − £322 | 28 |
| Chargeable gain | £350 |

The allowable cost of the shares is then reduced to £6,678 (£7,000 − £322) and the balance on the indexed pool to £7,245 (£7,595 − £350).

**Note**

(a) Other than for the purposes of corporation tax on chargeable gains, indexation allowance is frozen at its April 1998 level. Therefore, the indexation factor for April 1998 is used in respect of disposals in a later month (and expenditure incurred in April 1998 or later does not attract indexation allowance at all). See 210 INDEXATION.

### 224.9 BUILDING SOCIETY TAKEOVERS AND CONVERSIONS

#### (A) Cash received by investor on a takeover or conversion

Mr C Bagger opened a share account with the Toytown Building Society in August 1993. The society was taken over by High Street Bank plc in December 1997 and Mr Bagger received in that month a cash distribution of £13,000 which comprised a fixed payment of £500 and a percentage payment based on the higher of the balances on the account at two stated dates but restricted to $12\frac{1}{2}\%$ of £100,000. Mr Bagger's passbook showed the following account details.

| Date |  | Debit £ | Credit £ | Balance £ |
|---|---|---|---|---|
| 4.8.93 | Deposit |  | 50,000 | 50,000 |
| 31.3.94 | Net interest |  | 1,500 | 51,500 |
| 16.6.94 | Deposit |  | 75,000 | 126,000 |
| 31.3.95 | Net interest |  | 5,000 | 131,500 |
| 1.5.95 | Withdrawal | 25,000 |  | 106,500 |
| 31.3.96 | Net interest |  | 4,800 | 111,300 |
| 31.3.97 | Net interest |  | 5,300 | 116,600 |
| 1.6.97 | Withdrawal | 8,000 |  | 108,600 |
| 12.12.97 | Cash bonus on takeover |  | 13,000 | 121,600 |
| 12.12.97 | Closing interest |  | 2,800 | 124,400 |
| 12.12.97 | Balance transferred to deposit account at High Street Bank plc | 124,400 |  | Nil |

## 224.9 Shares and Securities

Relevant indexation factors are as follows

| | |
|---|---|
| August 1993 to March 1994 | 0.008 |
| March 1994 to June 1994 | 0.015 |
| June 1994 to March 1995 | 0.019 |
| March 1995 to May 1995 | 0.014 |
| May 1995 to March 1996 | 0.013 |
| March 1996 to March 1997 | 0.026 |
| March 1997 to June 1997 | 0.014 |
| June 1997 to December 1997 | 0.016 |

**The chargeable gain on the cash bonus is computed as follows**

| | Qualifying expenditure £ | Indexed pool £ |
|---|---:|---:|
| 4.8.93 acquisition | 50,000 | 50,000 |
| Indexed rise: August 1993–March 1994 | | |
| £50,000 × 0.008 | | 400 |
| 31.3.94 acquisition | 1,500 | 1,500 |
| | 51,500 | 51,900 |
| Indexed rise: March 1994–June 1994 | | |
| £51,900 × 0.015 | | 779 |
| 16.6.94 acquisition | 75,000 | 75,000 |
| | 126,500 | 127,679 |
| Indexed rise: June 1994–March 1995 | | |
| £127,679 × 0.019 | | 2,426 |
| 31.3.95 acquisition | 5,000 | 5,000 |
| | 131,500 | 135,105 |
| Indexed rise: March 1995–May 1995 | | |
| £135,105 × 0.014 | | 1,890 |
| | 131,500 | 136,995 |
| Disposal (no gain/no loss) | (25,000) | (26,045)* |
| | 106,500 | 110,950 |
| Indexed rise: May 1995–March 1996 | | |
| £110,950 × 0.013 | | 1,442 |
| 31.3.96 acquisition | 4,800 | 4,800 |
| | 111,300 | 117,192 |
| Indexed rise: March 1996–March 1997 | | |
| £117,192 × 0.026 | | 3,047 |
| 31.3.97 acquisition | 5,300 | 5,300 |
| | c/f 116,600 | 125,539 |

## Shares and Securities

|  | £<br>b/f 116,600 | £<br>125,539 |
|---|---|---|
| Indexed rise: March 1997–June 1997 | | |
| £125,539 × 0.014 | | 1,758 |
| | 116,600 | 127,297 |
| Disposal (no gain/no loss) | (8,000) | (8,734)** |
| | 108,600 | 118,563 |
| Indexed rise: June 1997–December 1997 | | |
| £118,563 × 0.016 | | 1,897 |
| 12.12.97 acquisition | 2,800 | 2,800 |
| | 111,400 | 123,260 |
| Disposal | (111,400) | (123,260) |

$$* \ £136{,}995 \times \frac{25{,}000}{131{,}500} = £26{,}045$$

$$** \ £127{,}297 \times \frac{8{,}000}{116{,}600} = £8{,}734$$

| | £ |
|---|---|
| Proceeds: | |
| Cash bonus | 13,000 |
| Balance of account | 111,400 |
| Total proceeds | 124,400 |
| Allowable cost | 111,400 |
| Unindexed gain | 13,000 |
| Indexation allowance £123,260 – £111,400 | 11,860 |
| Chargeable gain | £1,140 |

**Notes**

(a) A cash bonus received (in respect of a share account, but not a deposit account) on the takeover or conversion of a building society is within the charge to capital gains tax, but is reduced by indexation allowance based on the evolving balance of the account. (Revenue Press Release 27 March 1997, Tax Bulletin April 1998 pp 517–523).

(b) For the purpose of calculating the indexation allowance, each £1 deposited (or withdrawn) is treated in the same way as an acquisition (or disposal) of a share in a company.

## 224.9 Shares and Securities

**(B) Shares received by investor on a takeover or conversion**
Mr C Bagger in (A) above also has a share account (opened in November 1989) with the Farthing Wood Building Society which converted to plc status in May 1997. The balance of the account as at conversion was £27,000. Mr Bagger received no cash bonus but received a bonus of 1,600 ordinary shares in the new plc. On the first day of trading in the new shares, they opened at £3.55 per share. Mr Bagger retains his shares until February 2000 when he sells them for £7,800 (net of disposal costs).

**The chargeable gain on the sale of shares is computed as follows**

|  | £ |
|---|---:|
| Net proceeds | 7,800 |
| Cost of acquisition | Nil |
| Unindexed gain | 7,800 |
| Indexation allowance (none, as nil cost) | — |
| Chargeable gain 1999/2000 | £7,800 |

**Note**
(a) No chargeable gain arises in respect of the distribution of shares to members on a takeover or conversion of a building society. The shares are regarded as acquired for nil cost (and thus no indexation allowance can be due on a subsequent disposal). [*TCGA 1992, s 217*]. (Revenue Press Releases 21 March 1996, 27 March 1997, Tax Bulletin April 1998 pp 517–523).

# Shares and Securities — Identification Rules 225.1

## 225 Shares and Securities — Identification Rules

**Cross-reference.** See 224 SHARES AND SECURITIES.

### 225.1 IDENTIFICATION RULES AFTER 5 APRIL 1998 (OTHER THAN FOR CORPORATION TAX PURPOSES)

A has the following acquisitions/disposals of ordinary 25p shares in QED plc. Throughout their period of ownership by A, these shares are non-business assets for the purposes of TAPER RELIEF (226). QED ordinary 25p shares were worth 210p per share at 31 March 1982, and A has not made a global re-basing election (see 204 ASSETS HELD ON 31 MARCH 1982). Note that in 2001/02, A made no disposals of chargeable assets other than as shown below.

| Date | No. of shares bought/(sold) | Cost/(proceeds) £ |
|---|---|---|
| 1 May 1980 | 1,000 | 2,000 |
| 1 October 1983 | 2,000 | 4,500 |
| 1 December 1996 | 500 | 1,800 |
| 1 May 1999 | (1,000) | (3,900) |
| 25 May 1999 | 2,000 | 7,600 |
|  | 4,500 |  |
| 2 January 2000 | (2,000) | (9,000) |
| 1 July 2001 | (2,000) | (12,000) |
| Remaining holding | 500 |  |

Relevant indexation factors are

| | |
|---|---|
| March 1982 to April 1998 (note (*b*)) | 1.047 |
| October 1983 to April 1985 | 0.097 |
| April 1985 to December 1996 | 0.629 |
| December 1996 to April 1998 | 0.053 |

(i) **The disposal on 1 May 1999** is matched with 1,000 of the shares acquired on 25 May 1999 (under the 30-day rule — see note (*a*)). The resulting chargeable gain is as follows.

| | £ |
|---|---|
| Proceeds 1.5.99 | 3,900 |
| Cost (£7,600 × 1,000/2,000) | 3,800 |
| Chargeable gain (no taper relief due) | £100 |

## 225.1 Shares and Securities — Identification Rules

(ii) **The disposal of 2,000 shares on 2 January 2000** is matched firstly with the remaining 1,000 acquired on 25 May 1999 (LIFO), and secondly with 1,000 of the 2,500 forming the '*section 104* holding' as follows.

|  | No. of shares | Qualifying expenditure £ | Indexed pool £ |
|---|---|---|---|
| Pool at 6.4.85 | 2,000 | 4,500 | 4,500 |
| Indexation allowance to date: October 1983 – April 1985 £4,500 × 0.097 | | | 437 |
| | 2,000 | 4,500 | 4,937 |
| Indexed rise to December 1996: April 1985 – December 1996 £4,937 × 0.629 | | | 3,105 |
| Acquisition 1.12.96 | 500 | 1,800 | 1,800 |
| | 2,500 | 6,300 | 9,842 |
| Indexed rise to April 1998: December 1996 – April 1998 £9,842 × 0.053 | | | 522 |
| | 2,500 | 6,300 | 10,364 |
| Disposal 2.1.2000 | (1,000) | (2,520) | (4,146) |
| Pool carried forward | 1,500 | £3,780 | £6,218 |

Chargeable gains are as follows.

|  | £ | £ |
|---|---|---|
| Proceeds 2.1.2000 | 4,500 | 4,500 |
| Cost (£7,600 × 1,000/2,000) | 3,800 | |
| Cost (as above) | | 2,520 |
| Unindexed gains | 700 | 1,980 |
| Indexation (£4,146 – £2,520) | — | 1,626 |
| Chargeable gains | £700 | £354 |

Neither gain qualifies for taper relief. In each case, the shares acquired have been held for less than the requisite three complete years (for non-business asset taper relief) after 5 April 1998.

## Shares and Securities — Identification Rules 225.1

(iii) **The disposal of 2,000 shares on 1 July 2001** is matched firstly with the remaining 1,500 in the '*section 104* holding', and secondly with 500 of the 1,000 shares forming the '1982 holding'.

Chargeable gains are as follows.

|  | £ |
|---|---:|
| Proceeds of 1,500 shares on 1.7.01 | 9,000 |
| Cost (as per pool above) | 3,780 |
| Unindexed gain | 5,220 |
| Indexation (£6,218 − £3,780) | 2,438 |
| Chargeable gain subject to taper relief | 2,782 |
| Taper relief £2,782 × 10% (see below) | 278 |
| Chargeable gain | £2,504 |

|  | £ |  |
|---|---:|---:|
| Proceeds of 500 shares on 1.7.01 | 3,000 | 3,000 |
| Cost (£2,000 × 500/1,000) | 1,000 |  |
| Market value 31.3.82 500 × £2.10 |  | 1,050 |
| Unindexed gain | 2,000 | 1,950 |
| Indexation to April 1998: |  |  |
| £1,050 × 1.047 | 1,099 | 1,099 |
| Gain after indexation | £901 | £851 |

| | |
|---|---:|
| Chargeable gain subject to taper relief | 851 |
| Taper relief £851 × 10% (see below) | 85 |
| Chargeable gain | £766 |

Taper relief is at 10% as the shares are non-business assets and have been held for three plus one years since 5 April 1998, the one-year addition being by virtue of the fact that both the '*section 104* holding' and the '1982 holding' were acquired before 17 March 1998. [*TCGA 1992, s 2A(8)(9); FA 1998, s 121(1)*].

**Notes**

(*a*) Other than for the purposes of corporation tax on chargeable gains, disposals after 5 April 1998 are identified (1) with shares acquired on the same day; (2) with acquisitions in the following 30 days; (3) on a LIFO basis with post-5 April 1998 acquisitions; (4) with the 'section 104 holding' at 5 April 1998; (5) with the '1982 holding'; (6) on a LIFO basis with acquisitions on or before 6 April 1965; (7) with shares acquired after the disposal (and after the expiry of the 30-day period in (2) above) taken in the order in which such acquisitions occur. [*TCGA 1992, ss 105, 106A; FA 1998, s 124(1)(2)(7)*].

(*b*) Other than for the purposes of corporation tax on chargeable gains, indexation allowance is frozen at its April 1998 level. Therefore, the indexation factor for April 1998 is used in respect of disposals in a later month (and expenditure incurred in April 1998 or later does not attract indexation allowance at all). See 210 INDEXATION.

The indexed pool is upgraded as if the entire holding had been disposed of at the end of 5 April 1998 but is not adjusted for any subsequent indexed rise in expenditure. [*TCGA 1992, s 110A; FA 1998, s 125(2)(4)(5)*].

## 225.2 Shares and Securities — Identification Rules

225.2 **SHARE IDENTIFICATION RULES BEFORE 6 APRIL 1998 (AND CONTINUING FOR COMPANIES)** [*TCGA 1992, ss 104, 105, 107–110; FA 1994, s 93(6); FA 1998, s123*]

**(A) General**
B has the following transactions in 25p ordinary shares of H plc, a quoted company.

|  |  | Cost/(proceeds) £ |
|---|---|---|
| 6.6.78 | Purchased 500 at £0.85 | 425 |
| 3.11.81 | Purchased 1,300 at £0.80 | 1,040 |
| 15.5.82 | Purchased 1,000 at £1.02 | 1,020 |
| 8.9.82 | Purchased 400 at £1.08 | 432 |
| 1.2.86 | Purchased 1,200 at £1.14 | 1,368 |
| 29.7.87 | Sold 2,000 at £1.30 | (2,600) |
| 8.6.90 | Purchased 1,500 at £1.26 | 1,890 |
| 21.12.93 | Received 1,000 from wife (cost £1,250, indexation to date £250) | 1,500 |
| 10.5.97 | Sold 3,900 at £2.10 | (8,190) |

The shares stood at £1.00 at 31.3.82.

| Indexation factors | | |
|---|---|---|
| | March 1982 to May 1997 | 0.975 |
| | May 1982 to April 1985 | 0.161 |
| | September 1982 to April 1985 | 0.158 |
| | April 1985 to February 1986 | 0.019 |
| | February 1986 to July 1987 | 0.054 |
| | July 1987 to June 1990 | 0.245 |
| | June 1990 to December 1993 | 0.120 |
| | December 1993 to May 1997 | 0.106 |

**Disposal on 10 May 1997**

*The 'section 104 holding' pool immediately prior to the disposal should be as follows*

| | Shares | Qualifying expenditure £ | Indexed pool £ |
|---|---|---|---|
| 15.5.82 acquisition | 1,000 | 1,020 | 1,020 |
| Indexation to April 1985 | | | |
| £1,020 × 0.161 | | | 164 |
| 8.9.82 acquisition | 400 | 432 | 432 |
| Indexation to April 1985 | | | |
| £432 × 0.158 | | | 68 |
| Pool at 6.4.85 | 1,400 | 1,452 | 1,684 |
| Indexed rise: Apr. 1985 — Feb. 1986 | | | |
| £1,684 × 0.019 | | | 32 |
| 1.2.86 acquisition | 1,200 | 1,368 | 1,368 |
| | 2,600 | 2,820 | 3,084 |
| Indexed rise: Feb. 1986 — July 1987 | | | |
| £3,084 × 0.054 | | | 167 |
| | 2,600 | 2,820 | 3,251 |
| 29.7.87 disposal | (2,000) | (2,169) | (2,501) |
| c/f | £600 | £651 | £750 |

## Shares and Securities — Identification Rules 225.2

|  | Shares | Qualifying expenditure £ | Indexed pool £ |
|---|---|---|---|
| b/f | 600 | 651 | 750 |
| Indexed rise: July 1987 — June 1990 £750 × 0.245 |  |  | 184 |
| 8.6.90 acquisition | 1,500 | 1,890 | 1,890 |
|  | 2,100 | 2,541 | 2,824 |
| Indexed rise: June 1990 — Dec. 1993 £2,824 × 0.120 |  |  | 339 |
| 21.12.93 acquisition | 1,000 | 1,250 | 1,500 |
|  | 3,100 | 3,791 | 4,663 |
| Indexed rise: Dec. 1993 — May 1997 £4,663 × 0.106 |  |  | 494 |
|  | 3,100 | 3,791 | 5,157 |

The '1982 holding' is as follows

|  | Shares | Allowable expenditure £ |
|---|---|---|
| 6.6.78 acquisition | 500 | 425 |
| 3.11.81 acquisition | 1,300 | 1,040 |
|  | 1,800 | 1,465 |

(i) Identify 3,100 shares sold with '*section 104* holding'

|  | £ |
|---|---|
| Disposal consideration 3,100 × £2.10 | 6,510 |
| Allowable cost | 3,791 |
| Unindexed gain | 2,719 |
| Indexation allowance £5,157 − £3,791 | 1,366 |
| Chargeable gain | £1,353 |

(ii) Identify 800 shares sold with '1982 holding'

|  | £ | £ |
|---|---|---|
| Disposal consideration 800 × £2.10 | 1,680 | 1,680 |
| Cost $\frac{800}{1,800}$ × £1,465 | 651 |  |
| Market value 31.3.82 $\frac{800}{1,800}$ × £1,800 |  | 800 |
| Unindexed gain | 1,029 | 880 |
| Indexation allowance £800 × 0.975 | 780 | 780 |
| Gain after indexation | £249 | £100 |
| Chargeable gain |  | £100 |
| Total chargeable gain (1997/98) (£1,353 + £100) |  | £1,453 |

## 225.2 Shares and Securities — Identification Rules

**Notes**
- (*a*) Share disposals after 5.4.85 (31.3.85 for companies) and before 6 April 1998 (continuing after that date for companies) are identified firstly with the '*section 104 holding*' and secondly with the '1982 holding', both of which are regarded as single assets.
- (*b*) On share disposals after 5.4.88 identified with shares held at 31.3.82, the re-basing provisions have effect, and indexation is based on the higher of cost and 31.3.82 value. If an irrevocable election is made under *TCGA 1992, s 35(5)* for all assets to be treated as disposed of and re-acquired at their market value on 31.3.82, indexation must be based on the 31.3.82 value even if this is less than cost. [*TCGA 1992, s 55(1)(2)*].

# Shares and Securities — Identification Rules 225.2

**(B) Special rules — 'same day' transactions, 'ten day' rule and 'bed and breakfasting'** [*TCGA 1992, ss 105, 107(3)–(6); FA 1998, s 124(8)*].
C has the following transactions in 25p ordinary shares of J plc.

|  |  | Cost/(proceeds) £ |
|---|---|---|
| 16.12.84 | Purchased 20,000 at £1.92 | 38,400 |
| 5.8.87 | Purchased 12,000 at £2.40 | 28,800 |
| 3.4.88 | Sold 4,000 at £2.00 | (8,000) |
| 4.4.88 | Purchased 4,000 at £2.02 | 8,080 |
| 14.9.91 | Purchased 5,000 at £2.20 | 11,000 |
| 14.9.91 | Sold 1,000 at £2.19 | (2,190) |
| 30.4.97 | Purchased 2,000 at £2.55 | 5,100 |
| 3.5.97 | Purchased 2,000 at £2.58 | 5,160 |
| 8.5.97 | Sold 6,000 at £2.80 | (16,800) |
| 20.3.98 | Sold 7,500 at £3.00 | (22,500) |
| 23.3.98 | Purchased 7,500 at £2.98 | 22,350 |

Holding at 5.4.98 – 34,000

| Indexation factors | December 1984 to August 1987 | 0.124 |
|---|---|---|
|  | August 1987 to April 1988 | 0.036 |
|  | April 1988 to September 1991 | 0.271 |
|  | September 1991 to May 1997 | 0.166 |

## 1987/88
**Disposal on 3.4.88**

Establish '*section 104* holding' pool

|  | Shares | Qualifying expenditure £ | Indexed pool £ |
|---|---|---|---|
| 16.12.84 acquisition | 20,000 | 38,400 | 38,400 |
| Indexed rise: December 1984 — August 1987 |  |  |  |
| £38,400 × 0.124 |  |  | 4,762 |
| 5.8.87 acquisition | 12,000 | 28,800 | 28,800 |
|  | 32,000 | 67,200 | 71,962 |
| Indexed rise: August 1987 — April 1988 |  |  |  |
| £71,962 × 0.036 |  |  | 2,591 |
|  | 32,000 | 67,200 | 74,553 |
| 3.4.88 disposal | (4,000) | (8,400) | (9,319) |
| 4.4.88 acquisition | 4,000 | 8,080 | 8,080 |
| Pool carried forward | 32,000 | £66,880 | £73,314 |

| | | |
|---|---|---|
| Disposal consideration |  | £8,000 |
| Cost $\frac{4,000}{32,000} \times £67,200$ |  | 8,400 |
| Unindexed loss |  | 400 |
| Indexation allowance |  |  |

$\frac{4,000}{32,000} \times £74,553 = £9,319$

| | | |
|---|---|---|
| £9,319 – £8,400 |  | 919 |
| Allowable loss |  | £1,319 |

## 225.2 Shares and Securities — Identification Rules

**1991/92**
**Disposal on 14.9.91**
Match with acquisitions on the same day (note (*a*))

| | |
|---|---:|
| Disposal consideration | £2,190 |
| Cost $\dfrac{1,000}{5,000} \times £11,000$ | 2,200 |
| Allowable loss | £10 |

Add balance of 14.9.91 acquisition to pool

| | Shares | Qualifying expenditure £ | Indexed pool £ |
|---|---:|---:|---:|
| Pool at 4.4.88 | 32,000 | 66,880 | 73,314 |
| Indexed rise: April 1988 — September 1991 £73,314 × 0.271 | | | 19,868 |
| Balance of 14.9.91 acquisition | 4,000 | 8,800 | 8,800 |
| Pool carried forward | 36,000 | £75,680 | £101,982 |

**1997/98**
**Disposal on 8.5.97**
Match first with acquisition on 30.4.97 (note (*b*))

| | |
|---|---:|
| Disposal consideration 2,000 × £2.80 | £5,600 |
| Cost 30.4.97 | 5,100 |
| Chargeable gain | £500 |

Match next with 3.5.97 acquisition (note (*b*))

| | |
|---|---:|
| Disposal consideration 2,000 × £2.80 | £5,600 |
| Cost 3.5.97 | 5,160 |
| Chargeable gain | £440 |

Match finally with 'section 104 holding' pool

| | Shares | Qualifying expenditure £ | Indexed pool £ |
|---|---:|---:|---:|
| Pool at 14.9.91 | 36,000 | 75,680 | 101,982 |
| Indexed rise: September 1991 — May 1997 £101,982 × 0.166 | | | 16,929 |
| | 36,000 | 75,680 | 118,911 |
| Balance of 8.5.97 disposal | (2,000) | (4,204) | (6,606) |
| Pool carried forward | 34,000 | £71,476 | £112,305 |

# Shares and Securities — Identification Rules

Disposal consideration 2,000 × £2.80    £5,600

Cost $\dfrac{2,000}{36,000} \times £75,680$    4,204

Unindexed gain    1,396
Indexation allowance

$\dfrac{2,000}{36,000} \times £115,546 = £6,606$

£6,606 − £4,204 = £2,402 but restricted to    1,396

Chargeable gain    Nil

**Disposal on 20.3.98**
Match with acquisition on 23.3.98 (note (*c*))

Disposal consideration 7,500 × £3.00    £22,500
Cost 23.3.98    22,350

Chargeable gain    £150

Total chargeable gain 1997/98 (£500 + £440 + £150)    £1,090

**Notes**

(*a*)   Under *TCGA 1992, s 105*, a disposal of securities is matched as far as possible with an acquisition on the same day. It follows that no indexation can be available.

(*b*)   Subject to the overriding rule described in (*a*) above, and for disposals after 5.4.85 (31.3.85 for companies) and before 6.4.98 (continuing for companies), a disposal of securities is first matched with preceding acquisitions within a ten-day period on a first in/first out basis, and to the extent that they can be so matched, the securities are not pooled and no indexation allowance is due. [*TCGA 1992, s 107(3)–(6)*].

(*c*)   No special rules applied before 17 March 1998 where an acquisition *followed* a disposal, so the above did not affect a 'bed and breakfast' transaction. Disposals on or after that date (other than by companies) must first be matched with any acquisitions of securities of the same class within the next 30 days, taking earlier acquisitions before later ones. The advantages of 'bed and breakfasting' are thereby negated. [*TCGA 1992, s 106A(5); FA 1998, s 124(1)(8)*].

## 226.1 Taper Relief

# 226 Taper Relief

**Cross-reference.** See 225.1 SHARES AND SECURITIES — IDENTIFICATION RULES.

226.1 **THE BASIC RULES** [*TCGA 1992, s 2A, A1 Sch; FA 1998, s 121, 20 Sch*]

### (A) Computing the tapered gain

Brett acquired an asset in 1996 for £20,000 and sells it in September 2002 for £35,000. He makes no other disposals in 2002/03. At no time after 5 April 1998 was the asset used as a business asset. The indexation factor from date of acquisition to April 1998 (see note (*a*)) is, say, 0.060.

### The taxable gain is computed as follows

At the time of disposal, the asset has been held for four complete years after 5 April 1998. Because it was acquired before 17 March 1998, a further one year is added. Using the table at *TCGA 1992, s 2A(5)*, the taper relief for a non-business asset held for five complete years after 5 April 1998 is 15%.

|  | £ |
|---|---:|
| Proceeds | 35,000 |
| *Less* Cost of acquisition | 20,000 |
| Unindexed gain | 15,000 |
| Indexation to April 1998 £20,000 × 0.060 | 1,200 |
| Chargeable gain | 13,800 |
| *Less* Taper relief £13,800 × 15% | 2,070 |
| Taxable gain subject to annual exemption | £11,730 |

#### Note

(*a*) Other than for the purposes of corporation tax on chargeable gains, indexation allowance is frozen at its April 1998 level. Therefore, the indexation factor for April 1998 is used in respect of disposals in a later month (and expenditure incurred in April 1998 or later does not attract indexation allowance at all). See 210 INDEXATION.

### (B) Set-off of losses

Hannah made four disposals in 2005/06, as follows.

On Asset A, she realised a chargeable gain of £13,000 (after indexation to April 1998). This asset was acquired in 1995 and sold in May 2005 and was a non-business asset throughout its ownership.

On Asset B, she realised a chargeable gain of £2,000. This asset was acquired in December 2002 and sold in October 2005 and was a non-business asset throughout its ownership.

On Asset C, she realised a chargeable gain of £7,500. This asset was acquired in August 1999 and sold in December 2005 and was a business asset throughout its ownership.

On Asset D, she realised an allowable loss of £6,000.

# Taper Relief 226.1

**The gains qualify for taper relief as follows**

Asset A was held for seven complete years after 5 April 1998 and qualifies for a one-year addition as it was acquired before 17 March 1998. The gain thus qualifies for 30% taper relief.

Asset B was held for less than the minimum period of ownership necessary for a gain on a non-business asset to qualify for taper relief (three complete years).

Asset C was held for six complete years. It thus qualifies for 45% taper relief.

**The optimum set-off of losses is as follows**

It is beneficial to offset the loss on Asset D firstly against the gain attracting no taper relief, i.e. the gain on Asset B, with the balance against the gain attracting the lower rate of taper relief, i.e. the gain on Asset A.

|  | £ |
|---|---:|
| *Asset A* | |
| Chargeable gain | 13,000 |
| *Less* Allowable loss (balance) | 4,000 |
| | 9,000 |
| *Less* Taper relief £9,000 × 30% | 2,700 |
| Tapered gain | £6,300 |
| | |
| *Asset B* | |
| Chargeable gain | 2,000 |
| *Less* Allowable loss | 2,000 |
| | |
| *Asset C* | |
| Chargeable gain | 7,500 |
| *Less* Taper relief £7,500 × 45% | 3,375 |
| Tapered gain | £4,125 |
| | |
| Total taxable gains subject to annual exemption | £10,425 |

**Note**

(*a*)  Both current year and brought forward losses are set against gains in such a way as to maximise the taper relief due. [*TCGA 1992, s 2A(6); FA 1998, s 121(1)*].

## 226.2 Taper Relief

### 226.2 ASSETS WHICH ARE BUSINESS ASSETS FOR PART ONLY OF PERIOD OF OWNERSHIP [*TCGA 1992, A1 Sch 3; FA 1998, s 121(2)(4), 20 Sch*]

Penny acquired a freehold property in March 1990 and sold it on 30 September 2007, realising a chargeable gain (after indexation to April 1998) of £95,000. Between March 1990 and September 2001 inclusive, the property was used as business premises and qualifies as a business asset for taper relief purposes. From October 2001 to September 2007 inclusive, it was let to a tenant and was not a business asset. Penny made no other disposal in 2007/08.

**The gain qualifies for taper relief as follows**

The relevant period of ownership for the purposes of taper relief is the 9.5 years from 6 April 1998 to 30 September 2007. During that period, the asset was a business asset for 3.5 years (April 1998 to September 2001) and a non-business asset for the remaining six years. Therefore, 3.5/9.5 of the gain (£35,000) qualifies for the business assets taper and 6/9.5 of the gain (£60,000) qualifies for the non-business assets taper.

The number of complete years in the qualifying holding period is nine. However, there is a one-year addition as the asset was acquired before 17 March 1998. [*TCGA 1992, s 2A(8)(9); FA 1998, s 121(1)*].

**The taxable gain is computed as follows**

|  | Business asset £ | Non-business asset £ | Total £ |
|---|---|---|---|
| Chargeable gain | 35,000 | 60,000 | 95,000 |
| *Less* Taper relief 75%/40% | 26,250 | 24,000 | 50,250 |
| Taxable gain subject to annual exemption | £8,750 | £36,000 | £44,750 |

### 226.3 INTER-SPOUSE TRANSFERS [*TCGA 1992, A1 Sch 15; FA 1998, s 121(2)(4), 20 Sch*]

**Note.** See 215.1 MARRIED PERSONS as regards inter-spouse transfers generally.

**(A) Assets other than shares and securities**

Jack and Jill are a married couple living together. Jack owns a property which he acquired as an investment in May 1996 for £60,000. On 7 April 1999, he gives the property to Jill who thereafter uses it as offices in her profession as a solicitor. Three years later, Jill decides to rent larger office premises and sells the property on 8 April 2002 for £110,000. She makes no other disposals in 2002/03. The indexation factor for the period May 1996 to April 1998 (note (*d*)) is 0.063.

**Jack's disposal in 1999/2000 is at no gain/no loss as follows**

|  | £ | £ |
|---|---|---|
| Deemed consideration |  | 63,780 |
| *Less*: Cost of acquisition | 60,000 |  |
| Indexation allowance £60,000 × 0.063 | 3,780 | 63,780 |
| Gain/loss |  | Nil |

**The gain on Jill's disposal in 2002/03 is computed as follows**

| | £ |
|---|---|
| Proceeds | 110,000 |
| Less Cost of acquisition (as above) | 63,780 |
| Chargeable gain subject to taper relief | 46,220 |
| Less Taper relief (see below) | 14,733 |
| Taxable gain subject to annual exemption | £31,487 |

The qualifying holding period for taper relief is five years, i.e. four complete years after 5 April 1998 plus the bonus year for assets acquired before 17 March 1998. The relevant period of ownership is the four years from 6 April 1998 to 8 April 2002. During that period, the asset was a non-business asset for one year (6 April 1998 to 6 April 1999) and a business asset for three years (7 April 1999 to 8 April 2002). Therefore, one quarter of the gain qualifies for non-business asset taper relief and three-quarters for business asset taper relief (see also 226.2 above) as follows:

| | £ |
|---|---|
| (£46,220 × $\frac{1}{4}$ = £11,555) @ 15% | 1,733 |
| (£46,220 × $\frac{3}{4}$ = £34,665) @ 37.5% | 13,000 |
| Total taper relief | £14,733 |

**Note**

(a) Taper relief applies as if the time when the transferee spouse acquired the asset was the time when the transferor spouse acquired it.

(b) The question of whether the asset was a business asset at any specified time in the combined period of ownership after 5 April 1998 is determined by reference to the use to which it was put by the spouse holding it at that time.

(c) As regards that part of the combined period of ownership which falls *before* the inter-spouse transfer, the asset is also a business asset at any time if it then qualifies as such by reference to the spouse to whom it is eventually transferred, i.e. where an asset owned by one spouse is used in the other's business (not illustrated in this example).

(d) Other than for the purposes of corporation tax on chargeable gains, indexation allowance is frozen at its April 1998 level. Therefore, the indexation factor for April 1998 is used in respect of disposals in a later month (and expenditure incurred in April 1998 or later does not attract indexation allowance at all). See 210 INDEXATION.

**(B) Shares and securities**

George and Kelly are a married couple living together. George has his own trading company in which he owns 900 of the 1,000 issued ordinary £1 shares and thus 90% of the voting rights. Kelly owns the remaining 100 shares but does not work full-time for the company. They each acquired their shares at par on 30 April 1998 when the company was incorporated. On 29 April 2008, Kelly gives her shares to George. George wishes to retire from the business and, on 30 April 2009, he sells his entire shareholding for £25,000.

## 226.3 Taper Relief

**Kelly's disposal in 2008/09 is for a deemed consideration of £100 thus producing no gain and no loss.**

**The gain on George's disposal in 2009/10 is computed as follows**

|  | £ |
|---|---:|
| Proceeds (1,000 shares) | 25,000 |
| *Less* Cost of acquisition (£1 per share) | 1,000 |
| Chargeable gain subject to taper relief | 24,000 |
| *Less* Taper relief (£24,000 @ 75% — see below) | 18,000 |
| Taxable gain subject to annual exemption | £6,000 |

The qualifying holding period for taper relief is the eleven years from 30 April 1998 to 30 April 2009, so the gain qualifies for the maximum ten-year taper. The relevant period of ownership is the maximum ten years immediately preceding the time of disposal, i.e. the ten years to 30 April 2009. During the whole of that period, the company was a qualifying company by reference to George. Therefore, the whole of the gain qualifies for business asset taper relief which is at 75%.

**Notes**

(a) Taper relief applies as if the time when the transferee spouse acquired the asset was the time when the transferor spouse acquired it.

(b) As regards shares and securities, the question of whether the asset was a business asset at any specified time in the combined period of ownership is determined only by reference to the individual making the ultimate disposal.

(c) If, instead, George had given his shares to Kelly and she made the ultimate sale, the gain would have qualified for business asset taper relief only from the date of transfer as only from that date would the company be a qualifying company by reference to her (due to her share of the voting rights being at least 25%). The gain would have required apportionment using the method in (A) above.

## Taper Relief 226.4

226.4 **POSTPONED GAINS** [*TCGA 1992, A1 Sch 16; FA 1998, s 121(2)(4), 20 Sch*]

Gordon disposes of shares in A Ltd, his family trading company, in August 2000, realising a chargeable gain (after indexation to April 1998) of £25,000. He had held the shares since 1988 and they qualified as a business asset for the purposes of taper relief. He acquires shares in a Venture Capital Trust in March 2001 for £30,000 and makes a claim for deferral relief under *TCGA 1992, 5C Sch* (see IT 28.3(B) VENTURE CAPITAL TRUSTS). He makes no other disposals in 2000/01 and wishes to leave sufficient gains in charge to cover his annual exemption, which for that year is assumed to be £7,300.

The A Ltd shares were held for two complete years after 5 April 1998 and this is increased to three for taper relief purposes as they were acquired before 17 March 1998. [*TCGA 1992, s 2A(8)(9); FA 1998, s 121(1)*]. The taper is therefore 22.5% (see the table at *TCGA 1992, s 2A(5)*).

**The gain is computed as follows**

|  | £ |
|---|---|
| Gain before taper relief | 25,000 |
| *Less* Deferred on reinvestment in VCT (optimum amount) | 15,581* |
|  | 9,419 |
| *Less* Taper relief £9,419 × 22.5% | 2,119 |
| Tapered gain for 2000/01 covered by annual exemption | £7,300 |

* £7,300 × $\dfrac{100}{100 - 22.5}$ = £9,419.  £25,000 − £9,419 = £15,581.

In June 2007, Gordon sells his VCT shares. **The deferred gain becomes chargeable in 2007/08 and is computed as follows**

|  | £ |
|---|---|
| Deferred gain before taper relief | 15,581 |
| *Less* Taper relief £15,581 × 22.5% | 3,506 |
| Taxable gain for 2007/08 subject to annual exemption | £12,075 |

**Note**

(*a*) Taper relief on the deferred gain becoming chargeable is given by reference to the time and circumstances of the original disposal, not the disposal which brings the gain into charge. This applies in a number of circumstances in which gains are deferred or postponed, as listed at *TCGA 1992, A1 Sch 16*. For a further example, see 207.3(A) ENTERPRISE INVESTMENT SCHEME.

(*b*) A special rule applies in cases of serial EIS reinvestment. See 207.3(B) ENTERPRISE INVESTMENT SCHEME.

## 227.1 Wasting Assets

## 227 Wasting Assets

**Cross-references.** See also 213.3 LAND, 222.3 ROLLOVER RELIEF.

**227.1 GENERAL** [*TCGA 1992, ss 44–47*]

V bought an aircraft on 31 May 1995 at a cost of £90,000 for use in his air charter business. It has been agreed that V's non-business use of the aircraft amounts to one-tenth, on a flying hours basis, and capital allowances and running costs have accordingly been restricted for income tax purposes. On 1 February 2000, V sells the aircraft for £185,000. The aircraft is agreed as having a useful life of 20 years at the date it was acquired. The indexation factor for May 1995 to April 1998 (note (*b*)) is 0.087.

|  | £ |
|---|---:|
| **Amount qualifying for capital allowances** | |
| Relevant portion of disposal consideration $\frac{9}{10} \times £185,000$ | 166,500 |
| Relevant portion of acquisition cost $\frac{9}{10} \times £90,000$ | 81,000 |
| Unindexed gain | 85,500 |
| Indexation allowance £81,000 × 0.087 | 7,047 |
| Chargeable gain (subject to TAPER RELIEF (226)) | £78,453 |

| | | £ |
|---|---:|---:|
| **Amount not qualifying for capital allowances** | | |
| Relevant portion of disposal consideration $\frac{1}{10} \times £185,000$ | | 18,500 |
| Relevant portion of acquisition cost | | |
| $\frac{1}{10} \times £90,000$ | 9,000 | |
| *Deduct* Wasted £9,000 × $\frac{4y\ 8m}{20y}$ | 2,100 | 6,900 |
| Gain | | £11,600 |

The whole of the £11,600 is exempt.

The total chargeable gain is therefore £78,453

**Notes**

(*a*) Gains on tangible moveable property which are wasting assets not qualifying for capital allowances are exempt (and any losses would not be allowable). [*TCGA 1992, s 45*].

(*b*) Other than for the purposes of corporation tax on chargeable gains, indexation allowance is frozen at its April 1998 level. Therefore, the indexation factor for April 1998 is used in respect of disposals in a later month (and expenditure incurred in April 1998 or later does not attract indexation allowance at all). See 210 INDEXATION.

# Wasting Assets 227.2

## 227.2 OPTIONS [TCGA 1992, ss 44, 46, 146]

**Cross-reference.** See also 206.5 DISPOSAL.

### (A) Unquoted shares

On 1 July 1997, R grants C an option to purchase unquoted shares held by R. The cost of the option is £600 to purchase 10,000 shares at £5 per share, the option to be exercised by 31 December 1999. On 1 September 1999 C assigns the option to W for £500. The indexation factor for July 1997 to April 1998 (note (a)) is 0.032.

|  | £ | £ |
|---|---|---|
| Disposal consideration |  | 500 |
| Acquisition cost | 600 |  |
| *Deduct* Wasted £600 × $\frac{26}{30}$ | 520 | 80 |
| Unindexed gain |  | 420 |
| Indexation allowance £80 × 0.032 |  | 3 |
| Chargeable gain |  | £417 |

**Note**

(a) Other than for the purposes of corporation tax on chargeable gains, indexation allowance is frozen at its April 1998 level. Therefore, the indexation factor for April 1998 is used in respect of disposals in a later month (and expenditure incurred in April 1998 or later does not attract indexation allowance at all). See 210 INDEXATION.

### (B) Traded options

On 1 December 1999, C purchases 6-month options on T plc shares for £1,000. Two weeks later, he sells the options, which are quoted on the Stock Exchange, for £1,200.

|  | £ |
|---|---|
| Disposal consideration | 1,200 |
| Allowable cost | 1,000 |
| Chargeable gain | £200 |

**Note**

(a) The wasting asset rules do not apply to traded options. [TCGA 1992, s 146].

## 227.3 Wasting Assets

227.3 **LIFE INTERESTS** [*TCGA 1992, s 44(1)(d)*]

**(A)**
N is a beneficiary under a settlement. On 30 June 1986, when her actuarially estimated life expectancy was 40 years, she sold her life interest to an unrelated individual, R, for £50,000. N dies on 31 December 1999, and the life interest is extinguished.

**R will have an allowable loss for 1999/2000 as follows**

| | £ | £ |
|---|---|---|
| Disposal consideration on death of N | | Nil |
| Allowable cost | 50,000 | |
| *Deduct* wasted | | |
| $\dfrac{13y\ 6m}{40y} \times £50,000$ | 16,875 | |
| | | 33,125 |
| Allowable loss | | £33,125 |

**Note**
(*a*)  The amount of the cost wasted is computed by reference to the predictable life, not the actual life, of the wasting asset.

**(B)**
Assume the facts to be as in (A) above except that the sale of the life interest was on 30 June 1981 and N's life expectancy *at that date* was 40 years. The value of the life interest was still £50,000 at 31 March 1982.

**Calculation without re-basing**

| | £ | £ |
|---|---|---|
| Disposal consideration on death of N | | Nil |
| Allowable cost | 50,000 | |
| *Deduct* wasted | | |
| $\dfrac{18y\ 6m}{40} \times £50,000$ | 23,125 | |
| | | 26,875 |
| Loss | | £26,875 |

**Calculation with re-basing**

| | £ | £ |
|---|---|---|
| Disposal consideration | | Nil |
| Market value 31.3.82 | 50,000 | |
| *Deduct* wasted | | |
| $£50,000 \times \dfrac{17y\ 9m\ (31.3.82 - 31.12.99)}{39y\ 3m\ \text{(life expectancy at 31.3.82)}}$ | 22,611 | |
| | | 27,389 |
| Loss | | £27,389 |
| | | |
| Allowable loss 1999/2000 | | £26,875 |

**Wasting Assets 227.3**

**Note**
(*a*)   The second of the above calculations shows how the wasting assets provisions interact with the re-basing provisions of *TCGA 1992, s 35*. Where, by virtue of the re-basing rules, an asset is deemed to have been disposed of and re-acquired at its market value on 31 March 1982, that market value must be reduced in accordance with the period of ownership *after* that date and the predictable life of the wasting asset *at* that date.

# Table of Statutes

**1970 Taxes Management Act**
| | |
|---|---|
| s 59C | 212.1 |
| s 69 | 212 |
| s 86 | 211; 212.1 |
| s 88 | 212.1(B) |

**1979 Capital Gains Tax Act**
| | |
|---|---|
| s 44 | 210.1(D) |

**1980 Finance Act**
| | |
|---|---|
| s 79 | 204.2; 209.1(C) |

**1988 Income and Corporation Taxes Act**
| | |
|---|---|
| s 34 | 213.3(C) |
| s 122 | 216.1 |
| s 247 | 202.3 |
| s 249 | 224.7 |
| s 251(2)–(4) | 224.7 |
| s 282A | 215.2 |
| s 282B | 215.2 |
| s 291 | 207.3(A) |
| s 291B | 207.3(A) |
| s 312 | 207.3 |
| (1A)(a) | 207.2(B) |
| s 380(1) | 201.1(A) |
| s 575 | 214.2 |
| s 576 | 214.2 |
| (4) | 214.2 |
| (4A)(4B) | 214.2 |
| s 686(1A) | 223.1 |
| s 740(6) | 217.1(D) |
| Sch 18 para 1(5) | 224.6 |

**1988 Finance Act**
| | |
|---|---|
| s 34 | 215.2 |
| ss 130–132 | 217.2 |

**1991 Finance Act**
| | |
|---|---|
| s 72 | 201.1(A) |

**1992 Taxation of Chargeable Gains Act**
| | |
|---|---|
| s 2(2)(4)(5) | 201.2 |
| s 2A | 222.1(A)(C); 222.2(A); 226.1 |
| (1)(2) | 203.3(A)(B)(C) |
| (5) | 206.1(A); 206.4(E); 226.3 |
| (6) | 226.1(B) |
| s 2A(8)(9) | 206.4(E); 218.1; 225.1; 226.2; 226.3 |
| s 3 | 201.2; 223.1 |
| s 4 | 201.1; 215.1 |
| (1AA) | 223.1 |
| s 10 | 217.3 |
| ss 19, 20 | 202.4 |
| s 22 | 206.4 |
| (1) | 206.3 |
| s 23 | 206.4; 206.4(B)(C) |
| (1) | 206.4(E) |
| (2) | 206.4(D) |
| s 25 | 217.2; 217.3 |
| (1)(3)(8) | 217.3 |
| s 29 | 202.1 |
| s 30 | 202.2; 202.3 |
| s 31 | 202.3 |
| s 35 | 204.1; 213.3(E); 218.5; 227.3(B) |
| (1) | 204.1(A) |
| (2) | 203.1(A); 203.3(B); 204.1(A); 213.3(E) |
| (3) | 203.3(C); 204.1(A); 206.2(A) |
| (a) | 203.3(A)(B)(C); 213.3(E) |
| (b) | 203.1(B); 203.3(D) |
| (c) | 203.1(B); 204.1(B) |
| (d) | 204.2; 210.2(A) |
| (4) | 203.3(B); 204.1(A) |
| (5) | 203.1(A); 204.1(A)(B); 206.2(B); 218.1; 221.2(B) |
| (7) | 218.1 |
| s 38 | 206.1(A); 208.1(B) |
| s 39 | 206.1(A) |
| s 41 | 206.1(B); 217.3 |
| s 42 | 203.3(E); 206.2; 213.3(B); 215.2; 224.3 |
| (4) | 206.2(A) |
| (5) | 215.2 |
| s 44 | 206.5; 227.1; 227.2 |
| (1)(d) | 227.3 |
| s 45 | 227.1; 227.1(A) |
| s 46 | 206.5; 227.1; 227.2 |
| s 47 | 227.1 |
| s 53 | 207.1(B); 213.4 |

# Table of Statutes

*1992 Taxation of Chargeable Gains Act*

| | |
|---|---:|
| s 53(1) | 206.4(E) |
| (*b*) | 210.1(D) |
| (1A) | 206.4(E); 207.1; 207.3(A); 209.1(C); 209.3; 210.1(B) |
| (2A) | 210.1(D) |
| (3) | 206.4(E); 213.2(B) |
| s 54 | 210.1 |
| (1) | 207.1; 207.3(A) |
| (1A) | 207.1; 207.3(A); 209.1(C); 209.3; 210.1(B) |
| (4)(*b*) | 213.3(F) |
| s 55 | 210.1 |
| (1)(2) | 203.1(A); 203.3(A)(C); 204.1(A); 206.2(A); 210.1(C); 213.3(E); 225.2(A) |
| (5)(6) | 210.2(A)(C) |
| (7)–(9) | 210.2(C) |
| s 56 | 210.1 |
| (2) | 210.2(A)–(D) |
| (3) | 210.2(D) |
| (4) | 210.2(D) |
| s 57 | 206.4(E); 213.2(B) |
| s 58 | 210.2(A); 215.1; 215.1(B) |
| s 59 | 218.1 |
| s 62 | 210.1(C) |
| s 67 | 209.1(C) |
| s 70 | 223.3 |
| s 71 | 223.4 |
| (2)–(2D) | 223.4(B) |
| s 72 | 223.5 |
| s 76 | 223.5(B) |
| s 77 | 201.2; 223.1; 223.2; 223.3(B) |
| (2)–(5) | 223.1 |
| (6) | 223.2 |
| ss 78, 79 | 223.1; 223.2; 223.3(B) |
| s 86 | 201.2 |
| s 87 | 201.2; 217.1; |
| s 89(2) | 201.2 |
| s 91(3)–(5) | 217.1(C) |
| ss 91–93 | 217.1(B) |
| s 97 | 217.1(B)(D) |
| s 104 | 225.2 |
| s 105 | 205.2; 224.3(C); 225.1; 225.2; 225.2(B) |
| s 106 | 205.2 |
| s 106A | 220.1; 224.3(C); 225.1 |
| (5) | 225.2(B) |
| s 107 | 225.2 |
| s 107(3)–(6) | 225.2(B) |
| s 108 | 225.2 |
| (1) | 220.1 |
| s 109 | 225.2 |
| (2) | 224.3(C) |
| (4) | 203.1; 203.1(A) |
| (5) | 203.1 |
| s 110 | 225.2 |
| s 110A | 224.2(A)(B); 224.3(A)(B)(C); 224.7; 225.1 |
| s 115 | 220 |
| s 116 | 220; 220.2 |
| (10) | 220.2 |
| s 117 | 214.3; 220; 220.1 |
| (1) | 220.1; 224.6 |
| (7)(*b*)(8) | 220.1 |
| s 119 | 210.3 |
| s 122 | 224.4(A); 224.8(A); 224.8(B) |
| (2) | 224.8(B) |
| s 123 | 224.8(B) |
| (1) | 224.3 |
| s 126 | 224.1; 224.2 |
| s 127 | 220.2; 224.1; 224.1(A); 224.2; 224.3(C); 224.4(A) |
| s 128 | 220.2; 224.1; 224.2; 224.3(C); 224.7 |
| (4) | 224.3 |
| s 129 | 220.2; 224.1; 224.1(A) |
| s 130 | 220.2; 224.1; 224.1(B); 224.2 |
| s 131 | 224.1 |
| s 132 | 224.4(E); 224.6 |
| s 135 | 224.4; 224.4(A) |
| s 136 | 224.5 |
| s 137 | 224.4 |
| s 138 | 224.4; 224.5 |
| s 138A | 224.4(E) |
| s 140 | 217.4 |
| s 141 | 224.7 |
| s 142 | 224.7 |
| s 144 | 206.5 |
| s 145 | 206.5 |
| s 146 | 227.2; 227.2(B) |
| s 150A(1) | 207.2; 207.3; 207.3(B) |
| (2)(2A)(3) | 207.1; 207.2 |
| s 150D | 207.3(B) |
| s 152 | 205.2; 211.1; 222; 222.1 |

# Table of Statutes

| | | | |
|---|---|---|---|
| s 152(7)(9) | 222.2(B) | Sch 2 para 2(1) | 203.1(B) |
| s 153 | 222; 222.2(A) | 3 | 203.1 |
| s 154 | 222; 222.3 | 4 | 203.1; 203.1(A) |
| s 155 | 222 | | |
| ss 156–158 | 222 | 5 | 203.1 |
| s 162 | 209.2(A); 209.3 | 6 | 203.1 |
| s 163 | 221 | 7, 8 | 203.1 |
| (1)(2) | 221.1(B); 221.2(F) | 9–15 | 203.2 |
| | | 16 | 203.3; 203.3(D) |
| (3) | 221.1(B) | | |
| (4) | 221.2(F) | (3)–(5)(8) | 203.3(E) |
| (5)(7) | 221.1(C) | 17, 18 | 203.3 |
| (8) | 221.2(E) | 19 | 203.3 |
| s 164 | 221 | (1) | 203.3(C) |
| (3)–(5) | 221.2(C) | (2) | 203.3(D) |
| s 164A | 209.3 | (3) | 203.3(C)(D) |
| s 165 | 209.2; 221.3(D) | Sch 3 | 204.1 |
| s 171 | 210.2(C)(D) | para 1 | 210.2(A) |
| s 172 | 217.3 | 4(1) | 203.3(E); 206.2(B); 224.4(A) |
| s 176 | 202.5 | | |
| ss 185, 187 | 217.2 | (2) | 206.4(D) |
| ss 201–203 | 216.1 | 6 | 203.3(B) |
| s 217 | 224.9 | 7 | 204.1(A) |
| s 222 | 219.1; 219.1(B) | 8, 9 | 204.1(A) |
| (5) | 219.2 | Sch 4 | 204.2; 208.2(A); 208.3 |
| s 223 | 219.1 | | |
| (1) | 219.1(A)(B) | para 1(*a*) | 204.2 |
| (3)(*a*)(*b*) | 219.1(B) | 2 | 204.2 |
| (4)(7) | 219.1(A)(B) | 4 | 220.2 |
| s 225 | 223.4(A) | 5–9 | 204.2 |
| s 242 | 206.2(D); 213.1 | Sch 5B | 207.3 |
| (2) | 213.1 | Sch 5BA | 207.3; 207.3(B) |
| s 243 | 213.2; 213.2(B) | Sch 5C | 226.3 |
| ss 244–246 | 213.2 | Sch 6 | 221 |
| s 247 | 213.2; 213.2(A) | para 1 | 221.1(C) |
| s 248 | 213.2 | (2) | 221.2(F) |
| s 260 | 208.1; 223.3(A) | 2 | 221.1(D) |
| (5) | 209.1(B) | 3 | 221.1(B) |
| (7) | 208.1(C); 209.1(C) | 5(2)(4) | 221.1(B) |
| s 262 | 202.4 | 6 | 221.2(A)(B) |
| (2) | 207.1(A) | 7 | 221.2(A) |
| (3) | 207.1(B) | 8 | 221.2(B) |
| (4) | 207.1(C) | 10 | 221.2(D)(E) |
| s 283 | 210 | 11 | 221.2(F) |
| (1)(2) | 211.1 | 12 | 221.2(A)(B) |
| Sch A1 | 226.1 | (5)(6) | 221.2(F) |
| para 3 | 226.2 | 13 | 221.1(B); 221.2(C) |
| 13(3) | 206.5 | | |
| 15 | 226.3 | 14 | 221.3(A)(B) |
| 16 | 207.3(A); 220.2; 226.3 | 15 | 221.3(B)(D) |
| | | 16 | 221.3(C)(D) |
| Sch 1 para 2 | 223.1 | (3)(4) | 222.3(D) |
| Sch 2 para 1 | 203.1 | Sch 7 | 208.2 |
| 2 | 203.1 | para 5 | 208.2(A) |

## Table of Statutes

*1992 Taxation of Chargeable Gains Act*
| | |
|---|---:|
| Sch 7 para 7 | 208.2(B) |
| 8 | 208.2(A) |
| (3) | 208.2(B); 209.2(B) |
| Sch 8 para 1 | 212.3(A)(D)(E)(F) |
| (2) | 213.3(A) |
| (4)(*b*) | 213.3(F) |
| 2 | 213.3(B)(C) |
| 4 | 213.3(G)(H) |
| 5 | 213.3(C)(G)(H) |
| 5(2) | 213.3(G)(H) |
| Sch 11 para 10(1) | 202.2 |
| (2) | 202.3 |

**1992 Finance (No 2) Act**
| | |
|---|---:|
| s 23 | 201.1(B) |

**1993 Finance Act**
| | |
|---|---:|
| s 87 | 221; 221.1(C); 221.2(A)(B)(C)(F) |
| Sch 6 para 22 | 201.1(B) |
| Sch 7 para 1 | 208.2 |
| Pt I | 221; 221.1(C); 221.2(A)(B)(C)(F) |
| Sch 23 Pt III(7) | 221 |

**1994 Finance Act**
| | |
|---|---:|
| s 92 | 221; 221.1(B) |
| s 93(1)(2) | 206.1(B); 206.2(D); 206.3(C); 207.1(B); 210.1: 210.1(D) |
| (3) | 207.1(B); 210.1 |
| (4) | 210.1; 210.2(C) |
| (5) | 210.1; 210.2(A) |
| (6) | 225.2(A) |
| (11) | 210.1(D); 210.2(A) |
| s 194 | 212.1 |
| s 196 | 212.1 |
| s 199 | 212.1 |
| s 210 | 214.2 |
| Sch 12 | 210.1(C); 214.4 |
| Sch 15 para 28–30 | 207.1; 207.2; 207.3 |
| Sch 19 para 20 | 212.1 |
| 46 | 211; 211.2 |
| Sch 20 para 8 | 214.2 |
| Sch 26 Pt V(23) | 211 |

**1995 Finance Act**
| | |
|---|---:|
| s 50 | 220.1 |

| | |
|---|---:|
| ss 66, 67 | 207 |
| s 74 | 223.1; 223.2 |
| s 109 | 212.1 |
| s 110 | 212.1 |
| Sch 13 | 207 |
| para 2(1) | 207.1, 207.2 |
| (2) | 207.2 |
| (3) | 207.1 |
| 4(3)(4) | 207.3 |
| Sch 17 para 27–29 | 223.1; 223.2 |

**1996 Finance Act**
| | |
|---|---:|
| s 141(4)(6) | 213.2 |
| s 176 | 221 |
| Sch 6 para 27 | 201.1(B) |
| Sch 20 para 46 | 202.2; 202.3 |
| 47(*a*) | 202.2; 202.3 |
| 52 | 224.8(B) |
| 57 | 202.4 |
| 59 | 219.2 |
| 66 | 221.1(B) |
| (4) | 221.2(D)(E) |
| Sch 21 para 37 | 213.1 |
| 38 | 213.2 |
| 42(1)(2) | 203.1 |
| (3) | 203.3 |
| 43 | 204.2 |
| 44(1)(2) | 221.1(D) |
| (3) | 221.1(B) |
| (4) | 221.2(F) |
| (5) | 221.3(C)(D) |
| Sch 38 para 6(1)(2)(9) | 214.2 |
| Sch 39 para 5 | 223.5 |
| 7 | 221.3(A) |
| Sch 41 Pt V(10) | 219.2 |

**1997 Finance Act**
| | |
|---|---:|
| s 88 | 224.6 |
| s 89 | 224.4(E) |
| s 90 | 107.3 |
| s 92(5)(6) | 211.2 |

**1997 Finance (No 2) Act**
| | |
|---|---:|
| s 34 | 201.1(A) |
| Sch 4 para 24 | 201.1(A) |

**1998 Finance Act**
| | |
|---|---:|
| s 40 | 213.3(C) |
| s 74 | 207.2(B); 207.3 |
| s 80 | 214.2 |
| (3)(5) | 214.2 |
| s 120 | 201.1; 223.1 |
| s 121 | 206(E); 206.5; 207.3(A) |

# Table of Statutes

| | | | |
|---|---|---|---|
| s 121(1) | 203.3(A)(B)(C); 206.1(A); 207.1; 207.3(A); 222.1(A)(C); 222.2(A); 225.1; 226.1(B); 226.2; 226.3; 226.4 | s 125(2)(4)(5) | 224.2(A)(B); 224.3(A)(B)(C); 224.7; 225.1 |
| (2) | 207.1; 207.3(A); 220.2; 225.1; 226.2; 226.3 | s 126 | 224.7 |
| | | s 130 | 217.1(A) |
| | | s 144 | 206.5 |
| (3) | 201.2; 207.1; 207.3(A) | Sch 5 para 15 | 213.3(C) |
| | | 63 | 213.3(C)(G)(H) |
| (4) | 201.2; 203.3(A)(B)(C); 220.2; 225.1; 226.2; 226.3; 226.4 | Sch 13 para 6 | 207.3 |
| | | 12 | 207.2(B) |
| | | 24(1) | 207.1 |
| s 122(1) | 206.4(E); 209.1(C); 209.3; 210.1; 218.1 | 26–36 | 207.3; 206.5; 207.3; 220.2 |
| | | Sch 20 | 207.3(A); 226.1; 226.2; 226.3; 226.4 |
| (2) | 209.1(C); 209.3; 210.1 | Sch 21 para 2 | 201.2 |
| (3) | 209.1(C); 209.3; 210.1 | 3 | 201.2 |
| | | Sch 27 Part III(29) | 201.1 |
| (4) | 206.4(E); 218.1 | (31) | 221 |
| (5) | 206.5 | | |
| (6) | 210.1 | **1999 Finance Act** | |
| (7) | 206.4(E); 206.5 | s 26 | 201.1(A)(B) |
| s 123 | 225.2(A) | (3) | 223.1 |
| s 124(1) | 224.3(C); 225.1; 225.2(B) | s 72 | 207.3; 207.3(B) |
| | | s 73 | 207.3 |
| (2) | 224.3(C); 225.1 | s 75 | 223.4(B) |
| (7) | 224.3(C); 225.1 | Sch 7 | 207.3; 207.3(B) |
| (8) | 225.2(B) | Sch 8 | 207.3 |

# Index

This index is referenced to chapter and paragraph number. The entries in bold capitals are chapter headings in the text.

## A

| | |
|---|---|
| **Accrued income scheme** | **209.3; 220.1** |
| **Allowable and non-allowable expenditure** | **206.1** |
| **ANNUAL RATES AND EXEMPTIONS** | **201** |
| losses, interaction with | 201.2 |
| —attributed settlement gains | 201.2(B) |
| married persons | 215.1 |
| settlements | 223.1 |
| **ANTI-AVOIDANCE** | **202** |
| disposal to connected person | 202.4 |
| gains of non-resident trusts | 217.1 |
| groups of companies | |
| —depreciatory transactions | 202.5 |
| value-shifting | 202.1; 202.2; 202.3 |
| **Assets disposed of in series of transactions** | **202.4; 207.1(C)** |
| **ASSETS HELD ON 6 APRIL 1965** | **203** |
| buildings | 203.3(B) |
| chattels | 203.3(A) |
| land and buildings | 203.3(B) |
| land reflecting development value | 203.2 |
| part disposals after 5 April 1965 | 203.3(E) |
| quoted shares and securities | 203.1 |
| time apportionment | 203.3 |
| unquoted shares | 203.3(C)(D) |
| **ASSETS HELD ON 31 MARCH 1982** | **204** |
| deferred gains, relief for | 204.2 |
| general computation of gains/losses | 204.1 |
| no gain/no loss disposals | 210.2(A)(C) |
| part disposals before 6 April 1988 | 206.2(B) |
| partnerships, held by | 218.1 |
| private residences | 219.1(A)(B) |
| short leases | 213.3(E) |
| wasting assets | 227.1(B); 227.3(B) |

## B

| | |
|---|---|
| **Bondwashing** | **220.1** |
| **Building Societies** | |
| conversions and takeovers | 224.9 |
| **Business assets** | |
| deferment of chargeable gain on replacement of assets | 222 |
| disposal on retirement | 221 |
| gift of | 209.2 |
| taper relief | 226.2 |
| transfer to a company | 209.3 |

## C

| | |
|---|---|
| **Capital Allowances** | |
| capital gains, effect on | 206.1(B); 217.3; 226.1 |
| **Chattels** | **208.1** |
| held on 6.4.65 | 203.3(A) |
| **COMPANIES** (Capital gains of) | **205** |
| amalgamation and reconstruction | 224.4; 224.5 |
| capital losses | 205.1 |
| shares — acquisitions and disposals within short period | 205.2 |
| transfer of assets to non-resident company | 217.4 |
| **Companies (migration of)** | **217.2** |
| **Compensation** | |
| CGT on receipt of | 206.4; 213.2 |
| —taper relief | 206.4(E) |
| **Compulsory acquisition of land** | **213.2** |
| **Corporate bonds, qualifying** | **220; 224.6** |

## D

| | |
|---|---|
| **Deferment of chargeable gain** | |
| *See* Hold-over reliefs and Rollover relief | |
| **Deferred consideration** | **206.3(B)(C); 224.4(C)** |
| **Depreciatory transactions** | **202.5** |

# Index

| | |
|---|---|
| **DISPOSAL** | **206** |
| allowable expenditure | 206.1 |
| —effect of capital allowances | 206.1(B) |
| capital sums derived from assets | 206.3 |
| —deferred consideration | 206.3(B)(C); 224.4(E) |
| compulsory acquisition of land | 213.2 |
| connected persons | 202.4 |
| options | 206.5; 226.2 |
| part disposal | 206.2; 206.3(A); 207.1(C); 212.1; 213.2; 215.2 |
| —assets held on 6.4.65 | 203.3(E) |
| —small part disposals of land | 213.1 |
| premiums payable under leases | 213.3 |
| receipt of compensation | 206.4; 213.2 |
| —capital sum exceeding allowable expenditure | 206.4(D) |
| —compulsory acquisition | 213.2 |
| —indexation allowance | 206.4(E) |
| —part application of capital sum received | 206.4(C) |
| —restoration using insurance moneys | 206.4(B) |
| sets, assets forming | 207.1(C) |
| value passing out of shares | 202.1; 202.2; 202.3 |
| **Dividend income** | |
| capital gains tax rates, effect on | 201.1(B) |
| **Dwelling house, gains on** | **219** |

## E

| | |
|---|---|
| **Earn-outs** | **224.4(C)** |
| **Enterprise Investment Scheme** | |
| capital gains and losses | |
| —disposal more than five years after acquisition | 207.1; 207.2 |
| deferral relief | 207.3 |
| —serial investors | 207.3(B) |
| **EXEMPTIONS AND RELIEFS** | **208** |
| chattels | 208.1 |
| dwelling house | 219 |
| qualifying corporate bonds | 220 |
| tangible movable asset | 208.1 |

## G

| | |
|---|---|
| **Gifts** | **209** |
| assets held on 31 March 1982 | 204.2 |
| business assets | 208.2 |
| deferment of gain | 208.1; 208.2; 222.3 |
| **Groups of companies** | |
| depreciatory transactions | 202.5 |
| distribution followed by disposal of shares | 202.3 |
| intra-group transfers of assets | 210.2(C)(D) |

## H

| | |
|---|---|
| **HOLD-OVER RELIEFS** | **209** |
| *See also* Rollover Relief | |
| assets held on 31 March 1982 | 204.2 |
| chargeable lifetime transfers | 209.1(A) |
| disposal consideration | 209.1(B) |
| gifts | |
| —business assets | 209.2 |
| —chargeable lifetime transfers | 209.1 |
| IHT relief | 209.1(C) |
| transfer of business to company | 209.3 |
| **Husband and wife** | |
| *See* Married Persons | |

## I

| | |
|---|---|
| **INDEXATION** | **210** |
| allowance on receipt of compensation | 206.4(E) |
| assets held on 31.3.82 | 210.1(C) |
| general rules | 210.1 |
| indexation factor, calculation of | |
| —companies | 210.1(A) |
| —individuals, etc. | 210.1(B) |
| losses | 210.1(D) |
| no gain/no loss disposals | 210.2(A)–(D) |
| —inter-spouse transfers | 210.2(A)(B) |
| —intra-group transfers | 210.2(C)(D) |
| relevant securities, identification rules | 210.3 |

# Index

restriction 210.1(D)
shares and securities,
  identification rules 225.2
transitional relief 210.1(D)
**Inter-spouse transfers** **210.1(D);**
**210.2(A); 215.1; 215.2; 226.3**
taper relief 226.3
**Interest in possession**
termination of 223.4; 223.5
**INTEREST ON OVERPAID**
**TAX** **211**
pre-self-assessment 211.1
**INTEREST ON UNPAID TAX** **212**

## L

**LAND** **213**
compulsory purchase 213.2
development value, reflecting 203.2
held on 6.4.65 203.2; 203.3(B)
leases 213.3
—assignment of short
  lease 213.3(D)–(F)
—grant of long lease 213.3(B)
—grant of short lease 213.3(C)
—premiums on short
  leases 213.3(C)(G)(H)
—short leases which are not
  wasting assets 213.3(A)
—sub-lease granted out of
  short lease 213.3(G)(H)
small part disposals 213.1
**Leases**
*See* Land
**Loans to traders** **214.3**
**LOSSES** **214**
capital losses 205.1; 213
—indexation losses 210.1(D)
—tangible movable assets 207.1(B)
chattels 207.1(B)
interaction with annual
  exempt amount 201.2
unquoted companies 214.4
unquoted shares, capital losses available
  for set-off against
  income 214.4

## M

**MARRIED PERSONS** **215**
jointly owned assets 215.2
no gain/no loss
  transfers 209.1(D)(E);
  215.1; 215.2; 211.1(B)

retirement relief 221.3(C)(D)
taper relief 226.3
**Migration of companies** **217.2**
**MINERAL ROYALTIES** **216**

## N

**Non-resident, company**
**becoming** **217.2**
**Non-resident company, transfer**
**of assets to** **217.4**
**Non-residents trading through UK**
**branch or agency** **217.3**
**Non-resident settlements**
gains attributed to UK
  beneficiary 217.1

## O

**Options** **206.5; 226.2**
**Overdue tax**
*See* Interest on Overdue Tax *and* Interest
on Unpaid Tax
**OVERSEAS MATTERS** **217**
company migration 217.2
non-residents trading through
  UK branch or agency 217.3
overseas resident settlements 217.1
transfer of assets to non-
  resident company 217.4
UK beneficiary of an overseas
  resident settlement 217.1

## P

**Part disposals**
*See* Disposal
**Participators**
*See* Close Companies
**PARTNERSHIPS** **218**
accounting adjustments 218.3
assets 218.1
—distribution in kind 218.6
changes in partners 218.2–218.4
changes in sharing ratios 218.2–218.5
consideration outside
  accounts 218.4
disposal of partnership
  asset to partner 218.6
indexation 210.2(A)(C); 218.2
retirement relief 221.2(E)
revaluation of assets 218.3;
  218.5
shares acquired in stages 218.5

195

# Index

Premiums on short leases 213.3(C)(G)(H)
**PRIVATE RESIDENCES**     **219**
    capital gains tax exemption     219

## Q

**QUALIFYING CORPORATE**
    **BONDS**     **220**
    conversion of securities     224.6
    definition     220.1
    reorganisation of share
       capital     220.2

## R

**Repayments of tax, interest on**     **211.1**
**Residence**
    *See* Private Residences
**Residence and domicile**
    non-resident company, transfer
       of assets to     217.3
    non-resident settlements     217.1
**RETIREMENT RELIEF**     **221**
    amount of relief     221.3
    associated disposals     221.2(C)–(E)
    capital distribution     221.2(F)
    earlier business periods     221.3(A)
    extent of relief     221.1
    full-time working officer
       or employee     221.1(C)
    gains qualifying for relief     221.2
    gifts hold-over relief, interaction
       with     208.2
    ill-health grounds     221.1(B)
    married persons     221.3(C)(D)
    non-business chargeable
       assets     221.2(A)(B)
    partnerships     221.2(E)
    personal asset used by
       company business     221.2(D)
    qualifying period     221.1(B)
    separate disposals     221.3(B)
    share for share exchange     221.1(D)
    shares in holding
       company     221.2(B)
    trustees     221.2(C)
**ROLLOVER RELIEF**     **222**
    compulsory acquisition of
       land     213.2
    gifts     204.2; 208.1; 208.2; 223.3
    receipt of compensation not
       treated as disposal     206.4(B)–(E); 213.2
    replacement of business
       assets     222
    —nature of relief     222.1
    —partial relief     222.2
    —taper relief     222.1(C)
    —wasting assets     222.3
    transfer of business to a
       company     208.3
**Royalties and licences**
    mineral royalties     216

## S

**Self-assessment**
    interest on unpaid CGT     212.1
**SETTLEMENTS**     **223**
    annual exemptions     223.1
    creation of     223.3
    death of life tenant     223.5; 226.3
    interest in possession     223.5
    overseas resident     217.1
    person becoming absolutely entitled
       to settled property     223.4
    rates of tax     223.1
    settlor retaining an interest     223.2
    termination of an interest in
       possession     223.4; 223.5; 226.3
**SETTLEMENTS WITH INTERESTS**
    **IN POSSESSION**     **223.5**
    termination of an interest in
       possession     223.4; 223.5
    —losses     223.5(C)
**SHARES AND SECURITIES**     **224**
    acquisitions and disposals
       within short period     205.2
    amalgamations of
       companies     224.4; 224.5
    bonus issues     224.2
    capital distributions     221.2(F); 224.8
    conversion of securities     224.6
    corporate bonds, qualifying     220
    deferred consideration     206.3(B)(C); 224.4(C)
    earn-outs     225.4(C)
    holdings at 6.4.65
    —quoted     203.1; 224.1(G)
    —unquoted     203.3(C)(D); 224.8(C)
    qualifying corporate bonds     220
    reconstruction schemes     224.5

# Index

| | |
|---|---|
| reorganisation of share capital | 220.2; 224.1 |
| rights issues | 224.1; 224.3 |
| —sale of rights | 224.8(B) |
| scrip dividends | 224.7 |
| time apportionment — unquoted shares | 203.3(D) |
| transfer of business to a company for shares | 209.3 |
| unquoted shares | |
| —distribution in a liquidation | 224.8(C) |
| —losses relieved against income | 214.2 |
| —time apportionment | 203.3(D) |
| value passing out of | 202.1; 202.2; 202.3 |

| | |
|---|---|
| **SHARES AND SECURITIES— IDENTIFICATION RULES** | **225** |
| after 5 April 1998 | 225.1 |
| before 6 April 1998 | 225.2 |
| companies | 225.2 |
| qualifying corporate bonds | 220.1 |

## T

| | |
|---|---|
| **Tangible movable property** | **208.1** |
| **TAPER RELIEF** | **226** |
| basic rules | 226.1(A) |
| business assets, part use as | 226.2 |
| compensation | 206.4(E) |
| EIS deferral, interaction with | 207.3(B) |
| inter-spouse transfers | 226.3 |
| losses | 226.1(B) |
| postponed gains | 226.3 |
| rollover relief, interaction with | 222.1(C) |
| **Time apportionment** | **203.3; 224.7(C)** |
| **Transfer of business to a company** | **209.3** |
| **Trusts** | |
| *See* Settlements | |

## V

| | |
|---|---|
| **Value-shifting** | |
| anti-avoidance | 202.1; 202.2; 202.3 |

## W

| | |
|---|---|
| **WASTING ASSETS** | **227** |
| eligible for capital allowances | 227.1 |
| leases | 213.3 |
| —assignment of short lease | 213.3(D)–(F) |
| —grant of long lease | 213.3(B) |
| —grant of short lease | 213.3(C) |
| —short leases which are not wasting assets | 213.3(A) |
| —sub-lease granted out of short lease | 213.3(G)(H) |
| life interests | 227.3 |
| options | 206.5; 227.2 |
| rollover relief | 223.3 |

# Tolley

## Tolley's VAT Cases 1999

*By Alan Dolton, MA (Oxon) and Robert Wareham, BSc (Econ), FCA*

**21 Days Money Back Guarantee**

*"The bible of the UK VAT industry is Tolley's VAT Cases. No praise can be high enough for this book."* **THE TIMES**

Containing concise summaries of more than 3,000 essential court and VAT tribunal decisions relevant to current legislation, from 1973 to 1 January 1999, **Tolley's VAT Cases 1999** provides vital information in a readily accessible form. The specially designed format makes it easy to locate a relevant precedent and therefore to deal effectively with correspondence from Customs and Excise:

- Chapters are arranged alphabetically for ease of reference
- Cases are arranged into subject areas, rather than in chronological order
- Clear sub-headings identify the specific points at issue in each case
- Full case citations and references are also provided to allow transcripts of judgments to be consulted where necessary.

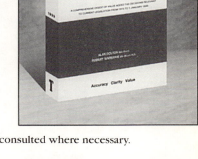

**No other single book contains concise summaries of all court and tribunal decisions relevant to the VAT legislation.**

### New to this Edition
Updated coverage provides you with the latest interpretations of the legislation.
- Introductory survey of leading 1998 decisions
- Expanded coverage of European Community law
- New chapter on "Trade Unions and professional bodies"

| Product Code: VC99 | Price: £81.95 | ISBN: 0 7545 0243 0 |

### How To Order
To order, please contact Butterworths Tolley Customer Service Dept:
Butterworths Tolley, FREEPOST SEA 4177, Croydon, Surrey CR9 5WZ
Telephone: 0181 662 2000   Fax: 0181 662 2012

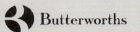

A member of the Reed Elsevier plc group
25 Victoria Street, London SW1H 0EX
VAT number: 730 8595 20
Registered Office Number: 2746621

NB: Your data may be used for direct marketing purposes by selected companies

**Butterworths Tax Direct Service** is the ultimate on-line service that provides you with instant access to the most authoritative information ... all via the internet.
For more information on all of our products, please visit our website at www.butterworths.co.uk

# Tolley

*All you need for effective capital tax planning...*

# Tolley's Capital Allowances

**Gary Mackley-Smith** FFA FIAB ATT AIMgt and **Kevin Walton** BA (Hons)

*"We recommend it to advisers to business, especially accountants and lawyers, who will find it excellent value"*  **TAX FILE**

Tolley's Capital Allowances 1999-2000 brings together in a single comprehensive volume, the law and practice regarding capital allowances. It has been designed so that practitioners and taxpayers can establish what types of allowance are available and how they can be claimed in order to achieve greater tax savings. This work was originally produced as a direct response to requests from tax practitioners for a book on this area of revenue law and shows the practitioner how to make the most tax-effective use of capital investments.

This edition of **Tolley's Capital Allowances** includes new material on:
- Changes from Finace Act 1999
- New cases
- Inland Revenue Tax Bulletins & Inland Revenue Guidance Manuals
- Updated worked examples and planning points

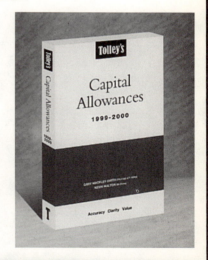

This highly practical guide also includes time-saving worked examples throughout, illustrating both complex points and basic queries to aid comprehension of how the law works in practice. Additional features include:
- Tables of cases
- Statutes and derivations
- Revenue Statements of Practice
- Extra-statutory concessions

**Product Code:** CAL00  **Price:** £44.95  **ISBN:** 0 75450 269 4  **Publication Date:** October 1999

## How To Order

To order, please contact Butterworths Tolley Customer Service Dept:
Butterworths Tolley, FREEPOST SEA 4177, Croydon, Surrey CR9 5WZ
Telephone: 0181 662 2000   Fax: 0181 662 2012

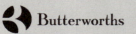

A member of the Reed Elsevier plc group
25 Victoria Street, London SW1H 0EX
VAT number: 730 8595 20
Registered Office Number: 2746621

NB: Your data may be used for direct marketing purposes by selected companies

**Butterworths Tax Direct Service** is the ultimate on-line service that provides you with instant access to the most authoritative information ... all via the internet.
For more information on all of our products, please visit our website at www.butterworths.co.uk

# Tolley

**21 Days Money Back Guarantee**

# Tolley's Tax Cases 1999

By Alan Dolton, MA (Oxon) and Glyn Saunders, MA (Cantab

*"concise but useful summaries of all the cases most of us would want to refer to...conveniently laid out, clearly written"* **BUSY SOLICITOR'S DIGEST**

## All the cases at your fingertips

**Tolley's Tax Cases 1999** contains brief, concise reports of more than 2,500 essential court cases and special commissions' decisions relevant to UK tax legislation from 1875 to 1 January 1999, including selected Irish cases.

Formatted in a way that enables you to avoid lengthy searches for relevant examples, **Tolley's Tax Cases 1999** includes:
- Cases arranged in subject areas
- Subjects arranged alphabetically
- Concise sub-headings identify specific points at issue
- Tables listing cases both alphabetically, under the names of both parties involved, and in chronological order of the relevant legislation
- Full case citations and references are provided to allow transcripts of judgments to be consulted where necessary

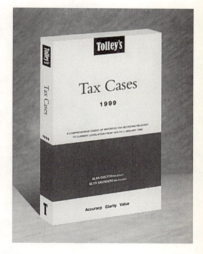

### New to this Edition
Updated coverage provides you with the latest interpretations of the legislation.
- Introductory survey of leading 1998 decisions
- Expanded coverage of European Community law

**Product Code:** TC99     **Price:** £48.95     **ISBN:** 0 7545 0242 2

## How To Order
To order, please contact Butterworths Tolley Customer Service Dept:
Butterworths Tolley, FREEPOST SEA 4177, Croydon, Surrey CR9 5WZ
Telephone: 0181 662 2000     Fax: 0181 662 2012

 **Butterworths**     **Tolley**

A member of the Reed Elsevier plc group
25 Victoria Street, London SW1H 0EX
VAT number: 730 8595 20
Registered Office Number: 2746621

NB: Your data may be used for direct marketing purposes by selected companies

**Butterworths Tax Direct Service** is the ultimate on-line service that provides you with instant access to the most authoritative information ... all via the internet.
For more information on all of our products, please visit our website at www.butterworths.co.uk